CISTERCIAN STUDIES SERIES: NUME

BECOMING FIRE

THROUGH THE YEAR
WITH THE DESERT FATHERS AND MOTHERS

CISTERCIAN STUDIES SERIES: NUMBER TWO HUNDRED TWENTY-FIVE

BECOMING FIRE

THROUGH THE YEAR WITH THE DESERT FATHERS AND MOTHERS

Edited by

Tim Vivian

Translations by

Apostolos N. Athanassakis, John Eudes Bamberger OCSO,
John Chryssavgis, Maged S. A. Mikhail, Birger A. Pearson,
Pachomios (Robert) Penkett, Norman Russell,
Armand Veilleux OCSO, Tim Vivian, & Benedicta Ward SLG

Preface by Stephen Emmel

Foreword by Aelred Glidden OSB

α

Cistercian Publications

LITURGICAL PRESS
Collegeville, Minnesota
www.litpress.org

A Cistercian Publications title published by Liturgical Press

Cistercian Publications
Editorial Offices
Abbey of Gethsemani
3642 Monks Road
Trappist, Kentucky 40051
www.cistercianpublications.org

Publication of this book was made possible by support from
Western Michigan University to The Institute of Cistercian Studies.

© 2008 by Tim Vivian.

1   2   3   4   5   6   7   8   9

Library of Congress Cataloguing in Publication Data

Becoming fire : through the year with the Desert Fathers and mothers /
edited by Tim Vivian ; translations by Apostolos N. Athanassakis . . .
[et al.] ; preface by Stephen Emmel ; foreword by Aelred Glidden.
         p.   cm. — (Cistercian studies series ; no. 225)
    Includes bibliographical references and index.
    ISBN 978-0-87907-525-5 (pbk.)
    1. Desert Fathers.   2. Spiritual life—Christianity—History—
Early church, ca. 30–600.   I. Vivian, Tim.   II. Athanassakis,
Apostolos N.   III. Title.   IV. Series.

BR195.C5B4313   2008
270.2—dc22
                                                              2008021411

To Gary
spiritual person, radical life
gospel life

To Hany N. Takla
founding president of
The Saint Shenoute the Archimandrite Coptic Society

To the founding members of
Remain Episcopal, Bakersfield,
now Grace Episcopal Church

In the morning, while it was still very dark, Jesus got up and went out to a deserted place, and there he prayed.   Mark 1:35

There is a big difference between merely collecting recipes and actually cooking and eating.   Sufi master Shaykh Fadhlalla Haeri

The spiritual life is the life of man's real self, the life of that interior self whose flame is so often allowed to be smothered under the ashes of anxiety and futile concern. . . . The life of the spirit, by integrating us in the real order established by God, puts us in the fullest possible contact with reality—not as we imagine it, but as it really is. It does so by putting us in contact with our own real selves and placing them in the presence of God.
     Thomas Merton OCSO, *No Man is an Island*

The work of the spiritual life is the radical remaking of the whole person.
     John Eudes Bamberger OCSO,
     Thomas Merton: Prophet of Renewal

In Navajo, the word for 'teach' does not translate as 'to tell' but literally means 'to show', 'to describe by action'.
     Joseph Epes Brown, *Teaching Spirits*

How could anyone really think that true reconciliation could avoid a proper confrontation?
     Archbishop Desmond Tutu, *No Future without Forgiveness*

That dangerous solitude.
     Tim Farrington, *The Monk Downstairs*

You cannot be a monk unless you become like a consuming fire.
     The Sayings of the Desert Fathers, Joseph of Panephysis 6

Let the monk's life be one that imitates the angel of the Lord, consuming sin with fire, for a monk's life is a whole burnt-offering for those who sin.
     Hyperechius, *Exhortation to the Monks* 25

*In the beginning there are a great many battles and a good deal of suf-
fering for those who are advancing towards God and, afterwards, ineffable joy. It is like those who wish to light a fire: at first they are choked
by smoke and cry, and by this means obtain what they seek (as it is
said: 'Our God is a consuming fire'). So we also must kindle the divine
fire in ourselves through tears and hard work.*

Sayings of the Desert Fathers, Syncletica 1

*A brother came to the cell of Abba Arsenius in Scetis. Waiting outside
the door, he saw the old man entirely like flame.*

The Sayings of the Desert Fathers, Arsenius 27

*Abba Isaiah called one of the brothers, washed his feet, put a handful
of lentils into the pot, and brought them to him as soon as they had
boiled. The brother said to him, 'They are not cooked, Abba'.*

*   The old man replied, 'Is it not enough simply to have seen the fire?
That alone is a great consolation'.*

The Sayings of the Desert Fathers, Isaiah 6

*Abba Lot went to see Abba Joseph and said to him, 'Abba, as far as
I can, I say my little office, I fast a little, I pray and meditate, I live in
peace and, as far as I can, I purify my thoughts. What else can I do?'*

*   Then the old man stood up and stretched his hands towards heaven.
His fingers became like ten lamps of fire and he said to him, 'If you
want to, you can become all flame'.*

The Sayings of the Desert Fathers, Joseph of Panephysis 7

TABLE OF CONTENTS

ACKNOWLEDGEMENTS

Most of the sayings and stories in this volume come from my own translations, published and unpublished. See 'Abbreviations, Sources, and Bibliography' and 'List of Sources' for details. I also wish, however, gratefully to thank the following translators for permission to use selections from their work—all published by Cistercian Publications:

- John Eudes Bamberger OCSO: *Evagrius Ponticus: The Praktikos & Chapters on Prayer.*
- John Chryssavgis and Pachomios (Robert) Penkett: *Isaiah of Scetis: Ascetic Discourses.*
- Norman Russell: *The Lives of the Desert Fathers: The* Historia Monachorum *in Aegypto.*
- Armand Veilleux OCSO: *Pachomian Koinonia*, volume 1, *The Life of Saint Pachomius and His Disciples.*
- Benedicta Ward SLG: *The Sayings of the Desert Fathers.*

I wish also to thank my co-translators:

- Apostolos N. Athanassakis: *The Life of Antony, The Life of Paesius/Bishoy,* and the *Systematic Apophthegmata.*
- Maged S. A. Mikhail: *The Life of John the Little.*
- Birger A. Pearson: the works by Paul of Tamma.

I also thank Fr John Behr for permission to use excerpts from *Four Desert Fathers: Pambo, Evagrius, Macarius of Egypt, and Macarius of*

Alexandria. Coptic Texts Relating to the Lausiac History of Palladius and *Saint Macarius the Spiritbearer: Coptic Texts Relating to Saint Macarius* (Crestwood, New York: Saint Vladimir's Seminary Press, 2004).

Translations from the Bible usually follow those of the New Revised Standard Version.

In addition, I wish to thank Prior Aelred Glidden OSB for agreeing to write the Foreword and Professor Stephen Emmel for permission to use as the Preface part of his keynote address at the Coptic Consultation of the American Academy of Religion in Washington, DC in November 2006. My thanks to the Rev'd Gary Commins for his suggestions about themes for the Church seasons. My thanks, too, to Gary Commins, Professor Jeffrey Russell, and Professor Miriam Raub Vivian for reading the Introduction and offering suggestions.

I relied on the biblical expertise of Chris Thomas, one of my students in Religious Studies at California State University Bakersfield, who spotted allusions to the Bible that I had missed. I wish to thank him for those and for his other suggestions.

Grateful thanks to Scott Porter, another Religious Studies student, wise in the ways of computers, for doing the indexes.

I also wish to thank my colleagues in the Department of Philosophy and Religious Studies at California State University Bakersfield, especially the Chair, Jacquelyn Kegley, and my colleagues in the Religious Studies Program, Steve Campagna-Pinto and Liora Gubkin, for their encouragement and support.

As always, great thanks to Dr. E. Rozanne Elder at Cistercian Publications for her editorial assistance and prompt answers to my numerous e-mails.

Again, as always, my deepest thanks to Miriam, Meredith, John, and David who put up with and support this 'monk' when he's at work in his 'cell'.

PREFACE[1]

WHEN I ASK MYSELF what it is that Coptology has that is, or might, or should be interesting to people well outside the discipline of Coptic studies, the answer I keep coming back to is: monastic spirituality. In our secular, consumption-oriented age, that might seem a strange answer. But I do not mean monastic spirituality presented in the first instance in the way that interests many scholars and university students today. Nor, in fact, do I mean anything specifically Christian about monastic spirituality. Rather I mean something that I perceive as the timeless, *human* essence of monastic spirituality, something that can speak to any human who is looking for meaning in this life. I mean the message that 'more, more, more' of one thing means less of something else that might be equally or even more important; the message that even though we cannot change the biological fact that we must consume in order to live, still we need not live merely in order to consume; the message that by consuming less, less, less, we might even discover something more meaningful than we can yet imagine.

I do not think that I am trying to say anything particularly profound here. I only mean to emphasize what many others have

---

[1] This Preface is a revised brief excerpt from 'A Vision for Coptic Studies: "Coptic Christianity" from Late Antique Egypt to the "Coptic Diaspora"', the keynote paper presented by Professor Stephen Emmel at the Coptic Consultation meeting of the American Academy of Religion in Washington, DC, November 19, 2006.

no doubt already thought about in one way or another: namely, that monastic spirituality has a message that is still relevant and perhaps even extremely important for the present and the future of humankind, apart from its Coptic Christian expression—I myself would say even apart from its *Christian* expression. Our access to that message is through a rich and diverse tradition full of interesting things that we can and should try to present to the world at large, but our access is also through an intellectually fascinating and challenging set of tasks that we must also present again and again to the world in ways that capture people's imaginations and interest. We can and must make people *think*, at the same time that we give them *information* to think *about.*

Stephen Emmel

Universität Münster

14

FOREWORD

A S WE LEARN MORE about the past we frequently discover that we know less than we thought and this is certainly true when dealing with the origins of christian monasticism. The tradition is that it all began when Saint Anthony of Egypt decided to move out into the desert to battle against the demons. The reality is unquestionably more complicated, but it is true to the extent that not only Anthony's contemporaries but all succeeding monks have continued to look to him and the other Elders of the Desert for inspiration. One of the reasons this is true for Benedictines is that Saint Benedict wrote in his Rule that, before the office of Compline each night, the monks should listen to readings from the *Lives* and *Sayings of the Desert Fathers* and the *Conferences* and *Institutes* of John Cassian—all of which were about the early monks of Egypt.

At Saint Gregory's Abbey we still follow the custom of reading from these sources before Compline, with special readings for particular feasts and for different seasons of the Church Year. During the month of July, when we have a Summer Vocation Program, I always interrupt our usual reading so that the men joining us for a few weeks to experience the monastic life can hear some of my favorites from the *Apophthegmata Patrum, The Sayings of the Desert Fathers.*

These 'Sayings of the Desert Fathers' consist of several collections of stories and sayings attributed to the early monks, mostly hermits or semi-hermits, in Egypt. All told, there are seven major and five minor different collections, and there are about six hundred stories common to all the collections that have been edited.

15

Some are arranged alphabetically by the name of the particular monk to whom the saying is attributed, while other collections are arranged by the particular virtue or principle promoted in the story. Ambrose Wathen, a monk of Saint Joseph's Abbey in Saint Benedict, Louisiana, refers to the selection of sayings that I choose for reading here at Saint Gregory's as 'The Aelred Collection'.

There is, then, not one collection of sayings and stories, but there are many collections, probably, the scholars say, edited not in Egypt but in Palestine several generations later to preserve the wisdom of the 'Golden Age'—and possibly to edit out elements that might be considered too much influenced by the thought of Origen and therefore heretical. For this collection of daily readings from the desert fathers, Tim Vivian has mined, in addition to the *Sayings*, most of the other significant sources,, including *The Life of Antony*, Evagrius Ponticus' *Praktikos*, Pachomius, and Isaiah of Scetis.

Many of these stories have the nature of peasant wisdom, whether originally or through judicious editing (or some combination of both), and the result is a collection of pithy insights which can cut through all our pretense and rationalizations and get to the core of what living the Gospel is all about. These desert ascetics regard self-awareness as similar to the 'mindfulness' to which Buddhists refer. Repeatedly they return to the importance of paying attention to what you are doing or to your thoughts and where they are leading you. To them 'discernment' means an immediate awareness of what is going on right now. Thus these sayings have been compared to zen koans—and one selection of sayings has been published with zen style illustrations which seem very appropriate.

Just as the monks in the desert passed on stories and the monks in Japan passed on stories, monks today still pass on stories. Spend social time with any monastic community and eventually you will hear about what Father or Sister or Brother or Mother So-and-So said or did. Frequently the stories are humorous, but almost always they will have some larger point, implicit or explicit. If the story is passed along in a private session, there will always be an important point, although the listener may not immediately discern it.

Many of these stories are not generally applicable to all pilgrims on the way. Their origin lies in a special relationship between a master and a disciple and the insights they provide were applied to an understanding of where that particular person was on the spiritual journey. On the other hand, some of the stories get repeated precisely because they seem appropriate in a new setting. In sermons or conferences or conversations I frequently say, 'As my Vocation Director told me, "People are different", but we keep acting as if everyone were like ourselves', or 'My Novice Master once told me never to let anyone else control my monastic vocation', or 'Abbot Benedict used to say, "If I were God, I wouldn't do things this way," or 'Brother Wilfrid always used to say, "They keep changing things!"' And sometimes I have even heard myself being quoted and, although, like as not, it is advice that I don't remember actually having given, it doesn't matter. If it helps someone, that is enough.

The sayings and stories gathered in this volume from the first monastics of the desert have a directness that makes them highly appropriate for the 'temporary monks' participating in our Summer Vocation Program to take in and reflect on. Of course, Saint Benedict was right in recommending these sayings to his monks, and it is good for members of the monastic community themselves to hear these stories again and again and ponder what they really mean about the way we live our lives.

But another reason that monks tell stories is that it is a way of passing along good advice without taking credit for it oneself, and thus telling stories is an exercise in that important monastic virtue, humility.

It is said that the devil once appeared to a brother in the guise of an angel of light, and said to him, 'I am the angel Gabriel and I have been sent to you'. The brother said to him, however, 'See if you aren't being sent to someone else. I certainly do not deserve to have an angel sent to me'. Immediately the devil disappeared.

A brother questioned Abba Poemen, saying, 'If I see my brother committing a sin, is it right to conceal it?' The old man replied, 'At the very moment we hide our brother's fault, God hides our own and at the moment we reveal our brother's fault, God reveals ours too.'

17

These stories can be extremely disconcerting for those who define morality as lists of right and wrong actions or who see monastic—or christian—life as a list of rules. For the early monks, knowing what you are doing seems to be more important than what you actually do. They teach that sin is a distortion of our ability to see things as they really are. This means that the first step in overcoming our sinfulness is an honest perception of the facts. A good illustration of this is one of my favorite Desert Father stories.

> It was said of Abba Ammonas that his goodness advanced to the point that he could no longer judge others. After he became a bishop, Abba Ammonas was visiting the other monks and there was a brother whom the other brothers hated. The monks, having heard that a woman had entered the brother's cell, gathered to punish him and asked Abba Ammonas to join them. Hearing them coming, the brother hid the woman in a large cask. Abba Ammonas, entering first, saw the cask, the only place that the woman could be concealed, and immediately sat down on top of the cask while the monks diligently searched the cell. When they had discovered nothing, Abba Ammonas rebuked them, saying, ' What have you done? May God forgive you!' and, after prayer, ordered them from the cell. After they had gone he went up to the brother and, taking him by the hand, said, 'Brother, have a care for yourself'. So saying, he departed.

Notice the different elements described or implied: the brother really does have a woman in his cell; but the other monks already hate their brother and somebody is bearing tales—gossip is the bane of all community. The focus of the story is not on sinful acts but on an habitual refusal to confront what one is actually doing—and this applies not only to the brother but to the other monks as well. One of the anonymous sayings is applicable here: 'Unawareness is the root of all evil' These monastics distrusted a pious spirituality detached from exterior reality. Any attempt at growth in the spiritual life that does not have a firm foundation of realistic self-understanding is always going to be prey to self-deception and illusion. Abba John the Little said, 'If you see a young man going up to heaven by his own will, grab his leg and pull him down again'.

Then there is the story of a young novice who was full of doubts; so he went to Abba Paphnutius who said to him, 'Stay in your cell and say one prayer in the morning and one prayer in the evening and one prayer at night. When you are hungry, eat. When you are thirsty, drink. When you are sleepy, sleep. And remain in the desert.' Well, this sort of common sense practical advice was not the magical mysticism that the novice wanted to hear, so he went to Abba John, who said, 'Don't bother trying to pray, just stay in your cell'. So the novice went to Abba Arsenius who told him just to do what he was told.

Thomas Merton once summarized the counsel of the Desert Fathers as 'Shut up and go to your cell!' and added, 'Now that's spiritual direction!' Notice that the concern and insight of these teachers is that the great temptation will be to come up with some reason to justify leaving.

At stake here is honesty, and not honesty in the abstract, but honesty about ourselves: who we are; what we can do; and what we can't do. How much food do I need? How much sleep? What is harmful self-neglect? What is harmful self-indulgence? We kid ourselves if we pretend that the answers to these questions are easy or obvious. Staying alone in your cell is being stuck with yourself and getting to know who you really are. It is no wonder that we spend so much of our time looking for distractions. Many of us do not really know ourselves and we suspect that if we did, we might not like what we find.

There is an anti-mystical strain in many of these desert stories from *The Lives of the Desert Fathers*. They have very little to say about experiences in prayer and—unlike the *Life of Anthony*—no graphic descriptions of struggles with demons. When an important visitor came to see Abba Poemen and immediately started talking about spiritual things, Abba Poemen had nothing to say to him—all he knew about were his own struggles against his own sinfulness. The same Abba Poemen was asked by a novice, 'How

19

do the demons fight against me?' and the elder answered, 'Our own wills become the demons and rise against us and attack us so we may overcome them'.

Many people have reacted against the ascetic tradition of the desert, thinking it excessive and an indication that the monks were trying to win their salvation. And it is true that there are stories about some extreme penances that the monks imposed on themselves. But the Elders were well aware of this problem. This is why Saint Benedict writes that any lenten observance a monk wishes to adopt must be approved by the abbot, 'lest it be attributed to vainglory'. And the Sayings always condemn excessive asceticism, preferring instead the humble heart. Abba Pambo said, 'If you have a heart, you can be saved', and having a heart is a quality not restricted to monastics.

Heretofore Tim Vivian has been known primarily as a scholar by other scholars as well as monastics, the same people who have been the primary students of the wisdom of the Desert. With *Becoming Fire*, you now hold in your hand, dear reader, something different: a collection of sayings not for historical study by scholars or emulation by cloistered monastics, but a day by day selection of readings from a wide variety of sources intended for regular reflection by everyone. I pray that these sayings will be as great a source of blessing to people in every walk of life as they have been in my own life as a monastic.

Aelred Glidden OSB

Saint Gregory's Abbey
Three Rivers, Michigan

INTRODUCTION

S OME YEARS AGO, on my first trip to Egypt, part of my responsibilities was to teach a course on Early Egyptian Monasticism. Almost all of my students were from conservative Evangelical Christian colleges. At our first class, I asked the students what they knew or—big mistake—thought about monks and monasticism. One young woman confidently told us that monasticism was 'the work of the Devil'. I knew then that this was going to be a tough crowd. I wondered why that student had come to an archeological dig in the Wadi al-Natrun (ancient Scetis) whose main purpose was to excavate and find out more about things monastic. She did, however, prompt—inspire, terrify—me into rethinking how on earth I was going to teach that course.

For our next session, I decided that instead of meeting as a 'class' and taking the usual classroom approach, we would gather in a small upstairs chapel. Since we were staying in a dormitory outside Deir Anba Bishoy, one of the most venerable, and still very active, monasteries in Egypt, the chapel was decorated in Coptic Orthodox fashion, replete with icons (a.k.a. 'idols' to some of my students). Our text for the day was *The Sayings of the Desert Fathers*—the translation used for this volume.

Instead of having us discuss the sayings as in a classroom setting, I had asked the students to read some of the book meditatively (I didn't give a page assignment; I just said 'Read'); that is, to read for wisdom, not knowledge. I asked them to read *slowly*, ruminating (to borrow a metaphor used by Saint Macarius the Great in this volume) on each saying; when they found one that spoke to, challenged, comforted, shocked, caressed, alarmed them,

21

they were to stop reading and sit quietly, silently, with the ancient words from the desert. If they read just one saying and reflected deeply on it, that was okay. That suggestion would surely make students happy!

When we met for class, instead of sitting in the usual pedagogical chairs facing Teacher, we sat on the floor in a circle in the center of the chapel, blessed (*I* thought) by an icon of the Pantokrator. I asked if someone would read aloud a saying that particularly spoke to that person. After the student read the saying, I said, we would sit in silence. (I joked that if no one spoke, we would have a real monastic experience—an hour of silence.) When someone else felt called—not called upon—to offer a personal reflection on that saying or to read aloud another one, that person would do so. In some small way, then, we were emulating the silence and speech of the desert fathers and mothers who had lived at the site of that very monastery some sixteen hundred years ago, who gave us the beginnings of the Sayings of the Desert Fathers and Mothers, who bequeathed us the sanctuary and sustenance of early desert monasticism, and who, therefore, continue to spiritually live today, both in their descendents, the coptic monks of the Wadi al-Natrun and the monastics of all Christendom—and of all religions—and in those who continue to appreciate their spiritual and temporal struggles and triumphs.

The 'class', I'm happy to say, worked. That is, we shared the sayings of the desert fathers and mothers in a fashion similar to the way they originally did: reflectively, prayerfully, alone and in community. Instead of critiquing, challenging, and complaining (the monks are 'escapist', 'sexist', 'narcissistic') we listened; instead of being content with the suzerainty of wonderful and limited reason, we explored, as the poet says, 'deep down things', digging down to the fountain of divinity that the mystics rightly and rightfully say bubbles up within each of us. That fount aches to burst through the mud and debris of our quotidian horror shows to wash away not only our sins and offenses but also, and perhaps just as importantly, at least more often, our fears, worries, doubts, insecurities, self-loathings, and projections that lead to so much offense and sin.

This book, then, I hope, will be for its readers a replication writ daily of that classroom experience. More importantly, I hope it will be a modest re-living of the desert experience, the monastic experience, the distillations and training of the Daily Office (times during the day set aside for communal or private prayer, meditation, liturgy, and reflective reading). It shouldn't be read through quickly, in gulps, but slowly, daily, savored, as its readings, and the reader's reflections on those readings, flavor and influence and enhance the day. A quiet cup of excellent coffee with a friend, not a 64-ounce soft drink grabbed solo and on the go from a convenience store. Perhaps we should, in fact, think of monasticism and monastic spirituality as an *inconvenience* store, like the parables of Jesus a storehouse of inconveniencing questions and truths that confront our comfortable certitudes and lazy hypocrisies. As Douglas Burton-Christie has observed with regard to Scripture and the first monks, the relationship between reader and text is symbiotic: the text influences and shapes the reader and the reader shapes and influences the text. Just as important, the reader *lives* the text. The text lives *through* the reader.

But why monasticism? Especially why the desert fathers and mothers? The latter question first: the desert mothers and fathers because, partly, they started it all—not the ascetic impulse, which lies within the Hebrew Bible and the New Testament (and, indeed, within many of the world's religions), but the specifically monastic impulse, organized asceticism, as it were (though some monks I know, living and dead, would call 'organized asceticism' an oxymoron). Contrary to some misshapen and atavistic ideologies, this does not mean that origins, whether in Buddhism, Christianity, Islam, or the United States Constitution, are inviolable and sacrosanct, offering one and only one 'original interpretation' (there is, in fact, no such thing). It means that those christian monks at the origins—the original margins—were attempting something new and groundbreaking—and breathtaking, living out the Gospel, not for the first or last time, but nakedly, to and at the bone. As Jerome of Jerusalem, a canonized and curmudgeonly monk, famously said, *sequere nudus nudum Christum*: 'Follow, naked, the naked Christ'.

There is a startling scene in the epic Inuit film *The Fast Runner* in which Atanarjuat, whose brother has just been savagely and cowardly murdered in his sleep, flees their attackers, naked across the frozen winter wastes of northern Canada. The filmmakers and actors, to their credit, do not fig leaf his flight: they show him naked, front and back, for a long time, close up, running for his life, framed against the vast white expanse of snow and sky, slipping on the ice, falling into frozen waters, leaving bloody footprints on the pristine snow.

In many ways, the desert mothers and fathers are like Atanarjuat: they are fleeing (withdrawing: in Greek *anachorein* > *anachoresis* > anchorite) from what they believed to be, both metaphorically and literally, a murderous world, even—horrible to say—a murderous Church; desperately, quietly, looking for sanctuary in the white expanses of the egyptian desert. Atanarjuat does eventually find shelter with another Inuit family, who hide him beneath a pile of seaweed. One of his trackers, his brother's murderer, not suspecting his prey's whereabouts, even takes a piss (the translated word used in the film) on the pile of seaweed sheltering Atanarjuat. That is a scene in the film that the ancient monks would appreciate, both for its jagged humor and its potential for incipient tragedy.

When Atanarjuat returns to his people, he does not—like Odysseus, like the many heroes of modern popular american revenge movies—kill his brother's murderers. In this way, like Jesus, he subverts the ancient and modern myth of the avenging hero. Through a clever, odyssean, ruse, Atanarjuat traps his three attackers in an igloo—but instead of killing them, he cries out, 'This killing must stop!' The killing does stop. *The Fast Runner* both subverts and enhances the hero story: after a council, the tribe strips the killer of his chieftainship, symbolized by a necklace of white animal teeth, sends him into exile, and bestows the necklace on Atanarjuat.

Like the desert monks, Atanarjuat has fled naked into an initially dangerous but now restored world, a world he has helped revivify. Since the desert monks lived in a desert and biblical world, their visions of restoration—unlike those of Atanarjuat, but like those in the Qur'an—are of fruit-bearing oases, renewed and restored Edens. But the two worlds, of desert and ice, though disparate and worlds apart, are alike in that both imagine and embody, literally, the restoration of Adam and Eve's lost paradise.

Atanarjuat brings, or restores, peace, harmony, reconciliation, forgiveness, and love to his tribe. But as Archbishop Desmond Tutu, reflecting on the horrors of apartheid in South Africa, wisely said about the post-apartheid healing he helped bring about, 'How could anyone really think that true reconciliation could avoid a proper confrontation?' Atanarjuat must confront his attackers, as Buddha confronted the renegade elephant set on him by his jealous brother, as Jesus confronted seemingly everyone, even, at the end, himself, in his own fears of death. Monks, both ancient and modern, and all those, of any religion, who seek to flee the world's many, often seductive, deaths in order to find peace, must face similar confrontations—with the hope, the belief, the faith, the practice, of eventual reconciliation.

So why do we focus on monks? Because monastics, whether robed or not, whether cloistered or not, by fleeing the enemy, in fact, regroup to confront him face-to-face.

After 9/11, both in the West and in the East, we have all too often made the enemy alien to ourselves, 'other'—and only other. The cartoon-strip character Pogo famously said, 'We have met the enemy and he is us'. Monastic spirituality knows this. The enemy, as our myriad conflicts show, is ourselves: our fear, our fears, our self-centeredness, our racism, our xenophobia, our bloody thirst for revenge. Monastics like the desert fathers and mothers confront their enemies, their demons both external and internal, and in doing so, restore, at least in faith, paradise. The resultant reconciliation, offered in the pages of this volume, teaches quiet withdrawal from the world's mad frenzies and trappings, peace, prayer and work as a loving couple (not, as for most of us, divorced from each other), humility, hospitality, simplicity, care for others, real community, and, finally, union with God. These, I believe, are worthy virtues (to use a monastic term); they are qualities, practices, to embrace, to learn, to grow into, and to let 'form' us (another monastic term).

This book has numerous predecessors back, at least, to the *catenae*, or chains, of the patristic and medieval age that gathered together excerpts—usually organized thematically—from the Bible or the Church Fathers. Two modern anthologies arranged for daily reading sit on my desk as I write: *Drinking from the Hidden Fountain: A Patristic Breviary. Ancient Wisdom for Today's World,* edited by Thomas Spidlik (Cistercian Publications), and *Blessings of the Daily: A Monastic Book of Days* (Ligouri/Triumph), edited by Brother Victor-Antoine d'Avila-Latourette—who also writes wonderful monastic cookbooks! One I have at home is *Through the Year with Thomas Merton: Daily Meditations from His Writings* edited by Thomas P. McDonnell (Galilee Trade).

In *Blessings of the Daily*, Brother Victor-Antoine offers a brief monastic quotation at the top of each day's page, and then his own, longer, reflections. In *Drinking from the Hidden Fountain*, Thomas Spidlik lets the texts speak for themselves each day. With this volume I have followed the second example, not because of sloth but because of humility and honest awareness: whatever I could possibly say could not even come close to what the desert mothers and fathers have to offer. So I have let them, in condensed form, speak for themselves.

All translation involves interpretation. In the case of the present volume, most—I won't credit myself with 'all'—organization involves interpretation. For the most part, I have chosen sayings and stories that speak to me—as a person of faith, as a teacher of many religious traditions, as an experienced reader in monasticism, as a journeyman translator of ancient monastic texts, and as one who has tried to emulate many of early monasticism's virtues. I have placed many—not all—sayings according to the themes of the seasons of the Church calendar; some sayings match up with selected feast days in Coptic Orthodox, Greek Orthodox, Russian Orthodox, Roman Catholic, Anglican, and Monastic, calendars.[1] Some sayings and stories share themes on the page; others do not.

---

[1] These calendars vary somewhat from place to place–e.g. the Roman Catholic calendar has some commemorations observed only in the American Church, and the calendars of the Church of England and The Episcopal Church are not identical.

My only hope is that my considerable years of living with the desert fathers and mothers have given me some ability, and some license, to speak for them, at least organizationally.

Some of these sayings and stories continue to amaze me with their wisdom and prescience; others startle me into saying 'Are you kidding me?' I have indeed passed over—omitted—some sayings and stories from the early desert monastics that strike me as abusive, either of self or of others. I don't agree with everything in this volume. For example, I get queasy over the early monastic delight in detailing the punishments of hell. (That said, I've long insisted in my translations of early monastic works that we capitalize the word 'Devil'. We can debate the physical or mythical or psychological or spiritual nature of the Devil, but by capitalizing the noun, we acknowledge—even if we do not accept—the early monastic understanding of the reality of evil.) I hope the sayings here startle, perplex, confront, challenge, anger. I also hope they quiet, soothe, comfort, relieve, hearten, encourage, and embolden. (Note that there are more verbs in the second group.) Maybe some sayings will do both. Each reader must decide.

The early monks, at least the anchorites (solitaries) and semi-anchorites who dominate these pages, were rarely programmatic and legalistic. The abbas and ammas (fathers and mothers) tailored the cut of each saying ('cut' meant several ways) to the individual disciple. Some apophthegms—sayings—in the Sayings of the Desert Fathers, like some passages in the Bible and the Qur'an, contradict one another. So too do some of the sayings in this volume. This book is not a Systematic Theology; there are plenty of those. But there is not, at least in English to my knowledge, a volume of early monastic sayings and stories like this one that offers the reader each day what Sister Joan Chittister calls 'wisdom distilled from the daily'.

Since the Church calendar and 'secular' calendar operate differently, I have tried to organize this volume by both. So, for example, although Advent is the beginning of the Church year, that season usually falls in December, so in this volume December is 'December/Advent/Christmas/Christmastide', a patchwork quilt of one secular and three ecclesiastical seasons; April is 'April/Lent/Easter'.

27

And so on. Such a system is not perfect, as, for example, when the final days of the Pentecost season fall in early December, or when Lent falls in March. The system used in this volume may be slightly cumbersome, but it will, I hope, allow readers to proceed by using the book according to either the secular or the sacred calendar. I have also added an Appendix with the major movable feasts: Ash Wednesday, Lent, Holy Week, Easter, and Pentecost.

Although the subtitle of this book is 'Through the Year with the Desert Fathers and Mothers', the sad reality is that there just aren't very many ammas, or mothers, in this volume. This reflects the dearth of women's sayings extant in the early written monastic tradition. Although we know of monasteries of women—apparently some of considerable size in Late Antiquity in Egypt—history and tradition have not left us much testimony from or about those women called to live the monastic life in the late roman period. The name *Apophthegmata Patrum*, 'The Sayings of the Desert Fathers', is reasonably accurate: only three *mothers*—Syncletica, Sarah, and Theodora—thrive and speak in its pages. The world of the desert fathers, at least the one bequeathed to us, was a man's world. I have been able to add some stories about female ascetics and monks, but the book, as far as our ability to hear women's voices, is admittedly still 'out of joint'.

Partly because of this imbalance and partly because we do not live in the Late Antique monastic world (roughly 300-600 CE) but must inhabit our own, I have decided to use inclusive language to a greater extent than the sources themselves. Wherever possible, I have used 'person', 'persons', or 'people' instead of 'man' and 'men'; instead of 'he who', I have used 'the one who', 'the person who', 'someone who', and 'anyone who' (Latin and Greek have generic terms for the human person—*homo, anthrōpos*—in distinction to a male—*vir, anēr*. In many languages, too, the masculine pronoun becomes generic unless there is reference to a specific male person.) This means that, in accordance with the policy of Cistercian Publications and with many today in academia and within and without the Church, and following my own inclinations, I have silently modified many of the translations used here—both those by myself and by others—to be inclusive. I have not, however, changed the masculine pronouns for 'God', nor have I, for the most part, attempted to change masculine pronouns referring to monks. The choice was 1) to make many nouns plural and thus avoid singular pronouns, 2) to use the cumbersome 'he/she', 'him/her', or 's/he', or, 3) like a good archeologist, to leave many masculine pronouns *in situ*. I have chosen the last option. Not all readers will like this compromise but, as an experienced translator, I think it best honors the texts. As I tell my students with regard to the Bible, our job now is to deal with these texts.

A Glossary at the end of the book defines many names and terms used in the translations. Some words, such as 'anchorite' or 'ascetic' may be familiar to some readers but not to others. Other terms, such as 'the Enemy' or 'the Deceitful One' for Satan, may be clear from context but are still glossed. More problematic are those words that have particularly monastic resonances and, therefore, slightly or completely different meanings from everyday use, such as: 'passion/s', 'movement', 'the world', or 'old man/men'. If a word or term doesn't quite make sense—or makes no sense— consult the Glossary.

And finally, titles for the sayings and stories are my own. A List of Sources at the end of the book following Abbreviations, Sources, and Bibliography gives the source for each saying or story. The feast days beneath the dates are commemorations observed on the calendars of the Coptic Orthodox (CO), Orthodox (O), specifically Greek Orthodox (GO) or Russian Orthodox (RO), Roman Catholic (RC), and Anglican/Episcopal (A) Churches, with additions from specifically Monastic (M) calendars. A Word Index and Scripture Index will, I hope, help readers find sayings they want to retrieve.

I welcome readers' comments: tvivian@csub.edu.

T.V.

Bakersfield, California
On the feast of Martin Luther King, Jr., 2008

JANUARY

CHRISTMASTIDE / EPIPHANY

THE MONK IS A DOVE

Question: What does the monk try to do?

Answer: The monk is a dove: when it's time for a dove to fly it spreads its wings and flies, but if it remains outside its nest too long it's set upon by wild birds and loses its dignity and beauty. It's the same with a monk: there comes a time for him at the public assembly to 'give wing' to his thoughts, but if he remains outside his cell too long he's set upon by the demons and his thoughts are darkened.

OBSERVE THE WATER

Someone related that three spiritual brothers, *philoponoi*, became monks. The first chose to bring peace to those who were fighting, according to what is proclaimed in Scripture: *Blessed are the peacemakers.*[1] The second chose to *visit the sick*,[2] while the third went away to live a life of contemplative quiet *in the desert*.[3] Although the first labored mightily to resolve conflicts between people, he was unable to remedy all of them. Discouraged, he went to see the one who was ministering to the sick; he found him dispirited and not even close to having *fulfilled the commandment*.[4] The two of

[1] Mt 5:9.
[2] See Mt 25:36.
[3] See Mk 1:35.
[4] See Mt 25:36.

them agreed: they went to see the hermit, told him their sorrows, and urged him to tell them what he had accomplished.

After remaining silent a short while, the hermit put water in a basin and said to them, 'Observe the water'. It was disturbed. A short time later he again said to them, 'Observe that the water is now calm'. When they looked closely at the water, they observed their own faces as if looking in a mirror. Finally he said to them, 'It is the same with someone in the midst of people. On account of disturbances, he does not see his own sins, but when he has contemplative quiet, especially in the desert, then he sees his own defects'.

January 2

NATIVITY OF TAKLA HYMENOT THE ETHIOPIAN (CO)
BASIL THE GREAT AND GREGORY NAZIANZEN,
BISHOPS AND DOCTORS (RC)

LOVING OTHERS

A brother went to Abba Matoës and said to him, 'How is it that the monks of Scetis did more than the Scriptures required in loving their enemies more than themselves?'

Abba Matoës said to him, 'As for me, I have not yet managed to love those who love me as I love myself'.

LIVING AND DEAD THOUGHTS

When Abba Cyrus of Alexandria was asked about the thought of fornication, he answered this way: 'If you do not have thoughts, you have no hope; if you do not have thoughts, you are doing it.

That is, whoever does not marshal his spirit against sin and oppose it physically will commit sexual sin. To be sure, whoever is actually committing sexual sin is not bothered by thoughts'.

So the old man asked the brother, 'Isn't it your habit to talk with women?'

The brother said, 'No, my thoughts paint old and new pictures of them: memories are what bother me, images of women'.

The old man said to him, 'Do not fear the dead but rather flee the living'.

January 3

WALK IN POVERTY

Walk in poverty and an unencumbered life, without worries and needs, and you will remain at peace.

Therefore, my son, since poverty and need are holdovers from passion, not worrying about these things is what saves a person.

HOW ACTING MERCIFULLY IS POWERFUL

A brother asked Abba Macarius, 'I want to know: how is acting mercifully powerful?'

Abba Macarius said to him, 'If the king banishes some men to a foreign and distant country, one of them acquires wisdom and counsel from those in authority; he grows powerful and sends gifts to that king, but the others do not do likewise. After a long time the king sends for those men and has them returned to their city and country. Will not the one who sent presents to the king rejoice more than the others because he will be made their champion? Will he not find greater freedom of speech than those who sent nothing at all? Does a commander-in-chief not have freedom of speech before the king of this world? So it is with mercy before Christ, the great king: it has great freedom of speech before him and offers a defense against everyone who accuses it'.

January 4
ELIZABETH ANN SETON (RC)[5]

THE CITY AND THE DESERT

Amma Syncletica said, 'Many of those living in a monastic community act like those living in cities and are lost while many of those living in cities do the works of the desert and are saved. Indeed, it is possible to live with a multitude and still be solitary in spirit just as it is possible to live as a solitary while one's thoughts are with the crowd'.

PLACING ONE'S FAITH IN GOD

One time a brother asked Abba Macarius, 'Tell me, my father, what is it to throw oneself down before God?'

---

[5] American Church calendar.

Abba Macarius said to him, '*It is written that our Lord did not speak to people except in parables.*[6] So, if an irrational wild beast leaps upon a domesticated animal and stands over it with great ferocity so that the animal beneath it weakly cowers before it, all its strength and hope depend on its master and it cries out in a loud voice, signaling to its master. If its master hears it, then he quickly takes pity on it and runs and helps it and saves it from being destroyed by the wild beast. If the master of this irrational animal takes pity on it and hurries until he saves it from the wild beast, then how much more is it true for us, the rational sheep of Christ's flock? If we put our faith in him, he will not allow the Enemy to do violence to us but will send his angel to us to save us from the Devil. Therefore, my children, throwing oneself down before God is when a person does not trust in his own strength alone but places his faith in the help of God, for it is he who saves us'.

January 5
SYNCLETICA, AMMA (O)
JOHN NEUMANN, BISHOP (RC)[7]

MAKE AN EFFORT AND PRAY TO GOD

A brother said to Abba Antony, 'Pray for me'.

The old man said to him, 'I will have no mercy upon you, nor will God have any, if you yourself do not make an effort and if you do not pray to God'.

[6] See Mt 13:14.
[7] American Church calendar.

37

WHAT I HAVE HEARD ABOUT YOU IS TRUE

Before Abba Poemen's group came to Scetis, there was an old man in Egypt who enjoyed considerable fame and repute. But when Abba Poemen's group went up to Scetis, men left the old man to go to see Abba Poemen. Abba Poemen was grieved at this and said to his disciples, 'What is to be done about this great old man, for people grieve him by leaving him and coming to us who are nothing? What shall we do, then, to comfort this old man?' He said to them, 'Make ready a little food and take a skin of wine, and let us go to see him and eat with him. And so we shall be able to comfort him'. So they put together some food, and went.

When they knocked at the door the old man's disciple answered, saying, 'Who are you?'

They responded, 'Tell the abba it is Poemen who desires to be blessed by him'.

The disciple reported this and the old man sent him to say, 'Go away. I have no time'.

But in spite of the heat they persevered, saying, 'We shall not go away till we have been allowed to meet the old man'.

Seeing their humility and patience, the old man was filled with compunction and opened the door to them. Then they went in and ate with him. During the meal he said, 'Truly, not only what I have heard about you is true, but I see that your works are a hundred-fold greater', and from that day, he became their friend.

ANTONY EMERGES, AS THOUGH FROM A SHRINE, INITIATED INTO DIVINE MYSTERIES AND INSPIRED BY GOD

Those friends who came to see Abba Antony, since he would not allow them to come inside the abandoned barracks he was living in, often remained outside day and night. They heard what sounded like mobs of people creating a ruckus and crashing around inside, letting loose their pitiful voices and crying out, 'Get away from what belongs to us! What are you doing in the desert? You will not be able to endure our connivings!'

Those outside at first thought some people who had gotten inside by means of ladders were in there fighting with him, but when they knelt down to look through a hole in the wall, they did not see anyone. At that point, realizing that the people inside were demons, they got scared, and started calling to Antony. Antony remained there, and suffered no harm from the demons, nor did he tire of struggling against them. For the increasing number of visions that came into his mind and the weakness of his enemies gave him great relief from his sufferings and provided him with even greater zeal.

Antony spent almost twenty years alone practicing his ascetic discipline this way, neither going out, nor being often seen by anyone. After awhile, many people yearned for his way of life and wished seriously to follow his ascetic practice, while others, his friends, came and forcibly tore down his door and forced him to come out. Antony emerged as though from some shrine, having been initiated into divine mysteries and inspired by God.

This was the first time that he came out of the barracks and appeared to those who came to see him. When those people saw him, therefore, they were amazed to see that his body had maintained

39

its natural condition, being neither fat from lack of exercise nor weakened from fasting and fighting with demons; they found him just as they had known him before his withdrawal. The character of his soul was pure, for it had neither been contracted by suffering nor dissipated by pleasure, nor had it been afflicted by laughter or sorrow. Moreover, when Antony saw the crowd, he was not bothered, nor did he rejoice at so many people greeting him. Instead, like someone guided by reason, he maintained his equilibrium and natural balance.

January 7
RAYMOND OF PENYAFORT, PRIEST (RC)

I NO LONGER FEAR GOD

Abba Antony said, 'I no longer fear God, but I love him. For *love casts out fear*'.[8]

THE COMPASSION OF CHRIST

Abba Macarius said, 'While we were still sitting in the cave one time, I heard a voice crying out like the voice of a falcon, and when I went outside I saw a huge serpent. When it saw me, it bent its neck and venerated me and afterwards it raised itself and turned its face toward me. When I looked at it, I saw that there

[8] Jn 4:18.

was something lodged in its right eye. When I thought about the compassion of my Lord Jesus Christ and the invincible power of the cross, I put some spittle on the serpent's face while saying, "My Lord Jesus Christ, *who opened the eyes of the man born blind*, have pity on this beast's infirmity and heal it".[9] When I said this, the fragment fell from its eye and after it bent its neck three times it kissed my feet and so I dismissed it. It left, giving glory to our Lord Jesus Christ for his numerous acts of compassion, for he even cares about wild beasts'.

January 8
THE ADORATION OF THE MAGI (CO)
GEORGE OF CHOZIBA, MONK (O)

DEATH AND LIFE, MONEY AND CHARITY

Just as death and life cannot be shared in at the same time, so also is it impossible for charity to exist in anyone along with money. For charity not only gets rid of money but even of this present life itself.

THEY WERE ALL EATING HONEY CAKES

It was told of a brother who came to see Abba Arsenius at Scetis that, when he came to the church, he asked the clergy if he could visit Abba Arsenius.

[9] Jn 9.

They said to him, 'Brother, have a little refreshment and then go see him'.

'I shall not eat anything', said he, 'till I have met him'.

So, because Arsenius' cell was far away, they sent a brother with him. Having knocked on the door, they entered, greeted the old man and sat down without saying anything.

Then the brother from the church said, 'I will leave you. Pray for me'.

Now the visiting brother, not feeling at ease with the old man, said, 'I will come with you', and they went away together.

Then the visitor asked, 'Take me to Abba Moses, who used to be a robber'.

When they arrived the Abba welcomed them joyfully and then took leave of them with delight. The brother who had brought the one said to his companion, 'See, I have taken you to the foreigner and to the Egyptian. Which of the two do you prefer?'

'As for me', he replied, 'I prefer the Egyptian'.

Now a father who heard this prayed to God, saying, 'Lord, explain this matter to me: for your name's sake the one flees from people, and the other, for your name's sake, receives them with open arms'.

Then two large boats were shown to him on a river and he saw Abba Arsenius and the Spirit of God sailing in the one, in perfect peace; and in the other was Abba Moses with the angels of God, and they were all eating honey cakes.

MAKING ONESELF A STRANGER

Abba Macarius also said, 'The monk who causes anger makes himself a stranger; the monk who causes his brother pain in anything makes himself a stranger'.

THE PERSON WHO SHED HIS SKIN LIKE A SNAKE

One time when our father Abba John the Little was heading out to the harvest there was brought to him for healing a person whose skin was completely pulled away with leprosy. Our father Abba John prayed over water in the name of Christ and poured it on the man, who shed his skin like a snake, and his previous color returned to him, and the man was cured and glorified God.

January 10
GREGORY OF NYSSA (O)

A LITTLE BIT OF ALL THE VIRTUES

A brother asked Abba Poemen, saying, 'Can a person put his trust in one single work?'

The old man said to him that Abba John the Little said, 'I would rather have a bit of all the virtues'.

MAKE FRIENDS WITH BULLIES

A brother going to market asked Abba Poemen, 'How do you advise me to behave?'

The old man said to him, 'Make friends with anyone who tries to bully you and sell your produce in peace'.

NO EXCUSES

The time of temptation is not the time to leave one's cell, devising plausible pretexts. Rather, stand there firmly and be patient. Bravely take all that the demon brings upon you. Indeed, to flee and to shun such conflicts schools the spirit in awkwardness, cowardice, and fear.

January 11

DIAMONDS ON THE SOLES OF HER SHOES

Blessed Melania talked to me one time about Abba Pambo: When I first arrived in Alexandria from Rome, Abba Isidore the priest told me about the virtues of Abba Pambo, and I begged him to lead me into the desert to where Abba Pambo lived so I could see him. And when he brought me to the monastic community, he spoke with him and took me further to the interior where he lived. When I threw myself to the ground and prostrated myself before him, he had me sit down. He himself was sitting and working with palm leaves. I opened my bag and gave him a silver chest with three hundred silver coins inside. I begged him to look inside and enjoy for himself some of my wealth. But he sat plaiting palm leaves, absorbed in his handiwork, nor did he raise his eyes to look at me, but instead spoke to me in a quiet voice: 'May the Lord bless you for your troubles and reward you in heaven'. And he spoke to me again: 'Put it on the windowsill'.

He called Theodore, his steward, and said to him, 'This woman has brought this for the stewardship of God; therefore take it and go, spend it, distribute it among the monks of the Cells and in Libya and among the brothers living in the rocks and on the islands, for those monasteries are poorer than all the others'. He ordered him: 'Do not distribute it among the monasteries of Egypt, because those other places', he said, 'have more physical needs than do the ones in Egypt'.

'As for me', she said, 'I stood there, expecting that he would perhaps honor me or praise me, and I didn't hear a single word from him. I said to him, "My father, I wish to inform you—so you know—that there are three hundred pounds of silver there".

'But he did not lift his head from his work but said to me in a firm voice: "He to whom you have given them knows their number; he doesn't need anyone to weigh them for him. He who 'weighs the mountains in a scale and the hills in a balance' *is not ignorant of the weight of this silver.*[10] Indeed, if you had given the money to me, then you'd do well to inform me about it, since I am a human being. But if you give the money to God, then there is no need to tell me. God, *who accepted the two small coins from the widow,*[11] will accept your offering too. As for yourself, be silent; do not boast". In this fashion, then, God set me at ease and I left him'.

From there she went into the great desert of Scetis and built a church for Abba Isidore the priest.

[10] Is 40:12.
[11] Mk 12:42.

45

I PUT HIS HEAD ON MY KNEES

Some old men came to see Abba Poemen and said to him, 'When we see brothers who are dozing at the synaxis, shall we rouse them so they will be watchful?'

He said to them, 'For my part, when I see a brother who is dozing, I put his head on my knees and let him rest'.

THOSE WHO ARE WITH US

It happened that Abba Moses was struggling with the temptation of fornication. Unable to stay any longer in the cell, he went and told Abba Isidore. The old man exhorted him to return to his cell. But he refused, saying, 'Abba, I cannot'.

Then Abba Isidore took Moses out onto the terrace and said to him, 'Look towards the west'.

Moses looked and saw hordes of demons flying about and making a noise before launching an attack.

Then Abba Isidore said to him, 'Look towards the east'.

Moses turned and saw an innumerable multitude of holy angels shining with glory.

Abba Isidore said, 'See, these are sent by the Lord to the saints to bring them help, while those in the west fight against them. Those who are with us are more in number than they are'.

Then Abba Moses gave thanks to God, plucked up courage, and returned to his cell.

TEACH YOUR MOUTH

Abba Poemen said, 'Teach your mouth to say what is in your heart'.

THE PARABLE OF THE SHEEPFOLD

Abba Macarius the Great said, 'One time when I was passing through Egypt I came upon a sheepfold with some sheep in it. I saw a sheep outside the sheepfold that had given birth and a wolf came and snatched her offspring and she was weeping, saying, "Woe is me! If I had not been outside the sheepfold, the wolf would not have found me and snatched my lamb!"'

While he was marveling at what the sheep had said, the brothers who were travelling with him asked him the meaning of what the sheep had said. He responded, saying, 'There will come a time when the monks will abandon the deserts where they live and will gather together and become a numerous people. If someone gets separated from them, the spiritual wolf will snatch that person's offspring, that is, his spirit, and he will become more unfeeling than the stones and irrational things, like animals that have no reason. Whichever of the brothers looks for him pridefully and without consulting others will not find him, even though he is right in their midst'.

WE HAVE BEEN SET FREE FROM CARE

Abba Euprepius said, 'Bodily things are compounded of matter. The person who loves the world loves occasions for falling. Therefore, if we happen to lose something, we must accept this with joy and gratitude, realizing that we have been set free from care'.

WALKING HIS VILLAGE AT NIGHT

A brother settled outside his village and did not return there for many years. He said to the brothers, 'See how many years it is since I went back to the village, while you often go up there'.

This was told to Abba Poemen and the old man said, 'I used to go back up there at night and walk all around my village, so that the thought of not having gone up there would not cause me vainglory'.

I WILL NOT LEAVE YOU ALONE

Abraham, Abba Sisoë's disciple, was tempted one day by the Devil and the old man saw that he had given way. Standing up, he stretched his hands towards heaven, saying, 'God, whether you will, or whether you will not, I will not leave you alone till you have healed him', and immediately the brother was healed.

THE PRIEST AND THE OLD ADAM

A priest of Pelusia heard it said of some brothers that they often went to the city, took baths, and were careless in their behavior. He went to the synaxis, and took the habit away from them. Afterwards, his heart was moved, he repented, and went to see Abba Poemen, obsessed by his thoughts. He brought the monastic habits of the brothers and told him about it. The old man said to him, 'Don't you sometimes have something of *the old Adam* in you?'[12]

The priest said, 'I have my share of the old Adam'.

The abba said to him, 'Look, you are just like the brothers yourself; if you have even a little share of the old Adam, then you are subject to sin in the same way'.

So the priest went and called the brothers and asked their pardon; and he clothed them in the monastic habit again and let them go.

January 16

GOOD WORKS

A brother asked an old man, 'What good work is there that I can do and live by doing it?'

---

[12] See Rom 5:12-22, Eph 4:22.

The old man said, 'God knows what is good. But I heard that one of the fathers asked this question of Abba Nisterus the Great, the friend of Abba Antony, and said to him, "What good work is there that I can do?" And he said to him, "Aren't all works equal? Scripture says that *Abraham was a friend to strangers and God was with him,*[13] Elijah loved contemplative quiet and God was with him, and David was humble and God was with him. Therefore, do whatever you see your soul desiring to do in accordance with God's wishes and keep watch over your heart"'.

TROUBLED BY THOUGHTS

It was said of Abba Longinus that, because he was often troubled by thoughts telling him to leave for the desert, one day he said to his disciple, 'Please, brother, whatever I do, put up with it and don't speak to me this week'.

Taking a palm staff, he began to walk around in his small court-yard. When he got tired, he sat down for a little and, standing again, would walk around. When evening came, he said to the thought, 'Whoever walks around in the desert does not eat bread but rather plants; you, therefore, on account of your weakness, eat some cut up vegetables'.

Doing this, he once again said to the thought, 'Whoever lives in the desert does not sleep on a bed but rather in the open air; you, therefore, do likewise'. And, laying himself down, he slept in his small courtyard.

Doing this for three days, walking around in his monastic dwell-ing, each evening eating a few chicory leaves, and sleeping at night in the open air, he got tired of it. So rebuking the thought that was troubling him, he refuted it, saying, 'If you are not able to do the works of the desert, remain in your cell with patient endurance, weeping for your sins, and do not wander about, for the eye of

---

[13] Gen 18:1–8.

God always sees our works and nothing escapes him and he works
with those who work for the good'.

January 17
ANTONY, MONK IN EGYPT (O, RC, A, M)

LIFE AND DEATH

Abba Antony said, 'Our life and our death is with our neighbor.
If we gain our brother, we have gained God, but if we scandalise
our brother, we have sinned against Christ'.

ANTONY'S CALL

After the death of his parents Antony was left alone with a very small
sister, and when he was around eighteen or twenty years old he had
to care for his home and his sister. Not six months had passed after the
death of his parents when—as was his custom—on his way to church
he was thinking to himself and reflecting on all these things: how the
apostles gave up everything and followed the Saviour, and how those
in Acts *sold their possessions and brought them and placed them at the feet of
the apostles for distribution to those in need*.[14] He was thinking about what
sort or what kind of hope was laid up for them in heaven.

Pondering these things, he went into the church; it happened
that the Gospel was being read at that time and he heard the Lord

[14] See Acts 4:32.

saying to the rich man, '*If you want to be perfect, go, sell all your posses-*
sions and give to the poor, and come follow me, and you will have treasure
in heaven'.[15] When Antony received from God the remembrances of
the saints and realized how that passage had been read for his sake,
he immediately left the church, and the possessions that he had inherited from his ancestors (there were three hundred fertile and very
prosperous acres) he freely gave away to people from his village so
they would not bother him or his sister about anything. He sold all
his remaining possessions and, collecting a considerable amount of
money, distributed it among the poor, keeping a little for his sister.

When Antony entered the church again and heard the Lord
saying in the Gospel, *Do not be concerned about tomorrow*,[16] he could
no longer bear to remain there, so he left and distributed his remaining things among those less well off. His sister he entrusted
to well-known and faithful virgins, giving her to them to be raised
in virginity, while from that time on he devoted himself to ascetic
discipline in front of his home, watching over himself spiritually
and practicing patient endurance.

January 18
ATHANASIOS AND CYRIL, PATRIARCHS OF ALEXANDRIA (GO)
BEGINNING OF THE WEEK OF PRAYER FOR CHRISTIAN UNITY

IS IT GOOD TO PRAY?

A brother asked Abba Poemen, saying, 'Is it good to pray?'

[15] Mk 10:21.
[16] Mt 6:34.

The old man said that Abba Antony said, 'This word comes from the mouth of the Lord, who said, "*Comfort, comfort my people*"'.[17]

WALKING ALONE WITH GOD AT YOUR SIDE

Allow yourself only one out of a thousand as an advisor[18] and you will be at peace all the days of your life.

You shall test the teaching that you follow, walking alone with God at your side.

For Elijah was at the river Chorath alone, God was with him, and the raven ministered to him.[19]

The prophet was also walking alone; *he took Paul's belt and bound himself.*[20]

A spirit of God also snatched Philip away and he was found in Azotus.[21] *And we are also built upon the foundation of the apostles and the prophets.*[22]

Now, then, God will remain with you as you walk alone and he will look for you in your cell and mysteries of God will be revealed to you there *as they were to Cornelius in his house.*[23]

Therefore, if you wear poverty in this world and humility, *you will be with the Son of God in his kingdom.*[24]

[17] Is 40:1.
[18] Sir 6:6.
[19] See 1 Kings 17:1-7.
[20] See Acts 21:11.
[21] See Acts 8:39-40.
[22] See Eph 2:20.
[23] See Acts 10.
[24] Lk 23:42.

THE GRACE THAT THE CELL PROVIDES

Our Lord, *although he was very rich, became poor for our sakes,*[25] and if you receive the grace that the cell provides, you will reach God.

HOW A PERSON SHOULD CONDUCT HIMSELF

A brother asked Abba Antony, 'How should a person conduct himself?'

The old man said to him, 'Let us consider Daniel: *no accusation was brought against him except with regard to the service he gave to God'.*[26]

WHAT LOVE IS

One time Abba Daniel once again went up to Alexandria with his disciple and he saw a blind person sitting naked in the square and he

[25] See 2 Cor 8:9.
[26] Dan 6:5-6.

was saying 'Give me something; have pity'. And the old man said to his disciple, 'Do you see this blind man? I tell you he is a great man. Do you want me to show you what sort of person he is? Stay here'. The old man went and said to him, 'Please do me a favor, brother. I don't have the means to buy myself palm branches so I can work and feed myself', and the blind man said to him, 'Why are you looking at *me*, Abba? You see me naked and begging and you tell *me* to buy palm branches for *you*? Wait here, however'.

The old man motioned to his disciple to follow him and they went to Saint Mark's Outside-the-City, for the blind man had a cell there, and the blind man said to the old man, 'Wait here for me, Abba', and he went inside and brought to the old man a small basket containing raisins, pomegranates, and dried figs and he took out of his pocket a *tremissis* and gave it to the old man, saying, 'Pray for me, Abba'. The old man went to his disciple and wept, saying, 'Look! How many hidden servants God has! As the Lord lives, I will never turn my back on almsgiving because that is what love is'.

After they left him, a few days later they heard that the Great Steward was suffering terribly with a liver ailment and was lying in Saint Mark's and Saint Mark the apostle appeared to him and said to him, 'Send for the blind man and bring him here and he will place his hand on the spot where you are suffering and you will be well again'. So the Great Steward quickly sent his servants and brought the blind man by force. After the blind man prayed and placed his hands on the man, the suffering immediately went away and news of what had happened spread throughout the city.

When the pope heard about it, he went to see the blind man and found him perfected in the Lord and news of his death spread throughout Scetis. And the old man went up with his disciple and other fathers and they received a blessing from their blessed fellow-brother. And almost the whole city turned out and, receiving a blessing from him, with hymns and celebration they bore his precious corpse out for burial. Thus was his life: if he received any kind of alms, he would buy apples, raisins, and pomegranates from the poor and would distribute them through someone else among the foreigners to the sick every Sunday. He kept up this virtuous service for forty-eight years, to the glory of God.

AS LONG AS THE POT IS ON THE FIRE

A brother said to Abba Poemen, 'Give me a word', and he said to him, 'As long as the pot is on the fire, no fly or any other animal can get near it, but as soon as it is cold, these creatures get inside. So it is for the monk; as long as he lives in spiritual activities, the Enemy cannot find a means of overthrowing him'.

ABBA PAMBO TEACHES ABBA PIHOR A LESSON

Abba Pihor the ascetic, the disciple of Abba Antony, wanted to pay Abba Pambo a visit one time. He had his bread with him and two olives so he could go see him. Abba Pambo said to him, 'What are these things, Pihor?'

Abba Pihor said to him, 'I decided to stay one day with you; therefore I've brought a few necessities with me'.

The old man in his wisdom understood that Pihor had vowed not to eat another person's bread, so later Abba Pambo wanted to teach him not to maintain his desire when he went to see the old men. Abba Pambo got up and paid a visit in turn to Abba Pihor. He moistened his bread before he went to see him and also took a bottle of water.

When he entered Abba Pihor's dwelling, Abba Pihor said to him, 'My father, what are these things?'

The old man said to him, 'It's my bread and my water. So I won't trouble you, I moistened my bread before coming to see you'.

Abba Pambo did this in order to silently teach him a lesson.

THE MIRACLE OF THE CAMEL

It happened one time, then, that the old servant of Maximus and Domitius was transporting a few of the blessed ones' baskets to Egypt after giving them a little bread in exchange, as was the custom. After getting a little bread for these saints, he loaded his camel and went to Scetis. When he reached the entrance to the swampy marshland, as he was walking with his camel he came to a steep slope and, through a scheme of the Enemy who hates all that is good, the camel slipped and fell and two of its legs were so badly broken that only the skin was holding them together. When this happened, the old man wept so bitterly and with such great sadness of heart that he tore his clothing and threw dirt on his head because he no longer had a camel. Then he gave thanks to God, saying, 'I give thanks to you, my Lord Jesus Christ, God of these saints'. He left the camel lying on the ground and went to the blessed ones' cave.

The old man told them what had happened with his camel. They, however, could not understand what he was saying but when they saw him weeping and saw his suffering, they went with him. When they approached the camel, it became afraid and cried out. It touched the ground with its head as though worshipfully greeting the saints. They said to the camel, 'Do not be afraid but get up and stand through the power of him who rose from the dead, Jesus Christ, God of the Christians'. After saying these words, they raised their eyes up to heaven, saying, 'God of our father Abba Macarius, listen to us, we pray to you, who love humankind!' Immediately the camel quickly got up; it stood on its feet, healed, as though nothing had happened to it.

They were walking home when Saint Domitius saw that the old man's face was covered with dust because he had thrown dirt on his head when the camel fell. Saint Domitius took the corner of his outer cloak that he was wearing in order to wipe off the old man's face. The old man, because of his great faith in them and in the miracle that he saw take place through the holy saints, took hold of the saint's hand and placed it over his afflicted eye in order to receive a blessing from him. When the saint's hand touched his eye, he could see immediately. The old watchman, the camel driver, glorified God greatly for the gift he had received. The saints commanded him, saying, 'See that you tell no one about this', and said to him, 'Do not imagine that this healing happened to you because of us, for we ourselves are sinners. No, this happened through the power of Christ'.

January 23
GREGORY OF NYSSA (CO)

WE FORGET OUR OWN SINS

This Abba John the Little also said for our benefit: 'We forget our own sins and judge our brother!'

IF PEOPLE MOCK YOU

If people mock you, saying, 'Why do you trouble yourself like this?' patiently say in return, 'This "trouble" is edification for me'.

THE BIRD WHO ABANDONS HER EGGS

Amma Syncletica said, 'If you find yourself in a monastery, do not go to another place, for that will harm you a great deal. Just as the bird who abandons the eggs she was sitting on prevents them from hatching, so the monk or the nun grows cold and their faith dies when they go from one place to another'.

WASHING COARSE CLOTHES

Blessed Syncletica was asked if poverty is a perfect good. She said, 'For those who are capable of it, it is a perfect good. Those who can sustain it receive suffering in the body but rest in the soul, for just as one washes coarse clothes by trampling them underfoot and turning them about in all directions, even so the strong soul becomes more stable thanks to voluntary poverty'.

[27] First woman priest in the Anglican Communion, 1944. American Church calendar.

THE OFT-TRANSPLANTED TREE

An old man said, 'Just as a tree cannot bear fruit if it is often transplanted, neither does a monk bear fruit when he moves from place to place'.

GLORY OR IGNOMINY?

Abba Abraham of Iberia asked Abba Theodore of Eleuthero-polis, 'Father, which is right? Ought I to seek glory for myself or ignominy?'

The old man said, 'As far as I am concerned, I prefer to seek glory rather than ignominy. If I do something good and praise myself for it, I can condemn my thoughts by saying to myself that I do not deserve the praise; but ignominy comes from evil deeds. How then can I appease my conscience if people have been shocked because of me? It is better, therefore, to do good and praise oneself for it'.

Abba Abraham said, 'Father, you have spoken well'.

I HAVEN'T EVEN BEGUN

It was said about Abba Pambo that as he was being perfected, at the very hour of his death, he said to the holy fathers standing around him, 'From the time I came to this place in the desert and built myself a cell and dwelled in it, I do not remember eating bread unless I earned it with my own hands, nor do I regret a single word I have spoken up to this very hour; even so, I go to God as one who has not yet begun to serve him'.

I SAW A MAN RADIANT WITH GLORY

I asked Abba Timothy, 'When you first came here to the desert, did you suffer a great deal?'

He said to me: 'Yes, I suffered a great deal, my son, so much that I threw myself to the ground on account of my pain and grief, crying out to the Lord on account of my many sins. I also suffered great pain from an infirmity laid upon me. Now I looked and saw a man radiant with glory standing beside me. He said to me, "Where are you sick?"

'My strength returned to me a little and I said to him, "Sir, it's my liver that hurts me."

'He said to me, "Show me where it hurts", so I showed him where my liver was hurting me. He stretched out his hand over me, with his fingers joined together, and he cut open my side as with a knife. He brought out my liver and showed me the wounds in it. He healed them and bound them up and put my liver back in its place again, and he smoothed over the spot with his hands

61

and rejoined the place which he had cut apart. He said to me, "*See, you are healed. Do not sin again that no worse evil happen to you.*[28] But be a servant of the Lord now and forever".

'Since that day all my insides have been healthy and the pain in my liver has gone away. I have lived here in the desert without pain. And he taught me about the bindings which he treated me with'.

January 27
ANGELA MERICI, VIRGIN (RC)
JOHN CHRYSOSTOM, BISHOP OF CONSTANTINOPLE (A)

EVAGRIUS, BECAUSE OF PRIDE AND ARROGANCE, LEAVES CONSTANTINOPLE

This person of whom we speak was a citizen of Pontus, which is where his family was from. He was the son of a priest from Iberia whom the blessed Basil, bishop of Cappadocia, had made a priest for the church in Caesarea. After the death of Saint Basil the bishop, and his father in God the priest, Evagrius went to Constantinople, a city filled with learning, for he walked in the footsteps of Saint Basil. He attached himself to Gregory of Nazianzus, the bishop of Constantinople, and when the bishop saw his learning and good intelligence, he made him a deacon, for truly he was a wise person, being in possession of himself and without passions, and was a deacon of steadfast character. Indeed, he himself attended the Council of Constantinople with our fathers the bishops at the

[28] Jn 5:14.

time of the synod that took place in Constantinople, and he was victorious over all the heretics. Thus this Evagrius and Nectarius the bishop debated with each other face to face, for truly Evagrius was very protective of the Scriptures and was well-equipped to refute every heresy with his wisdom. He was therefore well-known throughout Constantinople for having combated the heretics with forceful and eloquent language.

The whole city praised him greatly. After all this learning, on account of his pride and arrogance, he fell into the hands of the demon who brings about lustful thoughts for women, as he told us later after he had been freed from this passion. Indeed, the woman loved him very much in return. But Evagrius was fearful before God and did not sin with her because, in fact, the woman was married and Evagrius also followed his conscience because her husband was a member of the nobility and greatly honored and, furthermore, Evagrius thought deeply about the magnitude of shame and sin and judgement and realized that all the heretics whom he had humiliated would rejoice. He beseeched God continuously, praying that he help free him from the passion and warfare that he had been subjected to, for in truth the woman persisted in her madness for him to the point that she made a public spectacle of herself. He wanted to flee from her but could not summon up the courage to do so for in truth his thoughts were held captive by pleasure like a child. [29]

---

[29] Continued on 28 January.

EVAGRIUS BECAUSE OF PRIDE AND ARROGANCE, LEAVES CONSTANTINOPLE

God's mercy did not delay in coming to Evagrius but through his entreaties and prayers God came to him quickly. He comforted him through a revelation so that nothing evil could get at him with the woman. In a vision at night, the Lord sent angels to him dressed in radiant clothing who looked like soldiers of the prefect. They made him stand and seized him as though they were taking him before a judge, as though they had bound him in ropes along with other thieves, having put a collar around his neck and chains on his feet, acting as though they were arresting him but without telling him the charges or why they had seized him. But he thought in his heart that they had come after him on account of the affair with the woman, thinking that her husband had accused him before the prefect.

Afterwards he was utterly astonished, and the angel who had appeared to him changed form in front of him, taking on the appearance of one of his friends who had come to pay him a visit and comfort him. He said to Evagrius, who was bound with the thieves, 'Deacon Evagrius, why have you been arrested, sir?'

Evagrius said to him, 'The truth is, I don't know, but I think someone denounced me, perhaps because he was seized by ignorant jealousy. So I'm afraid that he's given money to the judge so he will quickly and violently destroy me'.

The angel said to him, 'If you will listen to me, who am your friend, then I will tell you: It is not good for you to stay in this city'.

Evagrius said to him, 'If God delivers me from this trouble and you still see me in this city of Constantinople, say "You deserve this punishment"'.

The angel who had taken on the appearance of a friend said to him, 'I will give you the Gospel; swear to me "I will not remain in this city", and that you will be concerned about the salvation of your soul. I will save you from this trouble'.

And he swore to him upon the Gospel, 'Give me one day to load my clothes on the boat and I swear to you I will leave this city'.

After he had sworn, he awoke from the vision he had seen at night and said, 'Even if I swore in a dream, nevertheless I have sworn this oath'. He immediately got up, loaded his things and his clothes on the boat, and set sail for Jerusalem.

January 29
DORMITION OF THE HOLY VIRGIN MARY (CO)
GREGORY OF NYSSA (CO)

A SINGLE LOAF OF BREAD

One time Abba Macarius told this parable when the brothers asked him about pity. The old man said to them:

There was a pitiless ruler in a town and one year a famine took place in that town so that the people despaired and thought they would die. A man approached this ruler and asked for bread because of the hunger in his belly and, *on account of his impudence toward that pitiless ruler*,[30] with numerous scornful words and causing great suffering, the ruler gave the man bread, but not without causing his blood to flow. This was the day of the dormition of her

[30] Lk 18:5.

who brought our Lord Jesus Christ into the world for us, Mary the holy Mother of God.

That very night, while that pitiless ruler was still asleep, his soul was suddenly taken away from his body and he was dragged away to be cast into bitter torments in order to be punished, and while he was being pitilessly dragged, a voice came from him who possesses numerous treasuries of mercy and compassion, he who alone is compassionate, our Lord Jesus Christ, our true God, he who blots out sins and forgives iniquities, saying, 'Return this soul to its body because this man gave bread to the man suffering from hunger and especially because today is the dormition of her who brought me into the world, the Virgin Mary'.

When that man awakened from death, he remembered the voice he had heard when he was being dragged to punishments and he said, 'On account of a single loaf of bread that I gave that man—and I did it in anger and even caused blood to flow from him—my Lord Jesus Christ has brought me out from bitter punishments. If I had distributed all my possessions, how much more would I have profited!' So he distributed his possessions even more, even so far as to also include his body, which he sold into slavery, and gave the price to the poor and the weak. Because of that man's love for other people and his upright intentions, he was invited into the priestly rank of the Church so that he was worthy of the episcopacy and celebrated the liturgy, giving glory to our Lord Jesus Christ.

HUMILITY

Abba Antony said, 'I saw the snares that the Enemy spreads out
over the world and, groaning, I said, "What can get through such
snares?" Then I heard a voice saying to me, "Humility"'.

MEETING THE NEEDS OF OTHERS

A hunter in the desert saw Abba Antony enjoying himself with
the brothers and he was shocked. Wanting to show him that it was
necessary sometimes to meet the needs of the brothers, the old
man said to the hunter, 'Put an arrow in your bow and shoot it'.
So he did. The old man then said, 'Shoot another', and he did so.
Then the old man said, 'Shoot yet again', and the hunter replied,
'If I bend my bow so much I will break it'. Then the old man
said to him, 'It is the same with the work of God. If we stretch
the brothers beyond measure they will soon break. Sometimes it
is necessary to come down to meet their needs'. When he heard
these words, the hunter was pierced by compunction and, greatly
edified by the old man, he went away.

THE BROTHER COVERED WITH MEAT

A brother renounced the world and gave his goods to the poor,
but he kept back a little for his personal expenses. He went to see
Abba Antony. When he told him this, the old man said to him, 'If
you want to be a monk, go into the village, buy some meat, cover

your naked body with it and come here like that.' The brother did so, and the dogs and birds tore at his flesh. When he came back the old man asked him whether he had followed his advice. He showed Abba Antony his wounded body, and Saint Antony said, 'Those who renounce the world but want to keep something for themselves are torn in this way by the demons who make war on them'.

January 31

OUR LIFE AND OUR DEATH

Abba Antony said, 'Our life and our death is with our neighbor. If we gain our brother, we have gained God, but if we scandalize our brother, we have sinned against Christ'.

STOP BREATHING

A brother came to see Abba Poemen and said to him, 'Abba, I have many thoughts and they put me in danger'.

The old man led him outside and said to him, 'Expand your chest and do not breathe in'.

The brother said, 'I cannot do that'.

Then the old man said to him, 'If you cannot do that, no more can you prevent thoughts from arising, but you can resist them'.

ACCEPTABLE PRAYER

Question: How can a person know *that his prayer is acceptable to God?*[31]

Answer: When a person makes sure that *he does not wrong his neighbor in any way whatsoever,* then let him be sure that his prayer is acceptable to God.[32] But if someone harms his neighbor in any way whatsoever, either physically or spiritually, his prayer is an abomination and is unacceptable. For the wailing of the one who is being wronged will never allow this person's prayer to come before the face of God. And if indeed he does not quickly reconcile with his neighbor, he will certainly not go unpunished his whole life by his own sins, for it is written that *whatever you bind on earth will be bound in heaven.*[33]

---

[31] 1 Pt 2:5.
[32] See Ex 20:16-17, Mt 19:19.
[33] Mt 18:18.

FEBRUARY

EPIPHANY

A CHEST FULL OF CLOTHES

Abba Isaiah questioned Abba Poemen on the subject of impure thoughts. Abba Poemen said to him, 'It is like having a chest full of clothes; if one leaves them in disorder they are spoiled in the course of time. It is the same with thoughts. If we do not do anything about them, in time they are spoiled, that is to say, they disintegrate'.

HUMILITY AND A HIPPOPOTAMUS

Then we saw another old man, called Abba Bes, who surpassed everyone in meekness. The brothers who lived round about him assured us that he had never sworn an oath, had never told a lie, had never been angry with anyone, and had never scolded anyone. This was because he lived a life of the utmost stillness, and his manner was serene, for he had attained the angelic state. He was extremely humble and held himself of no account. We pressed him strongly to speak a word of encouragement to us, but he consented to say only a little about meekness, and was reluctant to do even that.

Once when a hippopotamus was ravaging the neighboring countryside, the farmers called on this father to help them. He stood at the place and waited, and when he saw the beast, which was of enormous size, he commanded it in a gentle voice, saying, 'In the name of Jesus Christ I order you not to ravage the countryside any more'. The hippopotamus, as if driven away by an angel, vanished completely from that district. On another occasion he got rid of a crocodile in the same way.

February 2

THE PRESENTATION OF JESUS IN THE TEMPLE (O, RC, A)

AVARICE

Avarice suggests to the mind a lengthy old age, inability to perform manual labor (at some future date), famines that are sure to come, sickness that will visit us, the pinch of poverty, the great shame that comes from accepting the necessities of life from others.

DON'T DO THAT AGAIN

One of the Fathers related of Abba Sisoës of Calamon that, wishing to overcome sleep one day, he hung himself over the precipice of Petra. An angel came to take him down and ordered him not to do that again and not to transmit such teaching to others.

KNOWING WHEN TO OPEN YOUR MOUTH

Abba Cassian said: Abba Moses told us, 'It is good not to hide your thoughts but to confess them to spiritual and discerning elders, but not to those made venerable solely by time, because many, having regarded only the age of their confessors and having confessed their thoughts to them, instead of being healed have fallen into despair on account of the inexperience of those who heard their confession'. To give you an example, there was a certain brother, very serious and zealous, who, greatly troubled by the demon of sexual sin, went to a certain old man and declared to him his thoughts. When that old man, being inexperienced, heard the brother's confession, he rebuked him, calling him a wretch, and disparaged him, saying that he was unworthy of the monastic habit since he had entertained such thoughts.

When the brother heard these things, he despaired of himself and, abandoning his cell, returned to the world. According to the dispensation of God, however, Abba Apollo ran into him. When he saw that the brother was upset and thoroughly downhearted, he questioned him, 'Child, what is the cause of such great gloom?' The brother, however, was so dispirited that at first he could offer no reply. Later, after much encouragement by the old man, he confessed what had happened to him: 'Thoughts of sexual sin were bothering me, so I went and declared my thoughts to this old man and, as far as he's concerned, there's no hope of salvation for me. I've given up on myself, therefore, and am returning to the world'.

When Father Apollo heard these things, like a wise physician he encouraged and admonished the brother for a long time, saying, 'Do not be surprised at these thoughts, child, and do not give up hope for yourself; I myself, even as old and gray-haired as I am, am still very much bothered by these thoughts. Therefore do not lose heart when you are tested by a fire like this which is not healed so much by human effort as by God's mercy. Only, do me a favor today and return to your cell'.

The brother did as he was told.[1]

February 4

KNOWING WHEN TO OPEN YOUR MOUTH

Abba Cassian continued: After he left the brother, Abba Apollo went to the cell of the old man who had given up on the brother and, standing outside, he entreated God with tears, saying, 'Lord, you who bring temptations upon a person who will benefit from them, turn this warfare of the brother's back upon this old man so that, tempted in his old age, he may learn what in his long life has not been taught to him: to sympathize with those in the midst of battle'. When he finished the prayer, he saw an Ethiopian standing near the cell, shooting arrows at the old man; wounded by them, the old man was running here and there like a madman. Unable to bear the arrows, he left his cell and was heading for the world on the same road that the young man had taken.

Abba Apollo, however, understanding what had happened, went to meet the old man; advancing toward him, he said, 'Where are you going? What's the cause of this trouble that has its grips on

[1] Continued on 4 February.

you?' Fearful that Abba Apollo knew all about him, out of shame he said nothing. Abba Apollo said to him, 'Return to your cell and from now on recognize your weakness and consider yourself either ignorantly misled by the Devil or even despised, on account of either of which you have not been deemed worthy to do battle against him like those who are zealous. Why do I say "battle"? You have not been able to bear his assault for even a single day! This has happened to you because you received into your cell a young man besieged by our common enemy; instead of making him ready for combat, you drove him to despair, not taking account of that wise precept that says *Rescue those being led to death and do not shrink from redeeming those being slain*[2] nor of the parable of God our Savior that says *He will not break a bruised reed or put out a smoldering wick.*[3] For no one can bear the plots of the Enemy or put out nature's roiling fire, or even contain it, unless God's grace protects our human weakness. Therefore, since this saving dispensation has been accomplished for our sakes, let us supplicate God with our common prayers. For *it is he who causes suffering and restores one to health again; he hits and his hands heal;*[4] *he humbles and exalts; he causes death and brings one back to life; he leads one into Hades and brings one back up*'.[5]

After saying these things and praying for the old man, Abba Apollo immediately set him free from the war that had been waged against him and exhorted him to ask God to give him an educated tongue so he would know the appropriate time when he ought to open his mouth and speak a word.

[2] Prv 24:11.
[3] Is 42:3, Mt 12:20.
[4] Job 5:18.
[5] 1 Sam 2:6-7.

ONE WILL VERSUS MANY DESIRES

Abba Mark said to Abba Arsenius, 'Why do you flee from us?'

The old man said to him, 'God knows that I love you, but I cannot be with God and with people. The thousands and tens of thousands of heavenly beings have but a single will while human beings have many desires. Therefore I cannot forsake God to come be with people'.

CONSIDER THE FIRST BETRAYAL, THEN EXAMINE THE SECOND

There was a great hesychast in the mountain of Athlibeos. Some thieves fell upon him and the old man began to cry out. When they heard this the neighbors seized the robbers and took them to the magistrate who threw them into prison.

The brothers were very sorry about this and they said, 'It is through us that they have been put in prison'. They got up and went to Abba Poemen to tell him about it. He wrote to the old man, saying, 'Consider the first betrayal and where it comes from and then examine the second. In truth, if you had not first failed within, you would not have committed the second betrayal'.

On hearing Abba Poemen's letter read (for he was renowned in the entire district for not coming out of his cell), the old man arose, went to the city, got the robbers out of prison, and liberated them in public.

TRY TO THINK INWARDLY

One day when Abba Poemen was sitting down, Paesius fought with his brother till the blood ran from their heads. The old man said absolutely nothing to them. Then Abba Anoub came in and saw them; he said to Abba Poemen, 'Why have you let the brothers fight without saying anything to them?'

Abba Poemen replied, 'They are brothers, and they will make up again'.

Abba Anoub said, 'What do you mean? You saw them behaving like this, and all you say is "they will make up again!"'

Abba Poemen said to him, 'Try to think that inwardly I was not here to see it'.

GET UP, LET'S GO

It was said about Abba Agathon that he spent quite a long time building a cell with his disciples and, when they finished it, they came to live there from that time on.

During the first week he saw something that displeased him and said to his disciples, 'Get up, let's leave this place'.

But his disciples were very upset and said, 'If you had already decided to move, why did we go to all the trouble of building the cell? People are going to be scandalized and will say, "Look, they've moved again, those vagrants!"'

---

[6] February 5 on the American Episcopal Church calendar. Paul Miki and Companions on the RC calendar.

When he saw how weak-spirited they were, he said to them, 'If some are indeed scandalized, others, on the contrary, will be edified and will say, "Blessed are people like these! They have moved on account of God and have despised everything". But whoever wants to leave may go; as for me, I am going'.

So they threw themselves to the ground, begging him until he allowed them to travel with him.

February 7

YOU ARE BLESSED, ABBA ARSENIUS

Abba Theophilus, the archbishop of Alexandria, at the point of death, said, 'You are blessed, Abba Arsenius, because you have always had this hour in mind'.

WORKING A FIELD FILLED WITH THORN-APPLES AND THISTLES

A brother succumbed to temptation and on account of what was afflicting him quit keeping the monastic rule; wanting to start all over again, he was thwarted by his affliction and said to himself, 'When will I find myself like I once was?' Despondent, he was unable to begin his monastic work so he went to an old man and reported to him what was going on with himself. When the old man heard what had happened because of his affliction, he offered him the following story by way of illustration:

'A person had some land and through his carelessness it became overgrown and filled with thorn-apples and thistles. It finally occurred to him to cultivate the land and he said to his son, "Go and clear the land". When his son went to clear the land and saw that it was filled with thorn-apples and thistles, he got discouraged and said to himself, "How long will it take me to pull up all this stuff and clear everything here?" Giving up, he lay down and went to sleep. He did this for many days. Later, his father came to see what he had done; when he found that his son hadn't done any work, he said to him, "Why haven't you done any work yet?" and the young man said to his father, "I really was going to start work, father, but when I saw that the field was full of thorn-apples and thistles, I got overwhelmed by the task and so I laid myself down on the ground and went to sleep". Then his father said to him, "Son, if you had cleared each day an area equal to the bed you made for yourself, you would have made progress in your work and would not have got discouraged". When the young man heard this, he did as his father had advised and in a short time the land was cleared.

'So, brother, it's the same with you: do your work little by little and you won't get discouraged and God, through his grace, will restore you to your former condition'.

The brother left and with patient endurance sat in his cell and did what he had been instructed by the old man and in this way he found peace and made progress through Christ.

BE THEIR EXAMPLE

A brother asked Abba Poemen, 'Some brothers live with me; do you want me to be in charge of them?'

The old man said to him, 'No, just work first and foremost, and if they want to live like you, they will see to it themselves'.

The brother said to him, 'But it is they themselves, Father, who want me to be in charge of them'.

The old man said to him, 'No, be their example, not their legislator'.

THIS BARBARIAN IS AN IMAGE OF GOD

The barbarians invaded and ruled Scetis with tyrannical and despicable deeds, it was said, destroying the peace, tranquility, and way of life of our fathers, acting like wild beasts, threatening the monks and destroying the holy places.

But our holy father Abba John was meditating upon the saying of Christ who dwelled in him: *If they chase you from this town, flee to another.*[7] And with these words our father Abba John prepared to leave the place to go to Klysma, especially since this was according to God's plan so that other souls might also be saved through him in that other place, for the worship of idols still persisted there.

As our holy father was making haste to leave Scetis, it is said that all the brothers tearfully surrounded him, saying to him, 'Will you also leave, our father? Are you afraid of the barbarians?'

[7] Mt 10:23.

Our holy father Abba John answered them, 'By the name of Christ God, I am not afraid. No, the perfect goodness in God's presence does not allow each of us to pursue his own salvation alone; instead, according to an angelic purpose, each of us, especially the devout person, performs all his deeds while regarding his own good and that of his brother equally. This barbarian, even if he is separated from me by faith, nevertheless *is an image and creature of God* in the same way that I am.[8] If I resist this barbarian he will kill me and will go to punishment because of me'.

February 9
PAUL, THE FIRST HERMIT (CO)
LONGINUS, HEGOUMEN OF THE ENATON (CO)

FIRST THINGS FIRST

One day Abba Longinus questioned Abba Lucius about three thoughts, saying first, 'I want to go into exile'.

The old man said to him, 'If you cannot control your tongue, you will not be an exile anywhere. Therefore control your tongue here, and you will be an exile'.

Next Abba Longinus said to Abba Lucius, 'I wish to fast'.

The old man replied, 'Isaiah said, *If you bend your neck like a rope or a bulrush, that is not the fast I will accept; but rather, control your evil thoughts'*.[9]

---

[8] See Gen 1:26.
[9] See Is 58.

Abba Longinus said to him the third time, 'I wish to flee from people'.

The old man replied, 'If you have not first of all lived rightly with people, you will not be able to live rightly in solitude'.

WHY ARE YOU LOOKING FOR THAT OLD IMPOSTER?

A woman had an illness they call cancer of the breast; she had heard of Abba Longinus and wanted to meet him. Now he lived at the ninth milestone from Alexandria. As the woman was looking for him, the blessed man happened to be collecting wood beside the sea. When she met him, she said to him, 'Abba, where does Abba Longinus, the servant of God, live?' not knowing that it was he.

He said, 'Why are you looking for that old imposter? Do not go see him, for he is a deceiver. What is the matter with you?'

The woman showed him where she was suffering. He made the sign of the cross over the sore and sent her away, saying, 'Go, and God will heal you, for Longinus cannot help you at all'.

The woman went away confident in this saying, and she was healed on the spot. Later, telling others what had happened and mentioning the distinctive marks of the old man, she learned that it was Abba Longinus himself.

MY CONSCIENCE DEVOURS ME

A brother said to Abba Poemen, 'If I fall into a shameful sin, my conscience devours and accuses me, saying: "Why have you fallen?"'

The old man said to him, 'At the moment when a person goes astray, if he says, "I have sinned", immediately the sin ceases'.

THE HEALTH OF THE INTERIOR PERSON

Syncletica said, 'If illness troubles us, let us not be sorrowful as though, because of illness and the wounded nature of the body, we were unable to stand in prayer or say the psalms aloud. All these things are brought about for our benefit, for the diminution of our desires. Indeed, fasting and sleeping on the ground have been prescribed for us because of our most shameful pleasures. Therefore, if illness blunts these pleasures, the reason for the practices becomes superfluous. Why do I say "superfluous"? These fatal properties are abated by illness as though by a better and more powerful medicine. And this is the great ascetic practice: to persevere during illnesses and to offer up hymns of thanksgiving to the Almighty.

'Have we lost the use of our eyes? Let's not take it seriously. For we have cast away the organs of insatiable desire but with our interior eyes we behold the glory of the Lord. Have we become deaf? Let's give thanks, having finally gotten rid of a lot of silly talk. Do our hands hurt? We still have interior hands ready to wage war against the Enemy. Is our whole body gripped by illness? The health of the interior person will increase even more'.

SILENCE SPEAKS FOR ITSELF

Abba Theophilus, the archbishop of Alexandria, came to Scetis one day. The brothers who were assembled said to Abba Pambo, 'Say something to the archbishop, so he may be edified'.

The old man said to them, 'If he is not edified by my silence, he will not be edified by my speech'.

I STILL HAVEN'T FOUND WHAT I'M LOOKING FOR

A brother lived in Kellia and in his solitude was troubled so he went to Abba Theodore of Pherme and told him about the passion that was bothering him.

Abba Theodore said to him, 'Go, humble the thought that is bothering you and be obedient and stay with others'.

So he went to the monastic community and stayed with others, but returned to the old man and said to him, 'I don't find peace with people, either'.

The old man said to him, 'If you don't find peace alone, or with others, why did you come out here to be a monk? Wasn't it in order to endure afflictions? Tell me, how many years have you worn the habit?'

The brother said, 'Eight years'.

In reply the old man said, 'Truly, I have worn the habit for seventy years and I haven't found peace for even a single day. And you want to have peace after eight years?'

February 12
APOLLO, FRIEND OF APIP (CO)
HUMBELINA, NUN (M)

WEAVING WITHOUT CEASING

It was said of Abba John the Little that one day he was weaving rope for two baskets but he made them into one without noticing, until it had reached the wall, because his spirit was occupied in contemplation.

WE NEED WORKS, NOT WORDS

Abba James said, 'We do not need words only; at the present time, there are many words among people. Rather, we need works, for this is what is required, not words that do not bear fruit'.

February 13
APOSTLES AQUILA AND PRISCILLA (GO)
ABSALOM JONES, PRIEST (A)[10]

WHOEVER HAMMERS A LUMP OF IRON

Abba Antony said, 'Whoever hammers a lump of iron first decides what he is going to make of it: a scythe, a sword, or an axe. Even

[10] American Church calendar.

so we ought to make up our minds what kind of virtue we want to forge or we labor in vain'.

FERVENT IN THE SPIRIT

These, then, were the spiritual contests undertaken by Abba Bishoy, who was fervent in the Spirit: he did not eat bread all week; on Saturday his food was bread and salt. The rest of the week, instead of actual bread, he would enjoy spiritual bread. He used to continuously recite the prophecy of the divine Jeremiah and, they say, the prophet would often appear to him, explicating the secret parts of the prophecy and stimulating his mind through the hidden meanings to a love of the good things promised by God.

Since *he was always pushing forward to what lies ahead*,[11] he was not content with his former practices but insisted on finding other ones: to his former practice of fasting for one week he added another; fasting for two weeks, at the beginning of the third he would partake of a little bread with salt as his food. Even more remarkable is the fact that no one knew about his way of life equal to the angels except God alone, who sees what is hidden and has the unknown right before his eyes. And so Abba Bishoy's love for contemplative solitude became inexhaustible, but what he held dear seemed to be to offer prayers in solitude to God alone and to converse with him and be reconciled with the Supreme Judge and draw near to him through illuminations received in solitude.

[11] See Phil 3:13.

YOU DON'T HAVE A SHIP, SO HOW CAN YOU SAIL?

A brother came to Abba Theodore and began to converse with him about things that he had never put into practice. So the old man said to him, 'You have not yet found a ship nor put your cargo aboard it, and before you sailed you have already arrived at the city. Do the work first; then you will have the speed you are making now'.

THE PROSTITUTE AND THE KING

Our father Abba John used to tell this parable: 'A prostitute had for herself many adulterous friends. A king passed by her and saw her and took her as his wife. Because they feared the king, the adulterers would not approach her house again lest they themselves be killed, but they would gather at a distance from her house, whistling at her. Whenever she heard them she would run into her storehouse and shut the door behind her because of her fear of her husband and her fear that the glory that she obtained from him would be taken from her again'.

BE A COMFORT TO YOUR FATHER

Abba David said, 'One day Abba Arsenius called me and said, "Be a comfort to your father, so that when he goes to the Lord he may pray for you that the Lord be good to you in your turn"'.

BETTER MEAT THAN PRIDE

Isidore the Priest said, 'If you fast regularly, do not be inflated with pride, but if you think highly of yourself because of it, then you had better eat meat. It is better for a person to eat meat than to be inflated with pride and glorify himself'.

February 16

IF YOU DESIRE SALVATION

Abba Isidore said, 'If you desire salvation, do everything that leads you to it'.

DYING TO ONE'S NEIGHBOR

A brother asked Abba Moses, 'Here is a person who beats his servant because of a fault he has committed; what will the servant say?'

The old man said, 'If the servant is good, he should say, "Forgive me, I have sinned"'.

The brother said to him, 'Nothing else?'

The old man said, 'No, because from the moment he takes upon himself responsibility for the affair and says "I have sinned", immediately the Lord will have mercy on him. The aim in all these things is not to judge one's neighbor. For truly, *when the hand of the Lord caused all the first-born in the land of Egypt to die, no house was without its dead*'.[12]

The brother said, 'What does that mean?'

The old man said, 'If we are on the watch to see our own faults, we shall not see those of our neighbor. It is folly for a person who has a dead person in the house to leave him there and go weep over his neighbor's dead. To die to one's neighbor is this: To bear your own faults and not to pay attention to anyone else's, wondering whether they are good or bad. Do no harm to anyone, do not think anything bad in your heart towards anyone, do not scorn the person who does evil, and do not rejoice with the person who injures his neighbor. This is what dying to one's neighbor means.

'Do not rail against anyone, but rather say, "God knows each one". Do not agree with the person who slanders, do not rejoice at his slander, and do not hate the person who slanders his neighbor. This is what it means not to judge.

'Do not have hostile feelings towards anyone and do not let dislike dominate your heart; do not hate the person who hates his neighbor. This is what peace is.

[12] See Ex 11:4-6.

'Encourage yourself with this thought: "Affliction lasts but a short time, while peace is forever, by the grace of God the Word. Amen"'.

LET GO

Abba Poemen said to Abba Isaac, 'Let go of a small part of your righteousness and in a few days you will be at peace'.

DO NO EVIL, DO NOT JUDGE

Abba Paphnutius, the disciple of Abba Macarius, said, 'I begged the old man, "My father, tell me a word"'.

'He said to me, "Do not do anything evil and do not judge anyone, and you will be saved"'.

REVENGE RECYCLES

Abba Nilus said, 'Everything you do in revenge against a brother who has harmed you will come back to your mind at the time of prayer'.

I HAVE SEEN THEM

One day Macarius the Egyptian went from Scetis to the mountain of Nitria for the offering of Abba Pambo. The old men said to him, 'Father, say a word to the brothers'.

He said, 'I have not yet become a monk myself, but I have seen monks'.

February 19

THE DRUNKEN SISTER

Abba Daniel went up from Scetis one time with his disciple into the Upper Thebaid to Hermopolis; there was a monastery for women there called the Monastery of Abba Jeremiah, in which about three hundred sisters were living. So his disciple went and knocked and

93

the doorkeeper said to him in a faint voice, 'May you be saved. We are pleased that you have come. Why are you calling?'

He said to her, 'Call for me the mother archimandrite; I wish to speak with her'. She said, 'She never meets anyone, but tell me why you are calling and I will tell her'.

He said, 'Tell her "A certain monk wishes to speak with you"', and she left and told her. The abbess came and spoke to him, 'Why are you calling?'

The brother said, 'I'm calling to ask you to please do me a favor and allow me to sleep here, along with an old man; it's getting dark and we're afraid the wild beasts will eat us'.

The mother superior said to him, 'No man ever enters here. It would be better for you to be devoured by wild beasts outside rather than by those inside'.

The brother said to her, 'Abba Daniel, from Scetis, is outside'.

When she heard this, she opened the two gates and came running out, as did the whole community, and they spread their veils from the gate out to where the old man was. After they went inside the monastery, the mother superior brought a pan and filled it with warm water and herbs and stood the sisters in two choirs and they washed the old man's feet and those of his disciple in the water. She took a cup and, taking water from the pan, poured it over the brothers' heads and afterwards she poured it over her breast and over her head. One could see all of them standing there like stones upon stones, not moving or speaking. They moved only when the signal was given. So the old man said to the abbess, 'Do they honor us or are the sisters always like this?' She said, 'Your servants are always like this, master. Pray for them'.

One of the sisters lay asleep in the forecourt of the church, wearing rags that were in shreds. The old man said, 'Who is this sleeping?' One of the sisters said to him, 'She's a drunk, and we don't know what to do with her: we're afraid to take the responsibility of throwing her out of the monastery, and if we let her stay, she demoralizes the sisters'. The old man said to his disciple, 'Take the pan of water and throw it on her'. When he did as the old man had commanded, she stood up as though from a drunken stupor. The mother superior said, 'Master, this is how she always is'.

The mother superior took the old man and they went to the refectory and after she prepared dinner with the sisters she said, 'Bless your servants so they may eat in your presence', and he blessed them. Only she and her second-in-command sat with them. They set before the old man a small bowl containing some soaked lentils and raw vegetables and dates and water, while to his disciple they served boiled lentils and a small loaf of bread and wine mixed with water. To the sisters they served a number of foods, fish and wine in abundance, and they ate very well and no one spoke. After they got up, the old man said to the abbess, 'What is this you've done? *We* ought to have eaten well'. The superior said to him, 'You are a monk, and I served you a monk's food; your disciple is a monk's disciple and I served him a disciple's food. We, however, are novices and we ate novices' food'. The old man said to her, 'May your charity be remembered. We have truly profited from what you have done'.

As they were leaving the refectory, the old man stopped and said to his disciple, 'Go see whether the drunken sister sleeps where she was lying in the forecourt of the church', and he went and looked and returned and said to the old man, 'She sleeps by the exit to the toilets'. The old man said, 'Keep watch with me this night', and when all the sisters had gone to sleep, the old man took his disciple and went down behind the lattice and they saw that the drunken sister was standing up and was stretching her hands to heaven; her tears were like a river and she was offering up acts of contrition on the ground. Whenever she perceived a sister coming to use the toilet, she would throw herself to the ground and snore. She spent all her days this way.

The old man said to his disciple, 'Call the superior for me without anyone noticing'. He went and called her and her second-in-command and all night they watched what the sister was doing. The superior began to weep, saying, 'I don't know how many times I've treated her badly!' When the signal sounded, a rumor concerning her spread through the sisterhood and she perceived it and went without anyone noticing to where the old man slept. She stole his staff and cowl and opened the gate of the monastery and wrote a short note and put it between the bolt and the gate, saying, 'Pray, and forgive me whatever sins I have committed against you', and she disappeared.

When day came they looked for her and did not find her. They went to the entrance and found the gate opened and the note behind it, and the monastery erupted into weeping. The old man said, 'This was the very reason I came here, for God loves drunkards such as these'.

February 20
AGATHON, POPE OF ROME (O)

AVARICE

Abba Isaiah, when someone asked him what avarice is, replied, 'Not to believe that God cares for you, to despair of the promises of God, and to love boasting'.

CALUMNY

He was also asked what calumny is, and he replied, 'It is ignorance of the glory of God, and hatred of one's neighbor'.

ANGER

He was also asked what anger is, and he replied, 'Quarreling, lying, and ignorance'.

THE ENEMY REJOICES

A brother asked Abba Poemen, 'Why should I not be free to do what I want without manifesting my thoughts to the old men?'

The old man replied, 'Abba John the Little said, "The Enemy rejoices over nothing so much as over those who do not manifest their thoughts"'.

A RAT AND A LAMP FILLED WITH OIL

Abba Orsisius said, 'I think that if a person does not guard his heart well, he will forget and neglect everything he has heard, and thus the Enemy, finding room in him, will overthrow him. It is like a lamp filled with oil and lit; if you forget to replenish the oil, gradually it goes out and eventually darkness will prevail. It is still worse if a rat happens to get near the lamp and tries to eat the wick; it cannot do so before the oil is exhausted, but when it sees the lamp not only without a light, but also without heat, it tries to pull out the wick and it brings the lamp down. If it is earthenware it breaks, but if it is brass the master of the house will fill it with oil again'.

February 22
PAPHNUTIUS, ASCETIC (CO)
CHAIR OF PETER (RC)

SILENT FOR GOD'S SAKE

A brother asked Abba Poemen, 'Is it better to speak or to be silent?'

The old man said to him, 'The person who speaks for God's sake does well; but the person who is silent for God's sake also does well'.

DUST TO DUST

I, your brother Paphnutius, was thinking one day that I would go into the further desert so I could see whether there were any brother monks in the farthest reaches of the desert. So I walked four days and four nights without eating bread or drinking water. I continued walking on into the farther desert when finally after a number of days I came upon a cave. When I approached it, I knocked at the mouth of the cave at midday, but no one answered me. Now I thought to myself, 'There's no brother here', but then I saw a brother sitting silently inside. I took hold of his arm and it came off in my hands and disintegrated into dust. I felt his body all over and found that he was clearly dead and had been dead a long time. I looked up and saw a short-sleeved tunic hanging up. When I touched it, it fell apart and turned into dust. I stood up and I prayed, and I took off my robe and wrapped the body in it. I dug with my hands in the earth; I buried him, and I left that place.

DO NOT LOOK TOWARD PERSONS

Do not look towards persons.
Do not let a person look towards you.

THREE BISCUITS, SIX BISCUITS

There was an old man and each day he would eat three biscuits. A brother came to visit the old man and when they had sat down to eat, he set three biscuits before the brother. When the old man saw that the brother was still hungry, he brought him three more. When they had their fill and stood up, the old man condemned the brother and said to him, 'It is not fitting, brother, to serve the flesh'. The brother asked the old man's forgiveness and left.

The next day, when it was time for the old man to eat, he placed before himself, as was his custom, the three biscuits; after eating them he was still hungry but restrained himself. The following day the same thing happened to him. As a result, the old man began to lose his willpower and thought that he had been forsaken by God. Throwing himself before God, with tears he was imploring God for the reason why he had been forsaken and he saw an angel speaking to him, 'This has happened to you because you condemned the brother. Know, therefore, that when someone is able to exercise self-control or do any other good thing, he is able to do it not on his own power but because it is the grace of God that empowers each person'.

WHERE DO YOU WANT TO THROW HIM?

One day Abba Isaac went to a monastery. He saw a brother committing a sin and he condemned him. When he returned to the desert, an angel of the Lord came and stood in front of the door of his cell and said, 'I will not let you enter'.

But Isaac persisted, saying, 'What's the matter?' and the angel replied, 'God has sent me to ask you where you want to throw the guilty brother whom you have condemned'.

Immediately Isaac repented and said, 'I have sinned, forgive me'.

Then the angel said, 'Get up, God has forgiven you. But from now on, be careful not to judge someone before God has done so'.

HONEY, BREAD, AND DIRT

One day while our father Abba John was eating at the table with a number of monks, he had a revelation in the Spirit, and he saw this distinction among the brothers who were eating: some of them were eating honey, some were eating bread, and some were eating dirt.

While our father pondered this mystery, a voice came to him from heaven, saying, '*Those who eat honey are those who eat with fear and trembling*[14] and spiritual joy, *praying unceasingly*,[15] their way of life in heaven as their prayers ascend to God like acceptable incense; because of this they eat honey.

[13] American Episcopal Church calendar. 14 May on RC and other A calendars.
[14] Ps 2:11, Phil 2:12.
[15] 1 Thes 5:17.

Those who eat bread are those that eat in thanks, glorifying God for his great work and his gift that he has prepared for them.

Those who eat dirt are those that eat with murmuring, fault-finding, and slander, passing judgement that "This is bad" or "This is good". It is not fitting to think or speak like this at all. Much better is the person who glorifies God and blesses him with great thanks as we fulfill the Apostle's commandment: *Whether you eat or drink or do this or that, do everything for the glory of God*.[16]

February 25
JAMES THE APOSTLE (CO)

SEEK, THEN KEEP

Abba Arsenius said, 'If we seek God, he will show himself to us, and if we keep him, he will remain close to us'.

DISCERNMENT

It happened that several of the fathers went to the home of a friend of Christ; among them was Abba Poemen. During the meal, meat was served and everyone ate some except Abba Poemen. The old men knew his discretion and they were surprised that he did not eat it. When they got up, they said to him, 'You are Poemen, and yet you behaved like this?'

[16] 1 Cor 10:31.

101

The old man answered, 'Forgive me, my Fathers. You have eaten and no one is shocked; but if I had eaten, since many brothers come to me, they would have suffered harm, for they would have said, "Poemen has eaten meat; why should we not eat it ourselves?"'
So they admired his discernment.

February 26

HOW LONG HAVE YOU BEEN HERE?

A brother asked Abba Sisoës, 'Why did you leave Scetis, where you lived with Abba Or, and come to live here?'
    The old man said, 'At the time when Scetis became crowded, I heard that Antony was dead and I got up and came here to the mountain. Finding the place peaceful, I have settled here for a little while'.
    The brother said to him, 'How long have you been here?'
    The old man said to him, 'Seventy-two years'.

DO YOU SEE THIS ABBA ARSENIUS?

It was said of Abba Arsenius that once when he was ill at Scetis, the priest came to take him to church and put him on a bed with a small pillow under his head.
    An old man who was coming to see him saw him lying on a bed with a little pillow under his head and he was shocked and said, 'Is this really Abba Arsenius, this man lying down like this?'

Then the priest took him aside and said to him, 'In the village where you lived, what was your trade?'

'I was a shepherd', the old man replied.

'And how did you live?'

'I had a very hard life'.

Then the priest said, 'And how do you live in your cell now?' The other replied, 'I am more comfortable'.

Then the priest said to him, 'Do you see this Abba Arsenius? When he was in the world he was the father of the emperor, surrounded by thousands of slaves with golden cinctures, all wearing collars of gold and garments of silk. Beneath him were spread rich coverings. While you were in the world as a shepherd you did not enjoy even the comforts you now have, but he no longer enjoys the delicate life he led in the world. So you are comforted while he is afflicted'.

At these words the old man was filled with compunction and prostrated himself, saying, 'Father, forgive me, for I have sinned. Truly the way this man follows is the way of truth, for it leads to humility, while mine leads to comfort'.

February 27
GEORGE HERBERT, PRIEST (A)

MY HEART BECOMES LUKEWARM

A brother said to Abba Poemen, 'My heart becomes lukewarm when a little suffering comes my way'.

The old man said to him, 'Do we not admire Joseph, a young man of seventeen, for enduring his temptation to the end? And

God glorified him. Do we not also see Job, how he suffered to the end, and lived in endurance? Temptations cannot destroy hope in God'.

WE SOW A LITTLE POOR GRAIN

A brother said to Abba Poemen, 'If I give my brother a little bread or something else, the demons tarnish these gifts saying it was done only to please people'.

The old man said to him, 'Even if it is done to please people, we must give the brother what he needs'. He told him the following parable: 'Two farmers lived in the same town; one of them sowed and reaped a small and poor crop, while the other, who did not even trouble to sow, reaped absolutely nothing. If a famine comes upon them, which of the two will find something to live on?'

The brother replied, 'The one who reaped the small poor crop'.

The old man said to him, 'So it is for us; we sow a little poor grain so we won't die of hunger'.

February 28
JOHN CASSIAN (0)

CAPTIVITY AND CONFESSION

Abba Cassian said: Abba Moses told us about Abba Serapion who said, 'When I was a young man and was living with Abba Theonas, when I ate I would stand up from the table and, through the power of the Devil, would steal some bread and I would eat it without my abba knowing about it. When, therefore, I persisted in doing this for a while, I was dominated by desire and was unable to get control of myself; only I was condemned by my own conscience and was ashamed to speak to the old man. According to God's providence and loving-kindness, however, it happened that some brothers came to see the old man in order to profit from him and they were asking him about their own thoughts. The old man answered, "Nothing so harms monks and causes the demons to rejoice as when monks hide their thoughts from their spiritual fathers". He spoke to them also about self-control.

'While they were talking, I figured that God had informed the old man about me. Moved to compunction, I began to weep and from my breast pocket I pulled the biscuit that I had wickedly stolen by habit. Throwing myself to the ground, I begged their forgiveness for what had happened in the past and asked for their prayers to help keep me from stumbling in the future. Then the old man said, "My dear child, before I even said a word, your own confession freed you from this captivity, and by speaking out on your own you have slain the demon that was wounding you by means of your silence. Even if up to now you allowed him to rule over you when you neither spoke against him nor rebuked him, he no longer has hold of you, having been expelled from your heart".

'The old man had not even finished speaking when suddenly the power that had possessed me appeared like a flaming fire coming out of my breast and it filled the house with such a foul stench that those present thought the house was filled with burning sulfur. Then the old man said, "See, through this sign that has just taken place, the Lord has provided proof of the truth of my words and the fact that you are free"'.

MARCH

LENT

ON NOT JUDGING OTHERS

A brother did wrong one time at Scetis and when a council was called about it, they sent for Abba Moses, but he refused to come. So the priest sent someone to him, saying, 'Come, the community is waiting for you'.

He got up and went and, picking up a large basket with a hole in the bottom, filled it with sand, and carried it with him. When he arrived at the meeting, those who came out to meet him said to him, 'What's this, father?'

The old man said, 'My sins trickle out behind me and I do not see them and yet I have come today to judge someone else's sins'.

When they heard this, they did not say anything to condemn the brother but forgave him.

DYING EACH DAY

Abba Antony said, 'Children, let us, then, keep to our ascetic discipline and not lose heart. We have the Lord to help us, as it is written: *God helps everyone to do good who chooses to do good.*[1] Now with regard to losing heart, it is good for us to meditate on the Apostle's statement: *I die daily.*[2] If we too live our lives like this—

[1] See Rom 8:28.
[2] 1 Cor 15:31.

as though we are going to die each day—we will not sin. I am saying this so that if we awaken each day and think "I will not be alive until evening", and again when we are about to go to sleep, if we think "I am not going to wake up", then we will not take for granted that our life is so certain when we know that it is measured out each day by Providence'.

March 2
CHAD, MONK, BISHOP OF LICHFIELD (A)

THE MIRROR OF SINS

Abba Macarius said: If you look into a mirror to observe yourself, it will inform you of your beauty or of your ugliness. You cannot hide anything from it nor will it lie to you in any way; no, it produces a lifelike image and reflects back your own image and reproduces all your features and characteristics: if you smile, you see what sort of a smile it is; it will show you that your black hair is black and your gray hair is gray and it will reveal you to yourself and show you what you really look like.

It will be the same at the place of judgement, from which one cannot flee. There it is not a mirror made by human hands but deeds laid bare that show your likeness and reveal your sins like a noose around your neck. You cannot flee from them; no, they stand rebuking you without need of a witness. You are like a ladder in their midst: you are wretched, and words will not help you. The mirror of sins will teach you all of them and they are engraved in your heart like a silversmith's stamp, reproving you and making known to you one by one the deeds you have done: what time you did them, what season; when you did this or when you did that. Simply put, they are all shameful to you and cause you to be scorned in both worlds: with the inhabitants of heaven and with the inhabitants of earth, the place of fearful universal judgement. All the saints and all the heavenly ranks will be in mourning and will groan over you when they behold the great fall that has taken place in you on account of the ugly deeds you have done.

But our Lord Jesus Christ is merciful and full of compassion: our Lord Jesus Christ, the saviour of our souls and bodies, *who does not wish the death of a sinner so much as his conversion and life*.[3] Let us understand these things, brothers, and let us be wise from now on, seeing his love for humanity, just as formerly when *he had pity and wept over Lazarus, beseeching his Father's goodness while Mary and Martha, the sisters of the dead man, poured forth tears, and after four days he raised him from the dead*.[4] Let us draw near to him through prayers and holy tears so he will have pity on us and raise our souls from the death of sin that we might live by his mercy.

<hr />

March 3
JOHN AND CHARLES WESLEY, PRIESTS (A)

I AM SORRY FOR MY SIN

A brother questioned Abba Poemen, saying, 'What should I do?'

He said, 'It is written, *I confess my iniquity, I am sorry for my sin*'.[5]

---

[3] Ezek 33:11, 1 Tim 2:4, 2 Pet 3:9.
[4] Jn 11:1–44.
[5] Ps 38:18.

HE WILL SOON PLANT OTHERS

Abba Mark asked Abba Arsenius, 'Is it good to have nothing extra in the cell? I know a brother who had some vegetables and he has pulled them up'.

Abba Arsenius replied, 'Undoubtedly that is good but it must be done according to a person's capacity. If he does not have the strength for such a practice he will soon plant others'.

THAT IS A LOT

A brother questioned Abba Poemen, saying, 'I have committed a great sin and I want to do penance for three years'.

The old man said to him, 'That is a lot'.

The brother said, 'For one year?'

The old man said again, 'That is a lot'.

Those who were present said, 'For forty days?'

He said again, 'That is a lot'.

He added, 'I myself say that if a person repents with his whole heart and does not intend to commit the sin any more, God will accept him after only three days'.

REMEMBER HELL, BUT ALSO REMEMBER THE DAY OF RESURRECTION

Abba Antony said, 'As you sit in your cell, gather your thoughts: remember the day of your death; visualize the body's deadness at that time. Reflect on misfortune; accept suffering; condemn the world's foolish vanity. Be diligent about being gentle in your zealousness in order to maintain the same peaceful disposition at all times without weakening. Remember also the state of things in Hell and reflect on what it is like for the souls there, what sort of very bitter silence and utterly terrible groaning they endure, how great their fear and struggle, what their expectations are like as they anticipate ceaseless grief and the soul's unending tears. But remember also the day of resurrection and our appearance before God'.

JOHN HAS BECOME AN ANGEL AND IS NO LONGER AMONG MEN

Our all-holy father Abba John the Little was boiling with the fire of the Holy Spirit, always striving to emulate the way of life of the powers in the heights. One day he said to his older brother in zeal of the love of God, 'I myself desire, my brother, to be without care and to serve God without ceasing, like the angels, being continuously in the glory of his beauty and the light of his life'. So he took off his clothes and went out to the desert.

When he had spent a week without eating and drinking, he returned home to his brother through the special permission of God who wills the salvation of souls, laden with the fruits of humility in true repentance. When he knocked on his older brother's door, his brother did not open it to him, but said, 'Who are you?"'

John said to him, 'I am John'.

His brother said, "'You're John! John has become an angel and is no longer among men'. And he did not open the door to him but left him in front of the door from evening till morning.

When morning came, he opened the door of the dwelling and said to him, 'John, you need to realize that you are still a man and that you are still in the flesh; you still have to work to nourish yourself. What you've done is appropriate for the angels'.

Abba John begged his forgiveness, saying, 'Forgive me'.

March 5

A WANDERING HORSE

Abba Isaiah said, 'Lately I see myself as a wandering horse that has no master; whoever finds it sits on it and, when he leaves it, someone else takes it and sits on it'.

THE ENEMY WHO ENVIES THE FAITHFUL

One day Antony had a conversation with some people who had come to see him about the makeup of the soul and what sort of place it would have hereafter. That night, someone called to him from above, saying, 'Antony, get up! Come outside and look!' So he went outside (for he knew those he should obey) and looked up, and saw someone huge, incorporeal, and fearsome, standing and reaching to the clouds, while some beings were ascending as though they had wings. And he saw that giant stretch out his hands: some of those ascending were stopped by him while others flew on by and, having passed, finally flew on without any problem. Because of this, the giant was gnashing his teeth at those who escaped him and was rejoicing at those who were falling back. Suddenly a voice came to Antony: 'Understand what you are seeing!' When his mind was opened, Antony understood that this was the pathway for souls and that the giant standing there was the Enemy, who envies the faithful. He was seizing those who were accountable to him and preventing them from passing by, but those who were not obedient to him he was unable to seize; instead, they passed by and ascended.

When Antony saw this again, he remembered and fought still more each day *to advance to what lies ahead.*[6] He did not readily speak about these things, but while he persevered in his prayers, marveling privately at these events, those with him asked him about them and pressed him for an answer, forcing him to speak to them, like a father unable to hide things from his children.

<hr>

March 6
FINDING THE PRECIOUS CROSS BY SAINT HELEN (GO)

A RAG ON HIS CHEST

It was said about Abba Arsenius that his whole life while sitting and working with his hands he would have a rag on his chest on account of the tears that fell from his eyes.

[6] See Phil 3:13.

ABBA MACARIUS AND THE SKULL

It was said about Abba Macarius the Great that when he was out walking in the desert he found the skull of a dead person thrown on the ground. After moving it with his palm-tree staff, the old man said, 'Who are you? Answer me'.

The skull said to him, 'I was high priest of the pagans who lived here. And you—why, you're Macarius the Spiritbearer! Whenever you take pity on those being punished and pray for them, their punishments are assuaged a little!'

Abba Macarius said to him, 'What do you mean by "assuaged"?'

The skull said to him, 'As far distant as heaven is from the earth, just as great is the fire beneath our feet and over our heads. As we are standing surrounded by fire, it is not possible for anyone to see someone else face to face; rather, people are attached back to back. When you pray for us, therefore, each of us can partially see the other person's face'.

The old man wept and said, 'God have mercy on the day a person is born if this is what 'assuagement' from punishment means!' The old man once again said to the skull, 'Is there some other form of torture worse than this?'

The skull said to him, 'There is greater torture below us'.

Macarius said to the skull, 'And who are those who suffer this torture?'

The skull said to him, 'Those of us who did not know God have a little mercy shown to us, but others knew God and denied him and did not do his will; these are the ones below us'.

After these words, the old man took the skull, buried it in the earth, and continued his journey.

STONES IN THE MOUTH

It was said about Abba Agathon that for three years he placed a stone in his mouth until he had succeeded in keeping quiet.

THE CHICK-PEA IN THE ROAD

Abba Agathon was walking one time with his disciples. One of them, finding a small green chick-pea in the road, said to the old man, 'Father, may I take it?'

The old man stared at him in amazement and said, 'And did you put it there?'

The brother said to him, 'No'.

The old man said, 'Why, then, do you wish to take something that you did not put there?'

MAKE YOUR THOUGHTS LIKE A PRISONER'S THOUGHTS

A brother asked Abba Ammonas, 'Tell me a word'.

The old man said, 'Go, make your thoughts like those that evil-doers think who are in prison, for they are always asking people, "Where is the prefect?" and "When is he coming?" and they wail in expectation. In the same way the monk ought to attend to and reprove his soul at all times, saying, "God help me! How will I be able to stand before the judgement seat of Christ? How will I be able to offer him any defense?" If you attend to yourself this way at all times, you can be saved'.

THE ENCHANTER LURES THE WILD BEAST

Question: With what kind of thought does the Devil lure the monk out of his cell?

Answer: The Devil is an enchanter. With enticing words the enchanter lures the wild beast out of its lair and, catching it, drags it into the streets of the city where he releases it to people's laughter, and when later it grows old in his captivity he consigns it to the flames or tosses it into the sea. It's the same with a monk: his way of life suffers when, drawn outside by his thoughts, he abandons his cell.

A CROWING COCK, A SILLY TUG-OF-WAR, AND NAKED WOMEN

The demons also tried to shake Pachomius' cell to make him afraid that it should collapse upon him. Then against them he would recite the psalm, *God is our shelter, our strength, a help in the afflictions that try us exceedingly. So we shall not be afraid when the earth is shaken.*[7]

Another time, when he sat down to work, a demon came to tempt him in another way; taking the form of a cock, he crowed in his face. Or again they would bring into the middle of the place a tree leaf and tie it securely with thick ropes. Then they would stand on each side as though they were about to drag a big stone, shouting to each other, so that he would laugh with a relaxed heart and they would overcome him. When he saw it, he sighed at them, and since he paid no attention to them, they withdrew.

[7] Ps 45:1-2.

When he sat to eat, they would come in the form of naked women to sit with him to eat. But he closed the eye of his mind to them and the enemies disappeared without accomplishing anything against him. He was indeed preserved by the Lord who says to all the upright, *Do not be afraid, for I am with you.*[8]

March 9
POLYCARP OF SMYRNA (CO)
FORTY HOLY MARTYRS OF SEBASTEA (O)
GREGORY, BISHOP OF NYSSA (A)[9]

TEARS AND VAINGLORY

Abba Moses said, 'Through tears a person acquires the virtues and through tears comes remission of sins. When you weep, therefore, do not raise your voice with your groaning, and *do not let your left hand know what your right hand is doing.*[10] The left hand is vainglory'.

DANCING IN THE MIDST OF YOUR SOUL

Listen concerning the way you have asked about. Be attentive; stand with the Lord. If you keep these words, you will be one of the elect in all things.

---

[8] Gen 26:24; Is 41:10.
[9] American Church calendar.
[10] Mt 6:3.

For it is written: *Glory will go before those who are humble.*[11] And again, *The wisdom of the humble person lifts high that person's head.*[12] And again, *Whom will I look upon except the person who is humble and gentle and who trembles at my words?*[13]

And again it is written: *The bones of the humble will rejoice with you in every way.*[14] And again, *The prayer of a humble person is immediately heard.*[15]

Again it is written: *Look on my humility and my suffering and forgive all my sins.*[16]

See what sort of thing humility is: If you acquire it, you have acquired everything.

And again: Keep your body holy and the holy angels will come to you and give you joy, and you will see God.

It is written: *I have seen the Lord of Hosts with my eyes.*[17]

Again it is written: *I heard you with the hearing of the ears and just now I saw you with my eyes.*[18]

And the Holy Spirit will illumine all your members, and the twelve Virtues will dance in the midst of your soul, and the Cherubim and Seraphim will shelter you beneath their wings.

---

[11] Prv 29:23.
[12] Sir 11:1.
[13] Is 66:2.
[14] Ps 50:10 (LXX); 51:8.
[15] Sir 4:6.
[16] Ps 24:18 (25:18).
[17] Is 6:5.
[18] Job 42:5.

THE REMEDY

When Amoun was living as a solitary in Nitria, a child suffering from rabies was brought to him, bound with a chain. For a rabid dog had bitten him and given him the disease. His suffering was so unbearable that his whole body was convulsed by it. When Amoun saw the child's parents coming to entreat him, he said, 'Why are you troubling me, my friends, seeking something which is beyond my merits, when the remedy lies in your own hands? Give back to the widow the ox that you have killed surreptitiously, and your child will be restored to you in good health'. Their crime having thus been exposed, they happily did what they had been told; and when the father prayed, the child instantly recovered.

WHAT IS THE WORLD?

A brother asked Abba Isaiah, 'How ought I maintain contemplative quiet in my cell?'

The old man answered, 'In order to maintain contemplative quiet in your cell, you have to abandon yourself before God and do everything in your power to resist every thought sown by the Enemy. This, indeed, is what it means to flee the world'.

The brother said, 'What is the world?'

The old man answered, '"The world" is the distractions that come from *things*; "the world" is doing things that are contrary to nature and fulfilling your own fleshly desires; "the world" is thinking that you are going to remain in this present age; "the world" is having more concern for your body than for your soul and rejoicing in those things you leave behind. I have not said these things of my own accord; no, it is the apostle John who says these things: *Do not love the world or things in the world*.[19]

THE HOLY CROSS AND THE WOUNDS OF CHRIST

Our all-holy father and Spirit-bearing Abba John, *dead to sin but alive in Christ Jesus our Lord*,[20] boldly confessed pride in the Holy Cross and the wounds of Christ, walking in that which was pleasing to Christ's good will, purifying *a temple for the Holy Spirit*.[21]

THE ROCK IS YOUR FATHER

A brother asked Abba Macarius, 'Tell me what it is to live in obedience, my father'.

Abba Macarius said to him, 'It is like rock: if you use the rock to crush the wheat and extract all the filth from it, the wheat becomes pure bread. It is the same with you, my child: the rock is your father; you are the wheat. If you obey your father, he will intercede with the Lord on your behalf. He will extract all the filth of Satan from you and, instead of pure bread, you too will be a godly son'.

[19] 1 Jn 2:15.
[20] Rom 6:11.
[21] 1 Cor 6:19.

DEAF AND DUMB

Strive to render your mind deaf and dumb at the time of prayer and then you will be able to pray.

INVISIBLE NUBIANS

Now Abba Aaron and I rose and came out from the desert, and he took me to a priest to clothe me in the monastic habit. And when we called inside the priest's house he came outside and greeted us and took us inside his place. Right away my father told him about me and immediately the priest shaved the hair from my head and clothed me in the monastic habit. We rose and went home. Now my holy father Aaron spent a week in helping me lay the foundations for doing work in the service of God. After a week he said to me, 'Stay here while I go visit this brother and then I will come back and see you'. (Now he did not want me to know that he wanted to go keep his own monastic observances.) And I said to him, 'Will you come back today?' And he said to me, 'No, my dear brother. Give me until the Sabbath'.

He spent the first day and the second and the third and even the fourth and fifth away from me. As for me, demons were severely abusing me: 'Why did your father leave and leave you all alone? Why didn't he take you so you too could be blessed by that brother?' Now when they continued to trouble me, I rose and set

[22] Traditional date, used on American Church Calendar. September 3 on RC and other A calendars.

out into the desert to where I had found him the first time. He said to me, 'Why have you come here my son?'

I said to him, 'The Nubians have been tormenting me, and I've come to tell you'.

He smiled and said, 'Truly, they are invisible Nubians, my son'.

March 13

ME TOO

A brother sinned and was kicked out of church by the priest. Abba Bessarion stood up and went out with him, saying, 'I too am a sinner'.

SOME SORT OF WILD ANIMAL

Abba Cassian said that a brother visited Abba Serapion and the old man invited him, as was his practice, to offer a prayer. The brother, however, calling himself a sinner and saying that he was not worthy of the monastic habit, did not comply. Abba Serapion also wanted to wash his feet and the brother, making use of the same words, refused. The old man made the brother eat and while they were eating he began to admonish him in love, saying, 'Child, if you want to be profited, stay in your cell and pay attention to yourself and your handiwork. It's not good for you to go out because going out does not have as much benefit as staying home'.

When the brother heard these things he was so exasperated and his face changed so much that the old man could not help but notice, so Abba Serapion said to him, 'Up to now you have said, "I am a sinner", and accused yourself of not being worthy to live; and now, after I lovingly admonished you, you act like some sort of wild animal! If you want to be truly humble, therefore, learn to bear nobly what someone else has said to you and do not keep empty words to yourself'.

When he heard these things, the brother asked the old man's forgiveness and went away, having profited greatly.

March 14
BENEDICT OF NURSIA (O)

SOFTEN YOUR NATIVE RUDENESS

Pray first for the gift of tears so that by means of sorrow you may soften your native rudeness. Then having confessed your sins to the Lord you will obtain pardon for them.

TAKE OFF YOUR SHOES

If Moses, *when he attempted to draw near the burning bush, was prohibited from doing so until he removed the shoes from his feet*,[23] how should you not free yourself of every thought colored by passion, seeing that you wish to see the One who is beyond every thought and perception?

[23] See Ex 3:5.

A WISE GOLDSMITH

A brother asked Abba Macarius, 'Tell me the meaning of repentance'.

Abba Macarius said to him, 'Repentance does not consist only of kneeling, like the divining rod that indicates water by going up and down, but is like a wise goldsmith who wishes to craft a chain: with a link of gold and a link of silver, even with iron and lead, he lengthens the chain until he completes his work. This too is the form that repentance takes. All the virtues depend on it'.

THE CHILD OF DISOBEDIENCE

There was an old man in Scetis who, when he fell into a very serious illness, was ministered to by the brothers. When the old man saw how hard they were working, he said, 'I'll go to Egypt in order not to inconvenience the brothers', and Abba Moses said to him, 'Don't leave; if you go, you'll fall into sin'.

The old man was annoyed to hear this and said, 'My body has died, and you tell me this?' So he went to Egypt.

When the people heard, they were bringing the old man a lot of things, and a certain woman who was vowed to virginity came to minister to him. After a while, he got well and fell with her and she conceived in her womb and bore a son. The people asked her, 'Where did this come from?' and she said, 'From the old man', but they did not believe her. But the old man said, 'I'm the one who did it. Take care of the child I fathered', and they took care of it.

When the child had been weaned, the old man, carrying the infant on his shoulder, came down to Scetis when one of the feast days was taking place and went into the church and said to the brothers, 'Do you see this infant? He is the child of disobedience.

So watch out for yourselves, brothers; I did this as an old man. But pray for me'.

When they saw this, everyone wept, and he left and went to his cell and took up his former way of life.

March 16

THE PURE ANGELIC HABIT

Abba Macarius said, 'Like the carpenter who straightens what is crooked and bends what is straight, so it is with the repentance that our Lord Jesus Christ has appointed for us: it makes straight again what is crooked and rolls in the filth of sin and makes it pure *like virgins standing in the presence of our Lord Jesus Christ.*[24] Those who turn away from their sins and repent receive the pure angelic habit that is in heaven'.

THE SWEET OF ALL SWEETS

Abba Poemen said: I was sitting one time with some brothers beside Abba Macarius. I said to him, 'My father, what work must a person do in order to acquire life for himself?'

The old man said to me, 'I know that when I was a child in my father's house I used to observe that the old women and the young people were chewing something in their mouths so that

[24] See Mt 25:1-13.

it would sweeten the saliva in their throats and the bad breath of their mouths, sweetening and refreshing their liver and all their innards. If something fleshly can so sweeten those who chew it and ruminate it, then how much more the food of life, the spring of salvation, the fount of living water, the sweet of all sweets, our Lord Jesus Christ! If the demons hear his glorious name blessed by our mouths, they vanish like smoke. This blessed name, if we persevere in it and ruminate on it, opens up the spirit, the charioteer of the soul and the body, and drives all thoughts of evil out of the immortal soul and reveals to it heavenly things, especially him who is in heaven, our Lord Jesus Christ, *king of kings and lord of lords*,[25] who gives heavenly rewards to those who seek him with their whole heart'.

March 17
PATRICK, BISHOP OF IRELAND (O, RC, A)

WHAT IS SUFFICIENT

Question: *Is it good to possess two tunics?*[26]

Answer: To possess two tunics and not to possess evil that stains the whole body is a good thing, for the soul has no need of evil but the body needs clothing. *Since we have the things we need and they're sufficient, we are satisfied with them.*[27]

---

[25] 1 Tim 6:15, Rev 17:14.
[26] Mt 10:10, Lk 9:3.
[27] Prv 30:8 (LXX) and 1 Tim 6:8.

128

YOU CAN'T GO INSIDE

Abba Isaac of Thebes visited a cenobium and saw a brother doing wrong and condemned him. When he left for the desert, an angel of the Lord came and stood in front of the door to his cell and said, 'I will not let you go inside'.

Abba Isaac importuned him, saying, 'What's the matter?'

In reply the angel said to him, 'God has sent me to you, saying to me, "Say to him, 'Where do you order me to expel the brother who did wrong?'"'

Immediately Abba Isaac repented, saying, 'I have sinned. Forgive me'.

The angel said, 'Get up. God has forgiven you. But from now on guard against judging someone before God judges him'.

March 18
CYRIL, ARCHBISHOP OF JERUSALEM (O, RC, A)

THIS IS THE GREAT WORK

Abba Antony said to Abba Poemen, 'This is the great work of a person: always to take the blame for his own sins before God and to expect temptation to his last breath'.

I WILL NEVER GROW TIRED

Abba Macarius beseeched Christ, 'Jesus, Jesus, If my cries do not ring in your ears when I call out day and night to you in heaven

129

to have mercy on me and to pity me on account of my sins, I will still not grow tired of imploring you'.

FRUIT-BEARING STRUGGLES

A disciple of a great old man was once besieged by sin. When the old man saw him struggling, he said to him, 'Do you want me to entreat God to lift the warfare from you?'

The disciple said, 'No. Although I am struggling, I nevertheless see my struggles bearing fruit for me. Instead, entreat God in your prayers to give me the patient endurance to bear up under my struggles'.

His spiritual father said to him, 'Today I know that you are making progress and are surpassing me'.

March 19

APPARITION OF THE HOLY CROSS TO SAINT HELENA (CO)
MARTYRS OF SAINT SABAS MONASTERY, JERUSALEM (O)
JOSEPH, HUSBAND OF MARY (RC, A)

HIM TODAY, ME TOMORROW

When one of the fathers saw someone sinning, he wept bitterly and said, 'This fellow today and me tomorrow'.

FOUNDATION, STONES, AND RUBBLE

A brother asked an old man, 'If a monk falls into sin, he is afflicted like someone who goes from an advanced stage to a lower one and labors until he rises again, but the person who comes from the world makes progress like someone just starting out'. In reply the old man said, 'The monk who succumbs to temptation is like a collapsed house, and if he is completely vigilant with regard to his thoughts and wants to rebuild the collapsed house, he finds a large quantity of building material—the foundation, stones, rubble—and he is able to progress more rapidly than the person who did not trench and lay a foundation and made none of the necessary preparations but instead hoped that somehow the building might get finished. It is the same with building a monastic life: if someone succumbs to temptation and returns to a righteous way of life, he has a great deal of working capital: the meditative reading of scripture, psalmody, and manual work, which are the foundations. As long as he learns these things like a novice, the monk will regain his former position'.

March 20
CUTHBERT, BISHOP OF LINDISFARNE (GO, RC, A)

WALKING ALONE WITH GOD

You shall test the teaching that you follow, walking alone with God at your side.

For Elijah was at the river Chorath alone, God was with him, and the raven ministered to him.[28]

The prophet was also walking alone; *he took Paul's belt and bound himself.*[29]

WHEN YOU FELL INTO SIN YOU WON

A brother went to draw water from the river. He found a woman washing clothes and it happened that he fell into sin with her. After the sin, he took his water and was returning to his cell, but the demons, by means of his thoughts, trampled on him and afflicted him, saying, 'Where are you going? After this, there's no chance of your being saved! Why do you also want to inflict harm on everyone else?'

The brother, realizing that they wanted to utterly destroy him, said to the thoughts, 'Why do you burden and afflict me so I despair of myself? I haven't sinned!' Going to his cell, he lived a life of contemplative quiet as he had yesterday and the day before that.

The Lord, however, revealed to his neighbor, an old man, that such-and-such a brother, having fallen into sin, had defeated sin. So the old man went to the brother and said to him, "Brother, how are you doing?"

He said, 'Fine, Abba'.

The old man said to him, 'God revealed to me that when you fell into sin you won'. Then the brother told him everything that had happened to him. The old man said to him, 'Truly, brother, your discernment has crushed the power of the Enemy'.

[28] See 1 Kings 17:1-7.
[29] See Acts 21:11.

March 21

THE BROTHER AND THE DOVE

A brother was besieged by sexual sin. He happened to pass through a village in Egypt and when he saw a pagan priest's daughter he fell in love with her. So he said to her father, 'Give her to me as a wife'.

In reply the priest said to him, 'I cannot give her to you until I learn what my god wishes', and he went to the demon and said to it, 'Some monk has come, wishing to marry my daughter. Shall I give her to him?'

In reply the demon said, 'Ask him if he renounces his god and his baptism and his monastic vow'.

So the priest went and said to the monk, 'Do you renounce your god and your baptism and your monastic vow?'

The monk agreed to do so, and suddenly he saw something like a dove come out of his mouth and fly up into the sky.

So the priest entered the temple and went to the demon and said, 'Yes, he agreed to renounce these three things'.

The Devil then said to him in reply, 'Do not give him your daughter as a wife, for his god has not withdrawn from him but will still help him'.

So the priest went and said to the brother, 'I can not give her to you because your god is still helping you and has not withdrawn from you'.

When the brother heard these words, he said to himself, 'If God has shown such great goodness towards me even though I, wretch

[30] American Church calendar. See also June 8.

that I am, have denied him and my baptism and my monastic vow, isn't the good God still helping me right now, then?' [31]

THE BROTHER AND THE DOVE

So the brother came to himself and was restored to his right mind and he left and went into the desert and when he came to a great old man he related to him what had happened.

In reply the old man said to him, 'Stay with me in my cave and fast for three weeks and I will entreat God on your behalf'. And so the old man labored on the brother's behalf and entreated God, saying, 'I beg you, Lord, grant me this soul and accept his repentance'. And God heard him.

When the first week was completed, the old man went to the brother and asked him, 'Have you seen anything?'

The brother answered and said, 'Yes, I saw the dove up above in the highest heavens stationed above my head'.

The old man replied and said to him, 'Pay attention to what's going on inside you and fervently entreat God'.

After the second week, once again the old man went to the brother and asked him, 'Have you seen anything?'

The brother said, 'I saw the dove come down and light upon my head' [Mk 1:10]. So the old man commanded him, 'Be vigilant and pray'.

---

[31] Continues on 22 March.

134

And when the third week was completed, once again the old man went and asked the brother, 'Have you seen anything more?'

The brother replied and said, 'I saw the dove: it came and stood on my head and, stretching out my hand, I took hold of it and it flew up and went into my mouth'.

Then the old man gave thanks to God and said to the brother, 'Look, God has accepted your repentance. From now on, watch yourself'.

The brother replied and said to him, 'From now on I will remain with you, Abba, until I die'.

March 23
TURIBIUS DE MONGROVEJO, BISHOP, MISSIONARY (RC)
GREGORY THE ILLUMINATOR, BISHOP (A)

CONCEALING AND REVEALING

A brother asked Abba Poemen, 'If I see my brother's fault, is it good to conceal it?'

The old man said, 'At the very moment we conceal our brother's fault God also hides our own, and at the very moment we reveal our brother's fault God also reveals ours'.

SINNING IN THOUGHT AND SINNING IN DEED

It was reported that two brothers went into a village where they had been sent, and the demon attacked the older one five times in order to make him sin. And he contended with the attacks by saying a prayer each hour. They returned to their father and his face was troubled and he asked his father's forgiveness, saying, 'Pray for me, father; I have fallen into sin', and he related how his spirit had been attacked.

But the old man was perceptive and saw five crowns on the brother's head and said to him, 'Courage, child. When you came, I saw crowns on you. You haven't been defeated; rather, you have been victorious, seeing that you did not finish the act. It is a great struggle for a person to keep self-control when the opportunity to sin arises; he has a great reward because this warfare waged by the Enemy is very strong and bitter and it is difficult to flee from his snares.

'What do you think: *that the matter was easy for blessed Joseph*?[32] No, it was like a play in the theater: God and the angels were watching him fighting and the Devil and the demons were all the more making a ravenous beast of the woman. Therefore, when the athlete proved victorious, all the angels gave glory to God in a loud voice, saying, 'The athlete has gained an unusual victory!' It is good, therefore, not to do evil even in one's thoughts, but if someone is tempted, he does battle in order not to be defeated'.

THE DEFINITION OF HUMILITY

An old man was asked, 'What is humility?'
He said, 'If your brother sins against you and you forgive him even before he repents'.

[32] Gen 39:7-23.

FORGIVENESS AND REPENTANCE

Not long before, some robbers had come at night from some distance away to attack Abba Theon. They thought that they would find a considerable sum of gold hoarded by him, and intended to kill him. But he prayed, and they remained at the door, rooted to the spot, until daybreak. When the crowd came to him in the morning and proposed to burn these men alive, he was forced to speak a single sentence to them: 'Let them go unharmed; if you do not, my gift of healing will leave me'. They obeyed, for they did not dare to contradict him. The robbers at once entered the neighboring monasteries and with the help of the monks changed their way of life and repented of their crimes.

FRESH GRAPES

One time Macarius was sent some fresh grapes. He desired to eat them but, showing self-control, he sent them to a certain brother who was ill and who was himself fond of grapes. When the brother received them he was delighted but, wishing to conceal his self-mastery, he sent them to another brother, pretending he had no appetite for any food. When the next brother received the grapes he did the same in turn, although he too had a great desire to eat them.

When at length the grapes had been passed round a large number of the brothers without any of them deciding to eat them, the last one to receive them sent them again to Macarius, thinking that he was giving him a rich gift. Macarius recognized them and

137

after inquiring closely into what had happened, marveled, giving thanks to the Lord for such self-control among the brothers. And in the end not even he ate any of the grapes.

SIN AND PENITENCE, LOVE AND PRIDE

Abba Elias, the minister, said, 'What can sin do where there is penitence? And of what use is love where there is pride?'

A DEMON WITH A WINESKIN

Abba Elias said, 'I saw someone who was carrying a skin of wine on his arm and, in order to make the demon blush, for it was a fantasy, I said to the brother, "Of your charity take off your cloak". He took off his cloak, and was not found to be carrying anything. I say that so you may not believe even that which you see or hear. Even more, observe your thoughts, and beware of what you have in your heart and your spirit, knowing that the demons put ideas into you so as to corrupt your soul by making it think of that which is not right, in order to turn your spirit from the consideration of your sins and of God'.

BEING A WITNESS FOR GOD

Question: I want to be a witness for God.

Answer: If someone bears with his neighbor during a fit of temper, it is equal to *the furnace at the time of the three youths.*[33]

THE TUNIC AND THE PATCH

A brother asked Abba Macarius, 'My father, how can a person be free from the passions and be renewed in the Spirit?'

The old man said to him, 'I will give you *an analogy.*[34] It is like a tunic: if it is torn, a patch is put on it until it is made new once again. The tunic can be compared to the body, torn by sin and pleasure. The patch is the repentance that our Lord Jesus Christ gives to us'.

IT'S YOUR HUMILITY

When Abba Macarius was passing one time through the wadi to his cell, carrying some palm branches, the Devil met him on the path, carrying a scythe. He tried to strike Abba Macarius but was unable to, and said to him, 'You are powerful, Macarius! I can't do anything against you! Look—what you can do, I can do too: you fast and I don't eat anything at all; you keep vigil, and I don't sleep at all. There is only one thing at which you're better than me'.

[33] See Dan 3.
[34] 1 Cor 13:12.

Abba Macarius said to him, 'What is that?'

The Devil said to him, 'It's your humility. On account of your humility, there is nothing I can do to you'.

And when the saint stretched out his hands, the demon disappeared and Abba Macarius continued on his way, giving glory to God.

March 27
JOHN THE EGYPTIAN (RC)

DO WHAT YOU CAN

A brother in Scetis fell one time due to temptation and went to Abba Macarius the Alexandrian and told him about the temptation. After the old man punished him with the bonds of asceticism so he would repent and not open his door for a time, the brother left; he was troubled, however, because of the temptation and was in danger and was not able to carry out the order that Abba Macarius had bound him with. Distressed by battle, he went to the other Abba Macarius, the Egyptian. He told him about the transgression and about his inability to carry out the order that Abba Macarius had bound him with.

The old man calmed the brother's spirit and encouraged him in numerous ways, saying, 'Go, my child. What you're able to do, do; gird yourself not to ever commit that sin again'. This was his penance. The brother said to him, 'What shall I do? I am troubled on account of the order that Abba Macarius has bound me with'. The old man said to him, 'This order does not bind you; rather, it binds Abba Macarius'.

When Abba Macarius the Alexandrian heard that the old man had told the brother 'This order binds Abba Macarius', he fled into the marsh; he resolved to remain there, without coming into contact with anyone, until he completed the sentence that he had bound on the brother. He remained in the marsh many days until his body was swollen with mosquito bites.

Abba Macarius the Egyptian heard that the old man had fled to the marsh on account of what he had said. He went to the marsh and looked for Abba Macarius the Alexandrian until he found him. When he saw him, he said to him, 'Venerable sir, I said what I did in order to encourage that brother, and you, when you heard, *like a good virgin fled into the interior bedchamber.*[35] Get up, then, my father, return to your cell'. Abba Macarius the Alexandrian said, 'Forgive me according to the terms of what you told the brother, because what you said applies to me. Unless I complete the sentence that I bound on the brother, I will not leave'.

When Abba Macarius the Egyptian saw that he was firm in his decision to patiently endure his sentence, he encouraged him: 'No; come with me and I will show you what you need to do'. Persuaded, Abba Macarius the Alexandrian went with him. Abba Macarius the Egyptian spoke with him on familiar terms. He said to him, 'Go, spend this year eating once a week'.

This was not an order that he bound him with since before Abba Macarius the Egyptian had even spoken it, it was already the ascetic practice of Abba Macarius the Alexandrian to eat once a week.

[35] See Song 1:1-4.

EVERY BREATH WE TAKE

Abba Macarius said, 'Let us not slacken our resolve nor be without hope, for with every breath we take our Lord Jesus Christ gives us opportunity for repentance'.

SALTY WATER, SWEET WATER

He also said, 'Let us not cause that *fountain* to bubble up *which is salty* because of its single source, that is, the well of the heart, but let bubble up without ceasing *that which is sweet* all the time, that is, our Lord Jesus Christ'.[36]

CLOSE THE ONE DOOR, NOT THE OTHER

A brother came to see Abba Poemen in the second week of Lent and told him about his thoughts; he obtained peace, and said to him, 'I nearly did not come here today'.

The old man asked him why. The brother said, 'I said to myself, "Perhaps he will not let me in because it is Lent"'.

Abba Poemen said to him, 'We have not been taught to close the wooden door but the door of our tongues'.

[36] See Jm 3:11.

DRESS LIKE THE TAX COLLECTOR

Abba Evagrius said: I visited Abba Macarius and said to him, 'Tell me a word so I may live'.

He said to me, 'If I speak to you, will you listen and do it?'

I said to him, 'My faith and my love are not hidden from you'.

Abba Macarius said to me, 'Truly, I lack the adornment of virtue; you, however, are good. But if you cast off the pridefulness of this world's rhetoric and *clothe yourself in the humility of the tax collector*, you will live'.[37]

FRIENDS INDEED

A brother in a monastery was falsely accused of fornication and he arose and went to Abba Antony. The brothers also came from the monastery to correct him and bring him back. They set about proving that he had done this thing, but he defended himself and denied that he had done anything of the kind.

Now Abba Paphnutius, who is called Cephalus, happened to be there, and he told them this parable: 'I have seen a man on the bank of the river buried up to his knees in mud and some men came to give him a hand to help him out, but they pushed him further in up to his neck'.

Then Abba Antony said this about Abba Paphnutius: 'Here is a real man, who can care for souls and save them'.

[37] Lk 18:9–14.

All those present were pierced to the heart by the words of the old man and they asked forgiveness of the brother. So, admonished by the Fathers, they took the brother back to the monastery.

March 30
JOHN CLIMACUS (O, M)

THE REASON WE DO NOT MAKE PROGRESS

An old man said, 'The reason we do not make progress is because we do not know our own capacities and do not have patient endurance for the work we have undertaken. No, we want to acquire virtue painlessly'.

A SINNER, A PILLAR OF FIRE

It was said of Abba Mark of Egypt that he lived thirty years without leaving his cell: the priest would regularly come and celebrate Holy Communion for him. When the Devil saw the man's virtuous endurance, he hatched a plot to tempt him and got a demoniac to go to the old man under the pretext of asking for his prayers. Before the old man could say anything, the possessed person accosted him, saying, 'Your priest is a sinner; do not let him come see you!'

But Abba Mark said to him, 'Child, it is written, *Do not judge lest you be judged*.[38] Even if he is a sinner, the Lord forgives him

---

[38] Mt 7:1.

nonetheless. Look, I'm a greater sinner than he is'. In addition to saying this, the old man offered a prayer, drove the demon out of the person, and made him well.

When the priest came according to custom, the old man received him with joy. Seeing the old man's lack of malice, God showed him a certain wonder: when the priest was about to stand before the holy table, the old man himself related that 'I saw an angel come down from heaven and place his hand on the priest's head and the priest, standing for the holy offering, became like *a pillar of fire*.[39] I myself was filled with wonder at this sight and heard a voice saying to me, "Human, why are you marveling at this event? If an earthly emperor does not allow his nobles to stand before him with filthy clothing but only arrayed in glory, how much more will the divine power purify the ministers of the holy mysteries who stand before the heavenly glory?"'

Blessed Mark was deemed worthy of this grace because he had not condemned the priest.

March 31
JOHN DONNE, PRIEST, POET (A)

SEEN THE SIN BUT NOT THE REPENTANCE

An old man said, 'Even if someone sins in some way in your presence, do not judge him but consider yourself more of a sinner than he is, for you have seen the sin but you have not seen the repentance'.

[39] See Ex 13:21.

ABBA MACARIUS LEARNS ABOUT TRUE WORK

It was said about Abba Macarius the Great that, passing through Egypt one time, he came upon a threshing floor. He saw a heap of grain that had been threshed, its owner using it to pay wages to the workers. When the old man wished to test the grower, wanting him to talk about the nature of his work, he said to him, 'Please do me the kindness, my father, of giving me a little wheat'.

The grower said to him, 'If you have worked, I will pay you a wage, for whoever works receives a wage'.[40]

The old man said to him, 'You're right. Whoever works receives a wage'.

The grower said to him, 'Yes, just like I said: whoever works receives a wage'.

The old man said to him, 'This is just what I wanted to hear from you'.

When he was some distance away on his journey, Abba Macarius slapped himself in the face with his hands and said, 'Woe to you, Macarius! They have refused to give you a wage for the fleshly work of this world, since it is written, *Hasten to use the worker who has not been ashamed to do his master's work well.*[41] Woe to you, then, Macarius! You have failed to obtain that goodness of the master of the vineyard who says, *Call the workers, give them their wage, the last, the first, a measure to each,*[42] and *Whoever works, his wage is not reckoned to him a gift'.*[43]

And so the old man Macarius continued walking, mourning with tears and groaning.

[40] Lk 10:7.
[41] 2 Tim 2:15.
[42] Mt 20:1–16.
[43] Rom 4:4.

APRIL

LENT / EASTER

.

April 1

MARY OF EGYPT, PENITENT (O)
HUGH OF LINCOLN, MONK, BISHOP (M)
FREDERICK DENISON MAURICE, PRIEST (A)

TORN TO PIECES

A brother who had renounced the world and distributed what he owned among the poor, but who kept a few things for his own purposes, went to see Abba Antony, and when the old man learned what the brother had done, he said to him, 'If you want to become a monk, go to the village, buy some meat, cover your naked body with it, and come here like that'.

When the brother did what Antony had commanded, the dogs and the birds cut his body to pieces. When he went to meet the old man, Antony inquired if the brother had done as he had advised. When that brother showed him his lacerated body, Abba Antony said, 'Those who renounce the world and still want to keep some possessions are torn to pieces by the demons who wage war on them'.

WE'RE ALL IN SURGERY TOGETHER

Abba Isaiah said: We are all as if in surgery. One has a pain in the eye, another in the hand, a third in the veins, and whatever other diseases exist. Among these, some wounds are already healed, but when you eat something harmful, they return once again. This is what occurs to a person who is in repentance and yet judges or shows contempt toward others, because he must again return to repentance. Since those in surgery have different illnesses, if some-one cries in pain with regard to his own suffering, let no one else ask, 'Why are you crying out?' Is not each one concerned with his own pain? Therefore, if *the pain of my own sin is before me,*[1] I would not look at the sin of another, for everyone who lies in surgery observes the precautions of his own doctor, taking care not to eat whatever harms his wound.

April 2
FRANCIS OF PAOLA, HERMIT (RC)

ENDURING TEMPTATION

A brother asked Abba Poemen, 'Why is it that my heart despairs if a little suffering gets hold of me?'

The old man said to him, 'Do we not admire how *Joseph, just a little boy in Egypt, the land of idolaters, endured temptation?*[2] And God glorified him in the end. We also see that *Job did not stop holding fast to God to the end and the Enemy was unable to shake his faith*'.[3]

A GOLDEN CISTERN AND A LEPER

A priest visited an anchorite, celebrating for him the sacrifice of the holy mysteries. But another person came to the anchorite and

[1] Ps 51:3.
[2] See Gen 39–41.
[3] See Job.

made slanderous accusations to him that the priest was a sinner. When the priest came, therefore, as was his custom, to celebrate Communion, the anchorite was scandalized and would not let him in.

So the priest left and suddenly a voice came from God saying to the anchorite, '*People have taken my judgement into their own hands*'.[4] It was as if he were having a mystical vision: he saw a golden cistern and golden pail and golden rope and plenty of good water to drink; he also saw a leper drawing water and pouring it into a jar. He himself wanted a drink but did not take one because it was a leper drawing up the water. Suddenly the voice came to him again: 'Why do you not drink some of the water? What difference does it make who draws it up? That fellow only draws the water up and pours it into a jar'.

When the anchorite came back to himself and considered the power of the vision, he summoned the priest and had him consecrate the sacrifice of the holy mysteries for him as he had done before.

April 3
RICHARD OF CHICHESTER, BISHOP (A)

SAILORS FIGHTING A SURGING SEA

Amma Syncletica said, 'In the world, those who sin, even involuntarily, are thrown into prison; as for us, on account of our sins let us imprison ourselves so that such voluntary judgement may drive

---

[4] See 1 Sam 2:10, Mt 7:1.

off future punishment. Are you fasting? Do not pretend to be ill, for those who do not fast fall into real illnesses. Have you begun to do what is good? Do not fall back when the Enemy cuts off your advance, for through your patient endurance he is rendered impotent. Indeed, those who begin a voyage first unfold the sails and go before a favorable wind but later the wind becomes adverse and impedes them. The sailors, because of the chance winds, do not abandon ship, however; a little later, when they once again have calm or fight off the surging of the sea, they again gain control of the vessel. So it is with us, too: when an opposing spirit suddenly befalls us, let us stretch out the cross instead of sails and complete our voyage without hindrance'.

CUTTING THE DEVIL OFF AT THE KNEES

Question: What sort of virtues or commandments does a person need to possess in order to be saved?

Answer: There are four virtues prescribed for us: fasting, and prayer, and handiwork, and bodily chastity. When Satan overcame these virtues, *he drove Adam out of paradise*.[5] Deceiving Adam and dishonoring him by means of food, Satan drove him into hiding and away from the face of God so he would never ask God's forgiveness and have his sin forgiven.

When Adam had been driven out from paradise, on account of his idleness the Devil was intending to condemn him for another sin, expecting to gain possession of Adam because of the despair he felt for himself. But the loving and merciful Lord, knowing the wickedness of the Devil, gave work to Adam, saying, '*Work the earth from which you were taken*',[6] so that Adam, in his care for his work, might drive away the evil devices of the Devil.

[5] Gen 3:23; Rev 12:9.
[6] Gen 3:23.

The Devil, therefore, works against fasting, against prayer, and against handiwork, for handiwork cuts off at the knees the Devil's many evil devices. And he also opposes virtuous chastity. But if someone is deemed worthy of the labor of these four virtues, then he will gain mastery of all other virtues.

April 4
ISIDORE OF SEVILLE, BISHOP, DOCTOR OF THE CHURCH (RC)
MARTIN LUTHER KING, JR, CIVIL RIGHTS LEADER, MARTYR (A)[7]

ANGELS AND UNCLEAN SPIRITS

One of Abba Longinus' disciples had done some inappropriate things. When Abba Theodore of Enaton found out, he came to Abba Longinus with another elder. They implored him to expel the disciple. But Abba Longinus did not listen to them, thinking that perhaps his disciple would repent and God would forgive him; *he did not desire the death of the sinner but hoped he would repent and live.*[8] He said to them just these words: 'Woe to us because we renounce the world and have entered into the monastic life saying, "We are like angels", but in reality we are more evil than unclean spirits!'

NOTHING HANGING ON THE LINE

Pachomius' brother according to the flesh, who was called John, heard about him and came to him. Pachomius rejoiced greatly

[7] American Church calendar.
[8] See Ezk 33:11, Jm 5:20.

when he saw him, for he had never visited his relatives after his discharge from the army. John, choosing the same life, remained with him. And there they both were, having nothing save the law of God. For if they obtained anything from their labors, they gave the surplus to those in need, keeping for themselves what was necessary to live. In clothing, too, they were exceedingly poor, so poor that soon they did not have a second tunic to wear while they washed the one they wore.

April 5
MACARIUS THE GREAT (CO)
VINCENT FERRAR (RC)

ABBA MACARIUS WELCOMES REBUKE

It was said about Abba Macarius that if a brother came to him fearfully as though to a saint and great old man, he would say nothing to him. But if one of the brothers heaped scorn on him, saying, 'My father, when you were a camel-driver and stole nitre and sold it, didn't the guards beat you?' If someone said these words to him, he would speak with him with joy about whatever he asked him.

IMITATE THE DEAD

A brother paid a visit to Abba Macarius and said to him, 'Tell me a word: How can I be saved?'

The old man said to him, 'Go to the tombs. Curse the dead. Throw rocks at them'.

The brother left. He cursed the dead and threw rocks at them, and when he returned to the old man, the old man said to him. 'They didn't say anything to you, did they?'

The brother said to him, 'No, my father'.

The old man said to him, 'Go tomorrow and glorify them, saying, "You are apostles, you are saints and righteous"'.

He returned to the old man and said to him, 'I glorified them'.

The old man said to him, 'They didn't say anything to you, did they?'

He said, 'No'.

The old man said to him, 'You have seen how you cursed them and they did not say anything to you, and how you glorified them and they did not respond at all. It should be the same with you, too: if you wish to be saved, go, be dead, having no regard for people's contempt nor for their honors, like the dead, and you can be saved'.

April 6
METHODIUS, MISSIONARY TO THE SLAVS (O)

I DIED BEFORE HE DID

Abba Daniel told this story about Abba Arsenius: A magistrate came one time, bringing Abba Arsenius the will of a certain senator, a member of the abba's family who had left him a very large inheritance.

Taking it, Arsenius wanted to tear it up, but the magistrate threw himself at Arsenius' feet, saying, 'Do not tear it up! If you do, they will cut off my head!'

Abba Arsenius said to him, 'I died before my relative', and he gave the will back without accepting anything.

JUST STARTING OUT

Antony, knowing the people's practice of embalming and mummifying and afraid that they would do the same with his body, shared his plans with the monks on the outer mountain and then hastened away. So he went to the inner mountain and remained there, as was his custom, and after a few months he became ill. He summoned those who were with him (there were two of them who had stayed there with him for fifteen years, living ascetically and serving him on account of his old age). He said to them: 'As for me, as it is written, I am going the way of the fathers, for I see myself being called by the Lord. But as for you, be diligent and sober, and do not abandon the ascetic way of life that you have followed for so many years but, as though you were just now starting out, work hard at maintaining your zeal.

'You know that the demons are always hatching plots. You know how savage they are. But they are really weak and powerless. Therefore do not fear them but instead draw inspiration from Christ and believe in him. And live as though you were going to die each day, attentively observing yourselves, and remember the exhortations you have heard from me. Make every effort yourselves always to be united, especially with the Lord, and then with the saints, so that after your death they will receive you into the eternal habitations as friends and companions'.

STAYING WITH THE CROSS

I asked Abba Isaiah for a word and he replied: 'If you wish to follow our Lord Jesus Christ, keep his word. If you wish to *crucify the old person with him*,[9] you must remove those things that force you to descend from the cross. Prepare your heart to bear the contempt of the evil ones. They will humiliate you in order to rule your heart. Impose silence so that you do not judge someone whom you know in your heart'.

TRUE REPENTANCE

A brother asked an old man, 'If a person happens to fall into temptation because of some working of the Devil, what happens to those who are scandalized by it?'

The old man told him this story: There was a famous deacon in a cenobium in Egypt. A certain official, persecuted by a ruler, came to the cenobium with his whole household, and through the working of the Devil the deacon fell into sin with a woman and all the monks were ashamed. He left and went to an old man whom he loved and told him what had happened. Now the old man had a hiding place at the back of his cell and the deacon entreated him, 'Bury me alive here and tell no one!' So he entered that darkness and did true repentance.

Some time later, the water of the Nile did not rise, and when everyone was praying litanies it was revealed to one of the saints

[9] See Rom 6:6.

157

that unless the deacon who was hidden with that old man came out and prayed, the water would not rise. When they heard this they were amazed and they went and led him out of the place where he was. So he prayed and the water rose, and those who had once been scandalized were now all the more edified by his repentance and gave glory to God.

April 8

DO NOT LOSE HEART

Abba Poemen said, 'If a person has sinned and denies it, saying, "I have not sinned", do not reprimand him. That will discourage him. Instead, say to him, "Do not lose heart, brother, but be on guard in the future", and you will stir his soul to repentance'.

SEVENTY TIMES SEVEN

A brother asked Abba Poemen, 'If a brother is involved in sin and is converted, will God forgive him?'

The old man said to him, 'Will not God, who has commanded people to act thus, do as much himself and even more? For God *commanded Peter to forgive till seventy times seven*'.[10]

[10] Mt 18:22.

I GRIEVED YOUR IMAGE

When Abba John the Little was at the harvest with the brothers, he called out the name of one of the brothers in order for him to serve the brothers, but that one angrily cried out to our father, 'What! You too?'

Our father called to the brother, saying to him, 'Forgive me'. And immediately our father gave up his position, went to him, and asked the brother's forgiveness, saying to him, 'Forgive me, my son. For the sake of the Lord, forgive me'. And he returned again to the desert to his cell and spent that whole year there, fasting three days on bread with salt, and he petitioned God continuously, saying, 'Lord, forgive me, *for I grieved your image*'.[11]

April 9
DIETRICH BONHOEFFER, PASTOR, THEOLOGIAN (A)

THE TRUE GOD

It was said of Abba Milis that when he was living with his two disciples on the borders of Persia, two of the king's sons, blood brothers, came out, as was their custom, to hunt. Therefore, they put out nets for a distance of about forty miles so that, if something were found within the nets, they might hunt it and kill it with their pikes. Now the old man was present, with his two disciples, and when the king's sons saw him, hairy and frightful-looking, they

[11] See Gen 1:26; 1 Cor 11:7.

were struck with amazement and said to him, 'Are you a human being or a spirit? Tell us!'

He said to them, 'I am a human being, a sinner; I have come out here to weep for my sins and to entreat Jesus Christ, the son of the living God'.

They said to him, 'There is no God other than the sun and fire and water' (which they also worshipped). 'Come forward and offer sacrifice to them'.

He said to them, 'These are created things and you are in error, but I entreat you to convert and to acknowledge the true God, who created all things'.

They laughed and said, 'You're saying that the man who was condemned and crucified is the true god?'

The old man said, 'Yes, I say that *he who has crucified sin and killed death* is the true God'.[12]

But they tortured him, along with his disciples, and tried to force them to sacrifice. After subjecting the two brothers to numerous tortures, they beheaded them, but after subjecting the old man for days to numerous tortures, they finally, using their hunters' skills, stood him between them and shot arrows at him, one from the front and the other from behind. The old man said to them, 'Since you have agreed together to shed innocent blood, tomorrow at exactly this time, your mother will be childless and will be deprived of your love and with your own arrows you will shed one another's blood'.

Contemptuously dismissing what he said, they went out to hunt the next day. A deer sprang out from the nets and the king's sons, mounted on their horses, drove them forward and overtook it. Hurling their spears, they wounded each other in the heart and died, just as the old man had said.

[12] See Heb 2:14.

A TRAVELER WITH A SONG

Abba Hyperechius said, 'Let *a spiritual hymn*[13] be on your lips
and let the quiet recitation of psalms lighten the weight of the
temptations that assault you. Here is a clear example: with a song
a traveler who is loaded down cheats the weariness that comes
with travelling'.

FRUITS OF PARADISE

Saint Apollo was living in a cave in the mountain with five
brothers. He had recently come from the desert and these were
his first disciples. Easter came, and when they had finished giving
worship to God they ate whatever they happened to have. There
were a few dry loaves and some pickled vegetables. Then Apollo
said to them, 'If we have faith, my children, and are true sons of
Christ, let each of us ask of God what he desires to eat'. But they
entrusted the whole matter to him, considering themselves unworthy of such a grace. He therefore prayed with a radiant face
and they all said 'Amen'.

At once in the night a number of men arrived at the cave,
complete strangers to them, who said that they had traveled a
long distance. They were carrying things that the brothers had
not even heard of before, things that do not grow in Egypt: fruits
of paradise of every kind, and grapes and pomegranates and figs
and walnuts, all procured out of season, and honeycombs, and a
pitcher of fresh milk, and giant dates, and white loaves still warm

---

[13] Eph 5:19.

although brought to them from a foreign country. The men who brought these things delivered them simply with the message that they had been sent by a rich magnate, and immediately departed in a hurry. The brothers partook of these provisions until Pentecost and satisfied their hunger with them, so that they wondered and said, 'Truly these were sent by God'.

HIS PRACTICES, AND OURS

A brother came to Abba Poemen one time and said to him, 'What shall I do, father? I am bothered by sexual sin. You see, I went to Abba Ibiston and he said to me, "You must not allow it to hang around with you"'.

Abba Poemen said to him, 'Abba Ibiston's practices are above in heaven with the angels and he does not notice that you and I suffer from sexual sin. In my opinion, however, if a person masters his belly and his tongue, he can have confidence in himself'.

LIKE A NURSING MOTHER

A brother asked Abba Macarius, 'My father, I have committed a transgression'.

Abba Macarius said to him, 'It is written, my child, *I do not desire the death of a sinner so much as his repentance and his life*.[14] Repent, therefore, my child; you will see him who is gentle, our Lord Jesus Christ, his face full of joy for you, like a nursing mother whose face is full of joy for her child. When the child raises his hands and his face up to her, even if he is full of all kinds of uncleanness, she does not turn away from that bad smell and excrement but takes pity on him and lifts him up and presses him to her breast, her face full of joy, and everything about him is sweet to her. If, then, this created person has pity for her child, how much greater is the love of the creator, our Lord Jesus Christ, for us!'

April 12

THE COST OF LOVING PLEASURE AND MONEY

Abba Poemen said, 'It is impossible to live in accordance with God's wishes if you love pleasure and money'.

A DOG IS BETTER

Abba Xanthias said, 'A dog is better than I am, for he loves and does not judge'.

[14] Ezk 33:11, 1 Tim 2:4, 2 Pet 3:9.

IT IS BETTER TO DEPART

Abba Patermuthius went into the house where one of the sick brothers was and, finding him already dead, went up to the bed and prayed and kissed him and asked which he preferred, to go to God, or to continue to live in the flesh.

The brother sat up and said to him, '*It is better to depart and to be with Christ.*[15] To live in the flesh is not essential for me'.

'Then sleep in peace, my child', Abba Patermuthius said, 'and intercede with God for me'.

The brother, just as he was, immediately lay back and died.

All who were present were amazed and said, 'Truly this is a man of God!'

Then he buried him in a fitting manner, and spent the whole night singing hymns.

April 13
MARTIN I, POPE, MARTYR (RC)

GOOD AND BAD SMELLS

With regard to thoughts about sexual sin, another old man said, 'Be like someone who, passing by a tavern in the marketplace, catches the scent of cooking meat or something roasting. Whoever wishes to, goes inside and eats; whoever does not wish to, simply smells what is cooking, passes on by, and goes his way. It is the same with you: shake off what smells bad; get up and pray, saying, "Son of

[15] Phil 1:23.

God, help me!" Do this also for other thoughts, for our job is not to yank out thoughts by the roots but to struggle against them'.

LAYING DOWN YOUR LIFE FOR ANOTHER

Two brothers went to the marketplace to sell their wares, and when one of them left the other he fell into sin. When the other brother returned, he said to the brother who had sinned, 'Let's go to our cells, brother', but the other said to him, 'I'm not coming'.

The brother entreated him, saying, 'Why, brother?'

The brother who had sinned said, "When you left me, I fell into sin'.

Wanting to gain his brother, the brother began to explain to him, 'Me too. When I left you, the same thing happened to me. But let's go and repent with all our might and God will forgive us'.

When they returned, they explained to the elders what had happened to them; the elders prescribed penance for them and the one did penance for the other as though he too had sinned. When God saw the suffering that the one brother did out of love for the other, within a few days he revealed to one of the old men that because of the great love shown by the brother who had not sinned he had pardoned the brother who had sinned. Truly, this was an example of someone *laying down his life for his brother*.[16]

[16] Jn 15:13.

MY AMMA, AND YOURS

Abba Daniel once again went up with his disciple to Alexandria and while they were staying there, the following occurred: An abba of the Oktokaidekaton outside Alexandria had a son and his son had a wife, a young woman named Thomaïs, about eighteen years of age, and she lived with his son. His son was a fisherman. The enemy of our souls, the Devil, was waging carnal warfare against the abba with regard to his daughter-in-law and the abba was looking for an opportunity to have sexual intercourse with her and did not succeed. Therefore he began to kiss her constantly and the young woman accepted this, as from a father.

One day, then, fishermen came at night and took the young man in order to go out and fish. After the young man had left, the father got up and went over to his son's wife and the young woman said to him, 'What are you doing? Leave and cross yourself, for what you are doing is the work of the Devil'.

He refused to leave and the young woman, vigorously fighting him off, refused his advances. The young man's sword hung over the bed and, wanting to frighten her, the abba brandished the naked sword, saying, 'If you don't obey me, you will die!'

But she said, 'If I have to lose an arm, so be it; I will never obey you!'

He suddenly lashed out with the sword and pulled the young woman down by her hips and cut her in two.

Afterwards, Abba Daniel said to his disciple, 'Let us go and view the young woman's corpse'. When they came to the Oktokaideka-ton outside Alexandria, the fathers heard and came out to greet him. The old man said to them, 'As the Lord my God lives, her corpse shall not be buried except with the fathers'.

Many began to grumble. The old man said to them, 'This young woman is my amma, and yours: she died to protect her chastity. She is our fellow monk who died for her troubles'.

No one opposed the old man, and they buried the young woman with the fathers. The old man returned with his disciple to Scetis.

April 15

ONE'S REPUTATION AND ONE'S WORK

Abba Silvanus said, 'Unhappy is the person whose reputation is greater than his work'.

MOURNING THE DEAD

A brother did wrong one time in the cenobium. In that region there was an anchorite and he had not gone outside for a long time. The abbot of the cenobium went to the anchorite and reported to him the brother's wrongdoing. The anchorite said, 'Expel him'. Expelled from the cenobium, in great despair the brother threw himself into a gully and lay there weeping. Some brothers on their way to see Abba Poemen were passing by there and heard him weeping. Going down into the gully, they found him in great distress and urged him to journey to see Abba Poemen, but he refused, saying, 'I'm going to die here because I've sinned'.

When they came to Abba Poemen, the brothers told him about the brother and the old man comforted them and sent them back, saying, 'Say to him, "Abba Poemen sends for you"'. They left and brought him. When the old man saw him in such distress, he stood and embraced him and, graciously welcoming him, urged him to eat.

Abba Poemen then sent one of his brothers to that anchorite, saying, 'For many years I've desired to see you, hearing a lot about you, but because of our mutual laziness we haven't had a chance to meet each other. Now, therefore, both because God wills it and because the opportunity presents itself, please take the trouble to come here and let us see one another'.

The anchorite was not going to leave his cell but when he heard these words he said, 'If God had not advised the old man to send for me, he would not have done so'. So he got up and went to Abba Poemen and they embraced one another with joy and sat down. Abba Poemen said to him, 'Two people lived together and each of them had someone die. The first one left his own dead and went to mourn the other's'. When the old man heard this, he was filled with compunction at what Abba Poemen had said and remembered what he had done, and said, 'Poemen, you are up in heaven while I'm down below on the earth'.

April 16

THE HEART THAT DELIGHTS IN GOD

The wisdom of a wise person understands God's ways. His heart delights in God. God will give him peace in his cell.

TRIP, STUMBLE, AND FALL

Whatever you might do by way of avenging yourself on a brother who has done you some injustice will turn into a stumbling block for you at the time of prayer.

CONTEMPLATIVE QUIET IS GOOD

Abba Mark said, 'Contemplative quiet is good because it does not look at what is harmful. The mind does not receive what it has not seen, and that which does not occur in the mind does not trouble the memory with delusions. What does not trouble the memory does not excite passion, and when passion is not aroused, a person possesses deep calm and great peace within.'

April 17
ROBERT OF LA CHAISE-DIEU [ROBERT OF TURLANDE], MONK (M)

PRAY WITHOUT DISTRACTION

Go, sell your possessions and give to the poor,[17] *and take up your cross*[18] so that you can pray without distraction.

---

[17] Mk 10:21.
[18] Lk 14:27.

IS THE AXE ANY USE?

Abba Anoub asked Abba Poemen about the impure thoughts that a person's heart brings forth and about vain desires.

Abba Poemen said to him, '*Is the axe any use without someone to cut with it?*[19] If you do not make use of these thoughts, they will be ineffectual too.'

April 18

AN INHERITANCE

Abba Cassian related that a certain Abba John, who was the head of a monastery, attained greatness in his life. 'When this man', he said, 'was about to be perfected and was joyfully and eagerly departing this life to be with God, the brothers surrounded him and were asking him to leave them a brief and saving word as their inheritance by which they might become perfect in Christ. With a groan he said, "I have never followed my own will, nor have I ever taught anything that I myself had not done first"'.

GIFTS OF HEALING

It was said concerning Abba Macarius that Agathonicus, the procurator of Antioch, heard about him, that he had great powers and

---

[19] Is 10:15.

gifts of healing through our Lord Jesus Christ. He sent him his daughter, who had an unclean spirit, so Abba Macarius might pray over her. By the grace of God that was in him, when he prayed over her she was immediately healed and he sent her in peace to her parents. When her father and mother saw the healing that the Lord had brought about in their daughter through the prayers and intercessions of Saint Abba Macarius, they gave thanks, giving glory to our Saviour Jesus Christ.

April 19
ALPHEGE, ARCHBISHOP OF CANTERBURY, MARTYR (A)

STEADY WORK

Abba Matoës said, 'I want work that is light and steady, not work that is burdensome from the beginning and quickly given up on'.

WHOEVER NEEDS MONEY TAKE SOME

A great man came from a foreign country, bearing a large amount of gold with him to Scetis, and he urged the priest to give it to the brothers. But the priest said to him, 'The brothers do not need it'.

After making numerous attempts to force him to accept the money, the man placed the small basket at the door of the church, and the priest said, 'Whoever needs money can take some'.

No one came near it; some paid it no attention at all. And the priest said to him, 'God has accepted your alms. Go and give it to the poor'. And he left, greatly edified.

April 20

I AM SISOËS

They said of Abba Sisoës that when he came to Clysma he fell ill. While he was sitting with his disciple in his cell, someone knocked on the door. Then the old man understood and said to his disciple, 'Abraham, say to the person who is knocking, "I am Sisoës on the mountain and I am Sisoës on my bed"'.

Hearing this, the one who knocked disappeared.

THE NOONDAY DEMON

The demon of *acedia*—also called the noonday demon—is the one that causes the most serious trouble of all. He presses his attack upon the monk about the fourth hour and besieges the soul until the eighth hour. First of all he makes it seem that the sun barely moves, if at all, and that the day is fifty hours long. Then he constrains the monk to look constantly out the windows, to walk outside the cell, to gaze carefully at the sun to determine how far it stands from the ninth hour, to look now this way and now that to see if perhaps one of the brothers appears from his cell.

Then too he instills in the heart of the monk a hatred for place, a hatred for his very life itself, a hatred for manual labor. He leads him to reflect that charity has departed from among the brothers, that there is no one to give encouragement. Should there be someone at this period who happens to offend him in some way or other, this too the demon uses to contribute further to his hatred. This demon drives him along to desire other sites where he can more easily procure life's necessities, more readily find work, and make a real place that is the basis of pleasing the Lord. God is to be adored everywhere.

He joins to these reflections the memory of his dear ones and of his former way of life. He depicts life stretching out for a long period of time, and brings before the mind's eye the toil of the ascetic struggle and, as the saying has it, leaves no leaf unturned to induce the monk to forsake his cell and drop out of the fight. No other demon follows close upon the heels of this one (when he is defeated), but only a state of deep peace and inexpressible joy arise out of this struggle.

April 21
ANSELM, ARCHBISHOP OF CANTERBURY,
MONK, THEOLOGIAN (RC, A)

THROW IT OUTSIDE

Abba Isaac said, 'Abba Pambo used to say, "The monk should wear such clothing that he could throw it outside his cell and no one would take it"'.

I HAVE SOLD THE VERY WORD

An old man said: One of the brothers possessed only a book of the Gospels and he sold it and gave the money to feed the poor, making a statement that is worth remembering: 'I have sold the very word,' he said, 'that tells me *Sell your possessions and give to the poor*'.[20]

April 22
MARIA GABRIELLA SAGHEDDU, NUN, PATRON OF CHRISTIAN UNITY (RC, M)

SIT IN YOUR CELL

A brother came to Scetis to visit Abba Moses and asked him for a word.

The old man said to him, 'Go, sit in your cell, and your cell will teach you everything'.

THE POWER OF THE PARACLETE AT WORK

Abba Macarius said: I was passing through the desert one time when the Devil met me; his face was ugly and very fearful, and he said to me, 'You are powerful, Macarius! Your fame resounds in the east and in the west, like that of Antony the Great, the leader of

---

[20] Mt 19:21.

solitary monks, and you emulate him, *as Elisha emulated Elijah,*[21] for Antony himself was your teacher because it was he who clothed you in the monastic habit. Indeed, you have fought me with your humility because you received counsel from Antony in humility and esteemed him as a god through the love engendered by your authentic humility. When I fought you with my weapons, the passions, you would always say right away from the depths of your heart with a firm faith, "Behold, my doctor and my physician upon the mountain and the river'".

I said to him in response, 'I am truly blessed because the Lord Jesus, mindful of you, has strengthened my heart and faith in my teacher. The medicines of my lord and father Abba Antony are not fleshly; no, the power of the Paraclete is at work in his prayers. Spiritual medicines are acceptable to God like incense'.

When the Devil heard these things, he became like smoke and disappeared and I continued walking, giving glory to our Lord Jesus Christ.

April 23
GEORGE, MARTYR (O, RC, A)

ABBA JOHN AND THE COIN

One of the fathers told the story about Abba John the Persian that because of his great virtue he had attained the most profound innocence. He was living in Arabia of Egypt. One time he borrowed a gold coin from a brother and bought some thread in

---

[21] 1 Kings 19:19-21.

order to work. A brother came to him and said, 'Abba, loan me a little thread so I can make myself a cloak', and he gladly gave him some. Similarly, another brother also came and implored him, saying, 'Give me a little thread so I can make a headdress', and he gave him some also. Similarly, when others also asked, he freely and gladly gave them what they asked for. Later, the owner of the gold coin came and wanted it, so the old man said to him, 'I will bring it to you myself'.

Not having any way to return the money to its owner, he got up and went to Abba James the deacon to ask him to give him some money to repay the brother. While he was on his way, he found a solidus lying on the ground but did not touch it. Saying a prayer, he returned to his cell. Again the brother came, wanting to be paid his money, and the old man said to him, 'I will make it my only concern'. So the old man left once again and found the money lying on the ground where it had been before. Once again he offered a prayer and returned—and, once again, here came the brother, upset with him. And the old man said, 'Just give me one more chance and I will bring it to you'.

So once again he got up and went to that same place and found the coin lying there and he offered a prayer, picked it up, and went to Abba James and said to him, 'Abba, while I was coming to see you, I found this coin on the road. Please do me a favor and make it known in the region, in case someone lost it, and if its owner is found, give it to him'. So Abba James left and announced the discovery for three days, but no one was found who had lost it. Then the old man said to Abba James, 'If no one has lost this coin, give it to this brother here, for I owe him money. As I was coming to ask you for alms in order to pay back the debt, I found it in the road'.

The old man was amazed how Abba John, being in debt, had found the coin and had not taken it right away and paid off his debt with it. And this was equally amazing about Abba John: if someone came to borrow something from him, he did not supply it himself but would say to the brother, 'Go and help yourself to whatever you need'. If the brother returned it, Abba John would say to him, 'Put it back where you got it'. But if the person who took something did not return it, Abba John would not say anything to him.

THE AGGRIEVED TRAFFICKER

A brother came to Abba Theodore and spent three days begging him to say a word to him without getting any reply. So he went away grieved.

Then the old man's disciple said to him, 'Abba, why did you not say a word to him? See, he has gone away grieved'.

The old man said to him, 'I did not speak to him because he is a trafficker who seeks to glorify himself through the words of others'.

I GO WHEREVER I WANT

One of the fathers related a story, saying: When I was in Oxyrhynchus, the poor came there on Saturday evening to receive Christian charity. While they were sleeping, there was one person there who had only a single rush mat, half on top of him and half underneath him. It was very cold at that time.

When he went outside to urinate, I heard his teeth chattering on account of the cold and he was consoling himself by saying, 'I give you thanks, Lord. How many rich people are even now sitting in prison—some shackled in irons, while others have their feet held tightly in the stocks—unable even to urinate by themselves? I, however, am like an emperor, stretching my legs; wherever I want to go, I go'.

While he was saying these things I was standing there listening. I went inside and told the story to the brothers and they listened to it and benefitted from it.

LOVING YOUR NEIGHBOR

Our holy father Abba John went again to the harvest and was with the brothers as leader. With great mercy he allowed all of them to rest whenever necessary, and when he labored he would not straighten his back at all until he first clapped his hands and allowed the brothers to rest. Afterwards he also allowed himself to rest, saying, '*The law was given to us in the Scriptures to treat our friend as ourselves*, especially in honor.[22] Therefore, if I allow my brothers to rest, God will also allow me to rest'.

SIX BATCHES OF BREAD

Abba Theodore of Enaton said, 'When I was young, I lived in the desert. One day I went to the bakery to make two loaves, and there I found a brother also wanting to make bread, but there was no one to help him. So I put mine aside to lend him a hand. When the work was done, another brother came, and I did the same; and similarly one after the other, I baked for each of those who came. I made six batches. Later I made my own two loaves, since no one else came'.

[22] Mk 12:31 and parallels.

PRAYER IS SEED

Abba Nilus said, 'Prayer is the seed of gentleness and the absence of anger'.

PRAYER IS A REMEDY

He also said, 'Prayer is a remedy against grief and depression'.

THIS IS HUMILITY

A brother questioned Abba Motius, saying, 'If I go to dwell somewhere, how do you want me to live?'

The old man said to him, 'If you live somewhere, do not seek to be known for anything special. Do not say, for example, "I do not go to the synaxis"; or, perhaps, "I do not eat at the agape meal". These things make for an empty reputation and later you will be troubled because of this. People rush there where they find these practices'.

The brother said to him, 'What shall I do, then?'

The old man said, 'Wherever you live, follow the same manner of life as everyone else, and if you see devout persons whom you trust doing something, do the same and you will be at peace. For this is humility: to see yourself to be the same as the rest. When people see that you do not go beyond the limits, they will consider you to be the same as everyone else and no one will trouble you'.

EULOGIUS THE STONECUTTER

[*Abba Daniel and his disciple put in at a village in the Thebaid where they are greeted by 'an elderly lay person . . . a large man, completely gray-headed', named Eulogius. After Daniel and his disciple return to Scetis, Daniel tells him Eulogius' story.*]

That old man is called 'Eulogius'; by trade he is a stonecutter. He earns a *keration* a day from his manual labor, eating nothing until evening, and when evening comes he goes out to the village and takes home whatever foreigners he finds and feeds them, and the leftover fragments he throws to the dogs. When I was younger, I went up to sell my handiwork at that village and at evening he came and took me and other brothers with me, and gave us lodging. When I went there and saw the man's virtue, I began to fast every day of the week and entreat God to provide him with greater wages so he might have more money and do good for even more people.

After fasting for three weeks, I was half dead on account of my ascetic regimen, and I saw that it was as though I was standing in the Church of the Holy Resurrection. *A young man was sitting upon the holy stone*[23] and Eulogius was standing at his right. I then saw angels emptying a very large amount of money into Eulogius' lap and Eulogius' lap was able to hold it, however much they kept pouring. When I woke up I knew that I had been heard and I gave glory to God.

When Eulogius went out to do his work, he struck rock, heard a hollow-sounding thunk, so he struck again and found a small hole; again he struck the rock and found a cave filled with money. Amazed, Eulogius said to himself, 'What should I do with it? If I take it to the village, the owner will hear about it and will come

[23] See Mt 28:2.

and take it and I'll be in danger. It would be better if I go out into the countryside where no one knows me'. Hiring animals as though he were using them to haul stones, at night he hauled the money to the riverside and put the money in a boat and sailed to Byzantium. Justin, who was an old man, was emperor at that time. Eulogius gave a large amount of money to him and the emperor made him procurator of the holy praetorian guard. He also bought a large house and to this day it is called 'the house of the Egyptian'.

Two years later I saw that young man again in a dream in the Church of the Holy Resurrection, as before. A little later I saw Eulogius being dragged away by his hair from the young man by an Ethiopian. Waking up, I said to myself, 'God help me, a sinner!' Taking my sheepskin cloak, I left for the village in order to sell my handiwork, expecting to find Eulogius.

Late evening came and no one invited me home, so I got up and made inquiries of an old woman. Sitting down beside me, she said, 'Abba, sir, we used to have a certain stonecutter here and he used to do many good things for the foreigners. When God saw his works, he gave him grace, and today, so we hear, he is a patrician'.

When I heard these things, I said to myself, 'I committed this murder!' and I boarded ship and sailed to Byzantium. Diligently seeking the house of Eulogius the Egyptian, I sat in front of his gate until he came out. I saw him coming with great ostentation and I called out to him, "Have mercy on me! I wish to speak with you in private about some matter!" but he turned away from me and his escort beat me instead. I left in search of a ship and, finding one bound for Alexandria, I boarded ship alone and sat by myself, feeling discouraged.

Three months later, I heard that Justin had died and Justinian was now emperor in his place. Then a little later Hypatius and Dexikratius and Pompeius and Eulogius the procurator rose up against him. The first three were seized and beheaded and all their possessions were confiscated, as was Eulogius' estate. Eulogius fled Constantinople at night and the emperor ordered that he was to be killed wherever he was found. Then he fled and went to his own village and exchanged his clothing for that of the country folk who lived there. The whole village gathered to see Eulogius, 'It's good to have you back. We heard that you had become a patrician'. He said to them, 'Indeed. If I had become a patrician, you would be coming to me with petitions. No, that was another Eulogius, who is also from here. I was in the Holy Land'.

So Eulogius came to his senses and said, 'Eulogius, you wretch, get up, take your stonecutting tools, before you also lose your head. There is no royal court here!' A little later I went up to that village and when evening fell Eulogius came. Taking me, along with the others he had found, he washed my feet, as was his custom, and set a table for us. After we had eaten I said to him, 'How are you, Abba Eulogius?' He said to me, 'Abba, pray for me, sir. I am a wretch, having nothing to my name'. I said to him, 'I wish that you had not even had what you had!' He said to me, 'Why, abba, sir? What have I ever done to offend you?' I said to him, 'What haven't you done to offend me!' Then I laid out for him everything that had happened. Both of us wept and he said to me, 'Pray, abba, that God sends me what I need and from now on I will follow the right track'. I said to him, 'Truly, brother, do not expect Christ to ever entrust you with anything else as long as you are in this world except for this *keration*, the fruit of your labor'.

You see? God has now seen to it all these years that each day he has the strength to earn the *keration* from his manual labor.

AN UNBAKED BRICK

Abba Orsisius said, 'If an unbaked brick is put in the foundations near to the river, it does not last a single day, but baked, it lasts like stone. So the person with a carnal disposition of soul, who has not been in the fire *through fear of God like Joseph*,[24] utterly disintegrates when he accepts a position of authority'.

WHY ABBA NISTERUS WORE TWO TUNICS

A brother saw Abba Nisterus *wearing two tunics*[25] and he questioned him, saying, 'If a poor person came to ask you for a tunic, which would you give him?'

He replied, 'The better one'.

'And if someone else asked you for one, what would you give him?'

The old man said, 'Half of the other one'.

The brother said, 'And if someone else asked for one, what would you give him?'

He said, 'I would cut the rest, give him half, and gird myself with whatever was left'.

So the brother said, 'And if someone came and asked you for that, what would you do?'

The old man said, 'I would give him the rest and go and sit down somewhere until God sent me something to cover myself with, for I would not ask anyone for anything'.

[24] See Gen 39.
[25] See Lk 9:3.

WE, WHO HAVE NOTHING

Amma Syncletica said, 'Those who have endured the labors and dangers of the sea and then amass material riches, even when they have gained much they desire to gain yet more and they consider what they have at present as nothing and reach out for what they have not got. We, who have nothing of that which we desire, wish to acquire everything through the fear of God'.

IF SOMEONE OWNS A RUINED HOUSE

She also said, 'It is dangerous for anyone to teach who has not first been trained in the "practical" life. For if someone who owns a ruined house receives guests there, he does them harm because of the dilapidation of his dwelling. It is the same in the case of someone who has not first built an interior dwelling; that person causes loss to those who come. By words one may convert them to salvation, but by evil behavior one injures them'.

DO NOT CLING TO WEAKNESS

Do not cling to weakness, for weakness begets weakness.

DO NOT LISTEN

Do not give ear to anyone who speaks troubling things to you that cause you to be disturbed and to forsake your cell.

MAY

EASTERTIDE / PENTECOST/ ORDINARY TIME

May 1
JOSEPH THE WORKER (RC)
SAINT PHILIP AND SAINT JAMES, APOSTLES (A)

WITH THE GENTLENESS OF CHRIST

Some brothers asked our father Abba John, saying to him, 'Is it good, our father, to foster good habits with others?'

Abba John said to them, 'It is good to foster such habits toward our brother: God died for him, for us and for him at one and the same time, in the same unique way. With the gentleness of Christ let us gain our brother with all the purity of the Holy Spirit and let us exercise habit with courage against the enmity that separates us from God'.

MATTERS OF THE MARRIAGE CHAMBER

Our father Abba Macarius said: It is written, *Your fear, Lord, we conceived; we were in labor and gave birth to a spirit of salvation.*[1] See that you grasp what I am saying and not be someone who does not give birth. To be sure, my brothers, *these are matters of the marriage chamber,*[2] but they are also the fruits of *those who have done their work well,*[3] those who have *built their house on solid rock:*

[1] Is 26:18 (LXX).
[2] Mt 22:11.
[3] Mt 25:20-22.

compassion and faith.[4] Lord, let us not be lacking in your fear and wrath and let us not lack humility and mourning. Take heed of these things, which are salvation in our Lord, you who wish to live in peace. Amen.

GOD'S CONSUMING FIRE

Some old men questioned Abba Macarius the Egyptian: 'Whether you eat or whether you fast, your body is dried up'.

The old man said to them, 'Fire insatiably consumes the wood that is employed for kindling for the fire; likewise, if a person purifies his heart in the fear of God, the fear of God consumes his bones'.

THE ANGRY BROTHER AND THE WATER JUG

A brother was a hesychast in a cenobium and was often moved to anger so he said to himself, 'I will leave and go live by myself and, because I won't have anything to do with anyone and will be at peace, my passion will cease'.

So he left and lived in a cave by himself. One day he filled a small jug with water and put it on the ground and all of a sudden

[4] Mt 7:24.

190

it fell over. He picked it up and filled it a second time and again it fell over. Then he filled it a third time and it fell over. Enraged, he grabbed hold of the jug and broke it. When he came to himself, he knew he had been mocked by the demon and said, 'I've left and gone to live by myself and even here I've been defeated. Therefore, I will return to the cenobium. There needs to be struggle and patient endurance and God's help everywhere'. And he got up and returned to his cenobium.

May 3
PHILIP AND JAMES, APOSTLES (RC)

ABBA JOHN AND THE THIEVES

Through these great virtues of his, our father Abba John became *a great Israelite*[5] of Christ Jesus. As a result, while he was sitting in his cell one day, some men came and gathered up all the belongings he had in his dwelling and bound them in a bundle while Abba John sat there and did not speak. But those there did speak to him: 'Get up! Help us load this stuff'. Abba John got up and helped them load up, and when he had seen them off he sat back down.

When his brother came in he said, 'Where are our belongings?'

Abba John said to him, 'I don't know'.

His brother said to him, 'Show me our belongings; I don't know where they are'.

[5] See Jn 1:47.

But Abba John begged his forgiveness, saying to him, 'My brother, forgive me, I beg you. Remember, it has been three years since you laid me in the tomb'.

POSSESSING KNOWLEDGE OF OUR LORD JESUS CHRIST

Some brothers were sitting around Abba Macarius and openly asked him about *the mustard seed*: 'What is its interpretation?'[6]

He told them, 'The mustard seed can be compared to the spirit, for if a person possesses knowledge of our Lord Jesus Christ, it is said about him that his spirit is subtle. Just as the mustard seed is subtle and seasoned, in the same way it is said that the teacher is seasoned and his understanding is subtle'.

May 4
ENGLISH SAINTS AND MARTYRS OF THE REFORMATION (RC, A)[7]

WHAT EXILE MEANS

Abba Tithoës said, 'For us "exile" consists of a person gaining mastery over his tongue'.

---

[6] Mt 13:31//Lk 13:19; Mt 17:20//Lk 17:6.
[7] English Church calendars.

TRIPPING OVER MY TONGUE

Abba Sisoës spoke freely one time, 'Have courage. For thirty years now I have not prayed to God about sin, but I continue to say this prayer: "Lord Jesus, protect me from my tongue". To this very day I fall on account of my tongue and sin'.

May 5

THE MEANING OF SCETIS

Some old men inquired of Abba Macarius, 'What is the work of Scetis?'

He said to them, 'It resembles and is like *the four towns that God separated out for the children of Israel so that if an adulterer or murderer fled inside one of them he would be safe if he remained there*'.[8]

ANTONY'S FIRST SPIRITUAL DISCIPLINES

This was the way Antony initially occupied himself in that place. He resolved *not to think about his parents, nor was he mindful of his relatives*.[9] All his desire and all his energies he directed toward the great effort of ascetic discipline. So he worked with his hands,

---

[8] Num 35:11.
[9] See Mt 10:37.

having heard *Let the lazy person not eat.*[10] He would spend part of what he earned on bread and part of it he would give to those who were begging. He prayed all the time, having learned that it is necessary *to pray by oneself without ceasing.*[11] Indeed, *he paid such close attention to the reading of Scripture that nothing in the Scriptures was wasted.*[12] *He remembered everything,*[13] with the result that for him memory took the place of books.

May 6
JOB THE LONG-SUFFERING (O)

THE DEVIL'S FIRST ATTACK ON ANTONY

The Devil, who hates and envies what is good, could not bear to see such purpose in the young man so he now initiated his customary practices against Antony also. First, he attempted to lead him away from his ascetic discipline, filling him with memories of his possessions, his guardianship of his sister, the intimacy of his family, love of money, love of honor, the pleasure that comes from eating various kinds of foods, and the other indulgences of life, and finally the difficulty of living virtuously and the great suffering that that entails. He demonstrated for Antony the body's weakness and the long life ahead of him. In short, he raised up in

[10] See 2 Thes 3:10.
[11] See Mt 6:6, 1 Thes 5:17.
[12] See 1 Sam 3:19, 2 Kgs 10:10.
[13] See Lk 8:15.

Antony's mind a great dust cloud of thoughts, wanting to separate him from his ability to make correct choices.

But when the Enemy saw how weak he himself was in the face of Antony's resolve, and even more how he was being thrown to the ground by the determination of that man and tripped up by his faith and cast down by Antony's unceasing prayers, he then took courage from *the weapons strapped around his belly*.[14] Boasting about these (for these are the first snares that he lays against the young), the Enemy advanced against the young man, disturbing him at night and bothering him so much during the day that even those who were watching could see that there was a struggle being waged between the two of them.

The Devil whispered foul thoughts, but Antony rebuffed them with his prayers; the Devil titillated him, but Antony, as though he were blushing, fortified his body through faith and fasting. But the Devil stood his ground, the wretch, and now dared to take on the form of a woman at night and imitated all of a woman's ways, solely for the purpose of deceiving Antony. But Antony, reflecting on Christ in his heart and the goodness he had through him, and reflecting on the spiritual insight given to him by his soul, extinguished the Devil's deceitful coals. Once again, however, the Enemy whispered soft pleasures in Antony's ear, but Antony, as though angry and grieving, pondered in his heart *the threat of fire and the worm's punishment*.[15] Placing these thoughts in opposition to the Devil, Antony bypassed his insinuations unharmed. All these things happened to the shame of the Enemy. *He who had thought he would become like God*[16] was now mocked by a mere youth; he who had vaunted himself against flesh and blood was being rebuffed by a flesh and blood human being. For working with Antony was the Lord, who for us bore flesh and gave the body victory over

[14] Job 40:16 (LXX).
[15] See Jdt 6:17, Si 7:17, Is 66:24, Mk 9:48.
[16] Is 14:4, Ez 28:2.

the Devil so that each of those who struggle like Antony can say *It is not I but the grace of God that is in me.*[17]

THE NECESSITY OF TEMPTATIONS

Abba Antony also said, 'Whoever has not experienced temptation cannot enter into the Kingdom of Heaven'. He even added, 'Without temptation, no one can be saved'.

THOSE WHO ARE WORTHY OF ADMIRATION AND PRAISE

We were seven brothers, all of us foreign, who went up to see Abba John of Lycopolis. When he invited us to sit down, we thanked God for our meeting with him. He for his part, after welcoming us like his own dear children after a long absence, addressed us with a smiling face: 'Where are you from, my children? Which country have you travelled from to visit a poor man'.

We told him where we were from, adding, 'We have come to you from Jerusalem for the good of our souls, so that what we have heard with our ears we might perceive with our eyes'.

[17] 1 Cor 15:10.

The blessed John replied, 'And what remarkable thing did you expect to find, my dearest children, that you have undertaken such a long journey with so much labor in your desire to visit some poor simple men who possess nothing worth seeing or admiring? Those who are worthy of admiration and praise are everywhere: the apostles and prophets of God, who are read in the churches. They are the ones you must imitate. I marvel at your zeal', he said, 'how taking no account of so many dangers you have come to be edified, while we from laziness do not even come out of our cave'.

May 8
MARK THE EVANGELIST (CO)
JOHN THE THEOLOGIAN, APOSTLE (O)
JULIAN OF NORWICH (A)

NO ONE'S HOME

A magistrate came to see Abba Simon one day. When he heard of it, he put on his apron and went out to attend to a palm tree. When the visitors arrived they called out to him, 'Old man, where is the anchorite?'

He replied, 'There is no anchorite here'.

Hearing these words, they went away again.

EVAGRIUS' MYSTICAL ASCENT

A few days later Evagrius told us about the revelations he had seen. He never hid anything from his disciples. 'It happened', he said, 'while I was sitting in my cell at night with the lamp burning beside me, meditatively reading one of the prophets. In the middle of the night I became enraptured and I found myself as though I were in a dream in sleep and I saw myself as though I were suspended in the air up to the clouds and I looked down on the whole inhabited world. And the one who suspended me said to me, "Do you see all these things?" He raised me up to the clouds and I saw the whole universe at the same time. I said to him, "Yes". He said to me, "I am going to give you a commandment. If you keep it, *you will be the ruler of all these things that you see*".[18] He spoke to me again, "Go, be compassionate, humble, and keep your thoughts pointed straight to God. You will rule over all these things".

'When he had finished saying these things to me, I saw myself holding the book once again with the wick burning and I did not know how I had been taken up to the clouds. Whether I was in the flesh, I do not know; God knows. *Or whether I was in the mind, once again I do not know*'.[19]

And so he contended with the two virtues of compassion and humility as though he possessed all the virtues.

May 9
GREGORY OF NAZIANZUS, BISHOP OF CONSTANTINOPLE (A)

A PILLAGED VILLAGE

A brother was praised by the monks to Abba Antony. When the brother approached Abba Antony, the latter tested him to see if he

[18] See Lk 4:1-13.
[19] 2 Cor 12:2.

could bear dishonor and when he found that he could not bear it he said to him, 'You're like a village that's *magnificently decorated on the outside but which inside has been pillaged by robbers'.*[20]

SOLITUDE AND HELPING OTHERS

Antony healed people not by issuing orders but by praying and calling on the name of Christ. As a result, it became clear to everyone that it was not he who was doing these things but the Lord, who through Antony was demonstrating his love for humankind and healing those who were suffering. Antony prayed and practiced ascetic discipline alone, for that purpose sitting on the mountain. He rejoiced at the contemplation of divine things while at the same time he was saddened because he was being bothered by crowds of people and dragged away to the outer mountain. In fact even all the judges were asking him to come down from the mountain because it was not possible for them to go there because of all the people who accompanied the accused. So they asked him to come just so they could see him. Antony, however, turned away the petitioners and declined the invitations of those who journeyed to see him, but they persisted even more in sending him persons charged with crimes and they sent prisoners to see if he would come down on their account.

Compelled by necessity, and seeing those who were bewailing their fate, he came to the outer mountain. Once again his efforts were not without benefit, for he was able to help numerous people and his coming did a great deal of good. He helped the judges, especially advising all of them to make just decisions and to fear God and to realize that they were to be judged with the same judgement with which they judged.[21] But more than anything else, Antony loved spending his time on the mountain.

[20] See Mt 23:27.
[21] See Mt 5:27-28.

MY GOD, GIVE ME STRENGTH

It was related about Amma Sarah that for thirteen years she continued to be relentlessly warred upon by the demon of sexual sin and not once did she pray for the warfare to cease but said only, 'My God, give me strength'.

IT IS CHRIST WHO HAS DEFEATED YOU

Again it was said about her that the same spirit of sexual sin attacked her even more violently, whispering worldly vanities in her ear.

She, however, did not loosen herself from the fear of God and did not slacken her ascetic practice. She went up to her little cell to pray one day and the spirit of sexual sin appeared bodily to her and said to her, 'You have defeated me, Sarah'.

But she said to him, 'It is not I who has defeated you but my master, Christ'.

A SINGING SPARROW, RUSTLING REEDS

One time Abba Arsenius came to a place where there were some reeds and they were blowing in the wind. The old man said to the brothers, 'What is this rustling?'

They said to him, 'It's the reeds'.

The old man said to them, 'Truly, if someone living a life of contemplative quiet hears a sparrow singing, his heart no longer experiences the same peace. How much truer is this when you experience the rustling of these reeds?'

MERE SPITTLE

Abba Evagrius said: I was sitting one time with some brothers beside Abba Macarius. He was speaking to us about the sense of the Holy Scriptures and I asked the old man, 'What does this saying in the Gospels mean: *Whoever blasphemes against the Holy Spirit will not be forgiven, either in this age or in the age to come?*'[22]

The old man said to me, 'It is clear that if a person does not possess strong hope and firm faith every time he has a sinful desire, as the Lord said in the Gospel, "*If you have faith like a mustard seed, you will say to this mountain, 'Move from there,' and it will move and nothing will be impossible for you*",[23] but rather sins from his earliest days up to the end of his life and says in his heart, "If I return to God, there is no way he will forgive me or accept me," then this

[22] Mt 12:31-32; Mk 3:29//Lk 12:10.
[23] Mt 17:20//Lk 17:6.

person has blasphemed against the power of the Holy Trinity and has allowed Satan inside himself and a sin like this is unforgivable: he has not turned to God and repented with his whole heart. Again, it is like someone who has a physical malady: if he does not have faith in help from on high like *Job and like the paralytic*,[24] truly such a person blasphemes against the power of the Holy Trinity and, even worse, has allowed Satan inside himself, and sin like this is unforgivable: his sentence is to be cast eternally into Tartarus and *the outer darkness where there will be weeping and gnashing of teeth.*[25] But the repentance of all these persons is mere spittle spat in the presence of the mercy and compassion of him who possesses treasuries of compassion, our Lord Jesus Christ'.

May 12
NEREUS AND ACHILLEUS, MARTYRS (RC)

HIS SPEECH MAKES HIM WORTHY

Abba Joseph said, 'While we were sitting with Abba Poemen he mentioned Agathon as "abba", and we said to him, "He is very young, why do you call him 'abba'?"

'Abba Poemen said, "Because his speech makes him worthy to be called abba"'.

---

[24] Job 42; Mt 9:2.
[25] Mt 8:12.

THE SOUL THAT BEARS SPIRITUAL FRUIT

Abba Macarius said, 'Like *Aaron's staff, which brought forth flowers in a single night and bore fruit,*[26] thus it is with the soul of the monk: when the Lord comes to it, it puts forth spiritual flowers by means of the things that belong to Christ and bears the fruits of the Spirit and gives them to him who created it, Christ, its good King, the true and blessed God.'

May 13

A TIME IS COMING

Abba Antony said, 'A time is coming when people will go mad, and when they see someone who is not mad, they will attack him, saying, "You are mad, you are not like us"'.

A WORD OF DEATH OR A WORD OF LIFE

Abba Pambo spoke to them: 'From the day I came to this desert and built this cell and lived in it, I do not remember regretting a single word I've spoken or a single word that I should not have spoken, for unless I've ruminated on a word first and seen whether it is a word of death or a word of life, I have not spoken. *Nor am I aware of having eaten bread for nothing without working for it with my*

[26] Num 17, Heb 9:4.

hands.[27] And I have not allowed myself to think that I have spent a single day as a monk. Even now, as I am about to leave, I do not say that I have spent a single day serving God, but I reproach myself because I have not done the will of God.'

MACARIUS HEALS A HYENA PUP

One time while Abba Macarius was sitting in his cell, a hyena came to him, carrying her cub in her mouth. She placed the cub in front of his door and knocked on the door. The old man heard her knock and came out, thinking that a brother had come to see him. When he opened the door he saw the hyena. He was amazed and said, 'What do you seek here?'

She picked up her cub with her mouth and offered it to the old man, weeping. The old man took the cub in his hands with his customary simplicity; he turned the cub this way and that, inspecting its body to see where it might be hurt. When he examined the cub, he discovered that it was blind in both eyes. He took it, sighed, spit into its face, and made the sign of the cross on its eyes with his finger. Immediately the cub could see and left him for its mother and suckled. It followed her and they went into the river there and into the marshland and disappeared.

---

[27] 2 Thes 3:8.

The hyena let one day go by but the next day she came to the old man with a sheepskin, very plush and soft, hanging from her mouth as an offering, and knocked with her head on the door. The old man was sitting in the courtyard. When he heard the knock on the door, he got up and opened the door and found the hyena holding the skin as an offering. He said to the hyena, 'Where have you come from? Where did you get this unless you ate a sheep? What you have brought me has come from violence. I will not accept it from you. Unless you promise me you will not kill any living beast but will eat only carrion from now on, I will not accept the sheepskin. From now on, if you are weary from searching for food and are unable to find anything to eat, come to me here and I will give you bread, and do no violence to anyone from now on'.

The hyena prostrated herself to the earth, throwing herself on her knees, bending her paws, moving her head up and down, looking up into his face, as though she were giving him her promise. The hyena returned to her lair again and every few days would pay him a visit. If she was unable to find food, she would come to him and he would throw bread to her. She would often do this. The old man slept on the sheepskin until he went to his rest. I saw it with my own eyes.

PLEDGE, EXAMPLE, AND PROTOTYPE

One of the old men questioned Amma Theodora, saying, '*At the resurrection of the dead, how shall we rise?*'[28]

She said, 'As pledge, example, and prototype we have him who died for us and is risen, Christ our God'.

JESUS, SAVE ME!

Abba Elias said: An old man was living in a temple and the demons came to say to him, 'Leave this place, which belongs to us', and the old man said, 'No place belongs to you'. Then they began to scatter his palm leaves about, one by one, and the old man went on gathering them together with perseverance.

A little later the Devil took his hand and pulled him to the door. When the old man reached the door, he seized the lintel with the other hand, crying out, 'Jesus, save me!'

Immediately the Devil fled away. Then the old man began to weep. The Lord said to him, 'Why are you weeping?' and the old man said, 'Because the devils have dared to seize someone and treat him like this'.

The Lord said to him, 'You had been careless. As soon as you turned to me again, you see I was beside you'.

I say this because it is necessary to take great pains, and anyone who does not do so cannot come into the Kingdom of God'. For *he himself was crucified for our sake.*[29]

[28] See 1 Cor 15:12-28.
[29] See Gal 2:19-20.

HOLD OUT YOUR HANDS

When Chomai was about to be perfected, he said to his sons, 'Do not dwell with heretics, nor be friends with rulers, and do not hold out your hands in order to receive anything but instead hold them out in order to give'.

ABBA DANIEL FEEDS A LEPER

[*While kidnapped as a young man, Daniel kills one of the kidnappers and escapes; repentant for his sin, he visits several archbishops, asking for forgiveness. They tell him he has not sinned. Still repentant, he atones for the death by taking care of lepers.*]

The old man said to himself, 'I have hope, in God's merciful love for humankind, that His Goodness will not hold me responsible for this murder hereafter. From now on I pledge to Christ all the days of my life to serve one leper in return for the murder I committed'. So he took one leper to his cell and said to himself, 'If this leper dies, I will go up to Egypt and get another in his place'. All the monks of Scetis knew that the old man had a leper, but no one was able to see his face except the old man, and he alone.

One day, then, about noon, the old man summoned his disciple to serve him something to eat. Through God's divine agency it happened that the old man had forgotten that the door to his cell had been left open. He was sitting in the sun, treating the leper. The leper was completely eaten up by his many wounds. The old man's disciple returned from his duties and, finding the door open, observed how the old man was treating the leper. Because the leper had so completely rotted away, Abba Daniel kneaded the food and put it in the leper's mouth.

When the disciple saw the amazing work that the old man was doing, he was astonished and glorified God who was supplying such great patience to the old man to serve the leper like this.

TRUE SILENCE

Abba Poemen said, 'A person may seem to be silent, but if his heart is condemning others he is babbling ceaselessly. But there may be another who talks from morning till night and yet he is truly silent; that is, he says nothing that is not profitable'.

IS IT BECAUSE OF THE VOICES OF ANGELS?

Abba Poemen's brothers said to him, 'Let us leave this place, for the monasteries here worry us and we are losing our souls; even the little children who cry do not let us have interior peace'.

Abba Poemen said to them, 'Is it because of voices of angels that you wish to go away from here?'

May 18
JOHN I, POPE, MARTYR (RC)

DRIVING OVER THE DEVIL

A wise person in his cell is the winnower of the impious, and *he will drive a wheel over the Wicked One.*[30]

I SHALL FIND IT AGAIN

Abba Daniel said, 'At the point of death, Abba Arsenius sent us this message: "Do not trouble to make offerings for me, for truly I have made an offering for myself and I shall find it again."'

May 19
DUNSTAN, ARCHBISHOP OF CANTERBURY (A)

I GIVE THANKS TO YOU, MY GOD

Abba Arsenius was ill one time at Scetis and for his illness he did not have even a single loaf of wheat bread. Not having anything with which to buy any, he received some through someone's

[30] See Prv 20:26 (LXX).

charity and said, 'I give thanks to you, my God, because you have considered me worthy to receive charity in your name'.

THOUGHTS WEAVE CROWNS

An old man said: 'Once a brother was badly tempted by thoughts for nine years so that as a result he despaired of his own salvation and condemned himself, saying, "I have destroyed my soul. Since I've destroyed it, I'm going to return to the world".

'While he was on his way back to the world, a voice came to him on the road saying, "Those nine years that you were tempted were your crowns. Therefore return where you were and I will relieve you of your thoughts".

'Do you see that it isn't good for someone to fall into despair on account of thoughts? Instead, these thoughts weave crowns for us and place them on our heads if we successfully deal with them'.

May 20
MARK THE HERMIT (GO)
BERNARDINE OF SIENA, PRIEST (RC)
ALCUIN OF YORK, DEACON, ABBOT, SCHOLAR (A)

ABBA AARON AND THE MIRACLE OF THE FISH

On another occasion, some fishermen came to Abba Aaron, down-hearted, and they entreated him, saying, 'Please pray for us. We are being harassed by a certain nobleman about a large quantity of fish, which we have not been able to catch and deliver to him. We're afraid that he will hold us liable and sue us for damages beyond our ability to pay'.

Abba Aaron replied and said, 'Have you not heard that the Lord said to Peter, "*Cast your net on the right side of the boat, and you will catch something*"?[31] He did not say "on the left side", but "on the right side", which means that when someone abandons himself to evil thoughts, that is to say, to things that are on the left, he does evil. When he does the things of the right hand, that is, things that are good, everything that he asks from God will come to him. To be sure, the Lord spoke this way to those on the left: "*Depart from me, you accursed, into the everlasting fire that has been prepared for the Devil and his angels*".[32] But to those on his right hand he said, "*Come to me, you blessed of my father*".[33] And again he said, "*Come to me, everyone who is weary and burdened, and I will give you rest*".[34] And again, "*You will inherit the kingdom that has been prepared for you from the foundation of the world*".[35] Why? He said, "*I was hungry and you fed me; thirsty, and you gave me something to drink. I was naked, and you clothed me; I was a stranger and you accepted me among you. I was sick and you visited me; in prison, and you came to see me*".[36] All this means that if you cast your net on the right side, you yourselves shall catch many fish, according to your need'.

And they said to him, 'We swear by your salvation, our holy father, it's because of our poverty that we haven't had the leisure to go to church on the Sabbath and on the Lord's Day!' He said to them, 'Have I said to you, "You haven't been going to God's church?" If you ask him, he will have mercy on you, and he will not let you be in need of anything, for it is the duty of all Christians to go to the house of God first thing in the morning and pray to him to make ready the work of their hands'.

[31] Jn 21:6.
[32] Mt 25:41.
[33] Mt 25:34.
[34] Mt 11:28.
[35] Mt 25:34.
[36] Mt 25:35-36.

They prostrated themselves at his feet, saying, 'Pray over us, our holy father, and we will obey all your words'. So he prayed over them and gave them a bowl of water, saying, 'Sprinkle this over your nets, and you will catch something'. Now they left in faith and they caught a large number of fish. They gave the nobleman as many as he wanted and they kept the rest for the needs of their household. And they came to the righteous man and they gave thanks to God and to him for his holy prayers.

May 21
CONSTANTINE AND HELEN, EQUAL TO THE APOSTLES (O)
HELENA, PROTECTOR OF HOLY PLACES (A)
GODRIC OF FINCHALE (M)

IF WE TAKE AWAY TEMPTATIONS

Abba Evagrius said, 'Take away temptations and no one will be saved'.

THE PASSIONS OF THE SOUL

The passions of the soul are occasioned by human beings. Those of the body come from the body. Now the passions of the body are cut off by continence and those of the soul by spiritual love.

212

WHAT DO I DO IF SOMEONE HAS A GRIEVANCE AGAINST ME?

Abba Bitimius asked Abba Poemen, 'If someone has a grievance against me and I ask his pardon but cannot convince him, what is to be done?'

The old man said to him, 'Take two other brothers with you and ask his pardon. If he is not satisfied, take five others. If he is still not satisfied by them, take a priest. If even so he is not satisfied, then pray to God without anxiety that he may himself satisfy him, and do not worry about it'.

May 22
PACHOMIOS, FATHER OF EASTERN MONASTICISM (CO)

PACHOMIUS' CONVERSION

After the persecution of Diocletian, the great Constantine ruled. Making war against some tyrant, he ordered many conscripts to be impressed. Pachomius himself, who was then about twenty years old, was impressed. As the conscripts were sailing downstream, the soldiers who were keeping them put in at the city of Thebes and held them in prison there. In the evening some merciful Christians, hearing about them, brought them something to eat and drink and other necessities, because they were in distress. When the young man asked about this, he was told that Christians were merciful to everyone, including strangers. Again he asked what a Christian was. They told him, 'They are people who bear the name of Christ, the only begotten Son of God, and they do good to everyone, putting their hope in Him who made heaven and earth and us human beings'.

Hearing of this great grace, his heart was set on fire with the fear of God and with joy. Withdrawing alone in the prison, he raised his hands to heaven in prayer and said, '*O God, maker of heaven and earth, if you will look upon me in my lowliness*,[37] because I do not *know you, the only true God*,[38] and if you will deliver me from this affliction, I will serve your will all the days of my life, loving all people. I will be their servant according to your command'. After saying this prayer he set sail with them.

Constantine defeated his adversaries and the conscripts were discharged by an imperial edict. Pachomius went to the Upper Thebaid, and came to the church of a village called Chenoboskion. There he was instructed and baptized. The night he was made worthy of the mystery, he had a dream. He saw the dew of heaven descend upon him. When the dew had collected in his right hand and turned into solid honey and the honey had dropped to the ground, he heard someone say to him, 'Understand what is happening, for it will happen to you later'.

Then, moved by the love of God, he sought to become a monk.

---

[37] 1 Sam 1:11; see Lk 1:48.
[38] Jn 17:3.

THEY ARE NOT COOKED, ABBA

Abba Isaiah called one of the brothers, washed his feet, put a handful of lentils into the pot, and brought them to him as soon as they had boiled. The brother said to him, 'They are not cooked, Abba'.

The old man replied, 'Is it not enough simply to have seen the fire? That alone is a great consolation'.

GIVE ME SOME WHEAT

It was said of Abba Isaiah that one day he took a branch and went to the threshing-floor to thresh and said to the owner, 'Give me some wheat'.

The latter replied, 'Have you brought in the harvest, father?'

He said, 'No'.

The owner said to him, 'How then can you expect to be given wheat, if you have not harvested?'

Then the old man said to him, 'So then, if someone does not work, he does not receive wages?'[39]

The owner replied, 'No'. At that the old man went away.

Seeing what he had done, the brothers bowed before him, asking him to tell them why he had acted thus.

The old man said to them, 'I did this as an example: whoever has not worked will not receive a reward from God'.

[39] Lk 10:7, 2 Thes 3:10.

HOW CAN I BE SAVED?

When the holy Abba Antony lived in the desert, he was beset by *accidie* and attacked by many sinful thoughts. He said to God, 'Lord, I want to be saved but these thoughts do not leave me alone; what shall I do in my affliction? How can I be saved?' A short while afterwards, when he got up to go out, Antony saw a man like himself sitting at his work, getting up from his work to pray, then sitting down and plaiting a rope, then getting up again to pray. It was an angel of the Lord sent to correct and reassure him. He heard the angel saying to him, 'Do this and you will be saved.' At these words, Antony was filled with joy and courage. He did this, and he was saved.

WHAT DO YOU WANT WITH ME, YOU RUNT?

Our father Abba John came up from the field during the heat of the harvest with the brothers to allow them to cool off, and he met an old woman on the road lying flat on the ground, and a demon was flaying her mercilessly.

When our father Abba John saw her, he had pity on her and in spite of the heat stopped to pray over her. The demon called out from the woman, 'What do you want with me, you runt? I left you the desert. Now you've come here, too! Leave me alone!' And in that hour the demon came out of her and she was immediately cured. When the brothers saw what had happened through our righteous father, they glorified God.

A THOUSAND SILVER COINS, A SINGLE COPPER

While Abba Poemen was sitting beside him along with Abba
Paphnutius, the true and faithful disciple, Abba Evagrius asked
Abba Macarius about the purity of free will.

Abba Macarius told them, 'The purity of free will is the person
who will give a thousand silver coins to obtain what he wants
through his own free will, and these coins will be like a single
copper coin to him. If his free will acts so forcefully on account of
a single copper coin, he will suffer the loss of one thousand gold
coins on account of the force of his free will'.

They said to him, 'What do these words mean?'

Abba Macarius said to them, 'Search and see. Examine my
words'.

And when they examined his words, they found them to be
true, and after they asked his forgiveness, he prayed over them and
dismissed them while they gave glory to our Lord Jesus Christ.

COMPASSION AND PRAYER

Since it was necessary for Abba Macarius to take the road to see
those who were sick in order to pray for them, and since the
crowds bothered him, he dug in the earth below the church and
made a tunnel that he took to the hospice for the sick. He would
travel it beneath the earth twice a day to see them by means of the
hidden passage (no one knew about it), saying twenty-four prayers
while walking to see them under the earth and twenty-four prayers
with *metanoia* while returning from them under the earth until he
came to his church. And in this way he would visit them twice a
day, praying with them and petitioning God to heal them.

TRUST, NO REGRETS, AND RESTRAINT

Abba Pambo asked Abba Antony, 'What shall I do?'

The old man said to him, 'Do not put your trust in your own righteousness, have no regrets for something done in the past, and restrain your tongue and your belly'.

GOOD AND EVIL

One day Abba Macarius the Egyptian went up from Scetis to the mountain of Nitria. As he approached the place he told his disciple to go on ahead. When the latter had gone on ahead, he met a priest of the pagans. The brother shouted after him, saying, 'Oh, oh, devil, where are you off to?'

The priest turned back and beat him and left him half dead. Then picking up the stick, he fled. When he had gone a little further, Abba Macarius met him running and said to him, 'Greetings! Greetings, you weary man!'

Quite astonished, the priest came up to Abba Macarius and said, 'What good do you see in me that you greet me in this way?'

The old man said to the priest, 'I have seen you wearing yourself out without knowing that you are wearing yourself out in vain'.

The priest said to Abba Macarius, 'I have been touched by your greeting and I realize that you are on God's side. But another, wicked, monk who met me insulted me and I have given him blows enough for him to die of them'.

The old man realized that the priest was referring to his disciple. Then the priest fell at the old man's feet and said, 'I will not let you go till you have made me a monk'.

When they came to the place where the brother was, they put him on their shoulders and carried him to the church in the mountain. When the people saw the priest with Macarius they were astonished and they made him a monk. Through him many pagans became Christians. So Abba Macarius said, 'One evil word makes even the good evil, while one good word makes even the evil good'.

May 27
AUGUSTINE OF CANTERBURY, BISHOP (RC)

SEEING THE SIMPLE THINGS

Abba Poemen said, 'Because of our need to eat and to sleep, we do not see the simple things'.

YOU WHO CARE FOR ALL OF CREATION

When Abba Macarius was speaking openly to the brothers, he said: One time when I was in the wadi gathering palm branches, an antelope came up to me, tearing out its fur, weeping as though it were a he-goat, its tears flowing to the ground. It threw itself down on top of my feet and moistened them with its tears, and I sat down and stroked its face and anointed it with my hands, amazed at its tears, while it gazed back at me. After a while, it took hold of my tunic and pulled on me. I followed it through the power of our Lord Jesus Christ and when it took me to where it lived, I found its three young lying there. When I sat down, it took hold of them one by one and placed them in my lap and when I touched them I found that they were deformed: their chins were on their backs. I took pity on them as their mother wept; I groaned over them, saying, 'You who care for all of creation, our Lord Jesus Christ, who have numerous treasuries of mercy, take pity on the creature you made'.

After I said these words accompanied by tears before my Lord Jesus Christ, I stretched out my hand and made the saving sign of the cross over the antelope's young, and they were healed. When I put them down, their mother immediately gave them her attention. They went underneath to her nipples and sucked her milk. She rejoiced over them, delighting in them, looking into my eyes with great joy. I marvelled at the goodness of God and the love for humanity of our Lord Jesus Christ as shown by his tender mercies for me and for the other beasts that he cares about. I got up and walked, giving glory for the great goodness of our Lord Jesus Christ and the multitude of his mercies for every creature he has made.

May 28
GERMAIN OF PARIS (O)
LANFRANC, PRIOR OF BEC, ARCHBISHOP OF CANTERBURY (A)

CANNIBALISM

Hyperechius said, 'It is better to eat meat and drink wine and not eat the flesh of one's brothers through slander'.

THE WHISPERING SERPENT

Again he said, 'By whispering, *the serpent drove Eve out of paradise*.[40] Therefore, whoever slanders his neighbor is also like the serpent, for he destroys the soul of the person who listens to him and does not save his own soul'.

EVAGRIUS' CONTEMPLATIVE PRACTICES

With regard to sleep, Evagrius followed a rule: he would sleep a third of the night, but during the day he would not sleep at all. He had a courtyard where he would spend the middle part of each day walking, driving away sleep from himself, training his intellect to examine his thoughts systematically. When he had finished sleeping a third of the night, he would spend the rest of the night walking in the courtyard, meditating and praying, driving sleep away from himself, training his intellect to reflect on the meaning of the Scriptures.

May 29

I AM A SLAVE

Abba Silvanus said, 'I am a slave. My master says to me, "Do your work and I will feed you, but don't try to find out where your food comes from. Don't try to find out whether I have it or steal it or

[40] Gen 3:1-5.

221

borrow it. Just work, and I will feed you". Therefore, if I work, I eat what I have earned; but if I do not work, I eat charity'.

WATERING A PIECE OF DRY WOOD

It was said of Abba John the Little that he withdrew and lived in the desert at Scetis with an old man of Thebes. His abba, taking a piece of dry wood, planted it and said to him, 'Water it every day with a bottle of water, until it bears fruit'.

Now the water was so far away that he had to leave in the evening and return the following morning. At the end of three years the wood came to life and bore fruit. Then the old man took some of the fruit and carried it to the church, saying to the brothers, 'Take and eat *the fruit of obedience*'.[41]

May 30
JOAN OF ARC, VISIONARY (A)

WALK ON BY

Some fathers questioned Abba Poemen, 'If we see a brother sinning, do you want us to reproach him?'

The old man said to them, 'For my part, if I need to pass by where he lives and I see him sinning, I walk on by and do not reproach him'.

[41] See Gen 3:1-7.

THE DEMONS FIGHT AGAINST YOU?

Abraham, the disciple of Abba Agathon, questioned Abba Poemen, saying, 'How do the demons fight against me?'

Abba Poemen said to him, 'The demons fight against you? They do not fight against us at all as long as we are doing our own will. For our own wills become the demons, and it is these that attack us in order that we may fulfill them.'

May 31
THE VISITATION OF THE BLESSED VIRGIN MARY TO ELIZABETH (RC, A)

REMEMBERING THE RIGHT WRONGS

Abba Macarius said, 'If we keep remembering the wrongs that people have done us, we destroy the power of the remembrance of God. But if we remind ourselves of the evil deeds of the demons, we shall be invulnerable'.

BECOMING FIRE

Abba Lot went to see Abba Joseph and said to him, 'Abba, as far as I can, I say my little office, I fast a little, I pray and meditate, I live in peace and, as far as I can, I purify my thoughts. What else can I do?'

Then the old man stood up and stretched his hands towards heaven. His fingers became like ten lamps of fire and he said to him, 'If you want to, you can become all flame'.

JUNE

PENTECOST

ORDINARY TIME

THREE-HANDLED BASKETS

A certain old man, living in a village near the borders of Egypt, fell because of ignorance. He asserted that the duality of the Holy Trinity should be worshipped, that is, the Father and the Son, but that the Spirit should not be called 'God'. A large number followed him in thinking this way. God, however, did not want the old man's ascetic labor and sweat to be vainly squandered so he revealed the old man's ideas to the divine Bishoy, as well as showing him the region and location where the old man lived.

Abba Bishoy immediately got up and made a number of large baskets with three handles. He went to see that man and, when he found him, pretended to be a stranger. Many of the simpler people there shared the old man's wicked opinion. When those with him saw the three-handled baskets, not knowing who Bishoy was or where he was from, they were utterly astonished and had no idea how the baskets had been made. They asked him what they were and what he wanted to do with them. 'I want to sell them', he said. 'And why', they then asked, 'did you make them with three handles?'

'Because', he said, 'I am a friend and lover of the supremely holy Trinity, it is incumbent upon me to represent through my work the persons of the Trinity and to praise the Trinity in a three-fold fashion by making these three signs representing it. That one Nature expresses itself in three Persons. If someone understands this differently, he does not think correctly and should not hold such an opinion. Each basket has one nature with three *hypostases*, for in each of the three handles the entire essence of each basket manifests itself equally. In this way, then, the immaterial Nature and superessential Godhead is manifested in three forms or persons— the Father with the Son and the Holy Spirit—and the whole essence abides in each. Concerning the three, neither more nor less is spoken of, seeing that one does not claim to be greater in nature than another'.

June 2
MARCELLINUS AND PETER, MARTYRS (RC)
THE MARTYRS OF LYONS (A)

CHURCH CLOTHES

It was said of Abba Arsenius that just as none in the palace had worn more splendid garments than he when he lived there, so no one in the Church wore such poor clothing.

THE FRUITS OF THE SPIRIT

John of Lycopolis said, 'This is what it means to renounce the Devil and all his works. For through any sinful act or the onset of a perverse desire the Devil enters into our hearts, for vices are from him just as virtues are from God. So if there are vices in our heart, when their prince the Devil comes they give him room as their own creator and they introduce him to his own possessions. When this happens, such hearts can never have peace or stillness but are always thrown into disorder and held fast and oppressed, sometimes by an empty cheerfulness, sometimes by a vain sadness. For they have an evil occupant within them to whom they have given the means of entry through their passions and vices.

'On the other hand, for a mind that has truly renounced the world, that is, one that has cut off and severed itself from every vice and has left the Devil no means of entry, a mind that has checked anger, put down fury, avoided deceit, banished envy, and not only does not disparage its neighbor but does not even allow itself to think or suspect any evil of another and which takes to itself the joys of a brother and reckons his sadness as its own, a mind that observes these things and those like it, there will always grow therein the fruits of the Spirit, which are joy, happiness, love, patience, long-suffering, and goodness. This is what the Lord said in the Gospel: *A good tree cannot bear bad fruit, nor can a bad tree bear good fruit.*[1] *For a tree is known by its fruit*'.[2]

[1] Mt 7:18.
[2] Mt 12:33.

WATCH YOUR MOUTH

Do not let your mouth give you so much difficulty that, in its lack of restraint, it delivers you into the hands of your enemies.[4] *For great and numerous are its slaughters and the deadly snares that come from it.*[5]

THREE DEMONS ACCOST ABBA MACARIUS AT NIGHT

When Abba Macarius was asleep one night, three demons appeared and said to him, 'We are saints. Get up so we can pray'.

He remained sitting and said to them, '*Go to the darkness where there will be tears*'.[6]

They said to him, 'You blaspheme the saints? Get up so we can pray! A demon will not say to a person "Pray". But look, there are three of us, a type of the Trinity'.

Again, however, he cursed them in the name of the Lord. When they drew near to him, he began to slide himself back with the mat that was under him and cried out, 'My Lord Jesus, help me!' Immediately they became like smoke and disappeared.

HOW TO PRAY

Abba Macarius was asked, 'How should one pray?'

[3] Charles Lwanga and companions on the RC calendar.
[4] See Jm 3:5-8.
[5] See Sir 5:14.
[6] See Mt 8:12.

The old man said, 'There is no need at all to make long discourses; it is enough to stretch out one's hands and say, "Lord, as you will, and as you know, have mercy". And if the conflict grows fiercer say, "Lord, help!" He knows very well what we need and he shows us his mercy'.

June 4
PETROC, ABBOT OF PADSTOW (A)

THE WORLD'S ENTANGLEMENTS

May the world's entanglements not seize you, my beloved.

RUNNING IN VAIN

If you desire to pray as you ought, do not sadden anyone. Otherwise you run in vain.

TWO DAYS VS. SIXTY YEARS

An anchorite became a bishop. This man, out of piety, would rebuke no one, patiently bearing everyone's faults. The bishop's administrator, however, was not managing the church's business as he was supposed to, so some people said to the bishop, 'Why do you not rebuke the administrator for being negligent?'

The bishop postponed the rebuke to the next day; as a result, those who were opposed to the administrator, irritated with the bishop, came to see him. When the bishop learned about it, he hid himself somewhere and when those people came, they were unable to find him. They learned from the bishop's associates where he was hidden and they found him and said to him, 'Why did you hide yourself?'

He said, 'Because you wish to strip away in two days what it has taken me sixty years to accomplish by praying to God'.

June 5
DOROTHEOS OF GAZA, MONK (O)
BONIFACE (WYNFRITH), APOSTLE TO GERMANY, MARTYR (RC, A)

IF THE CUSHION DOES NOT SPEAK

One of the brothers said that a question arose in the laura of Egypt and everybody spoke, both great and small. Only one monk did not speak. When all the monks left, one of the brothers asked him, 'Why didn't you speak?'

Forced by the brother to say something, he told him, 'Forgive me. I said to myself, "If the cushion under me does not speak, do not speak". So I didn't say anything'.

DEMON CANNOT DRIVE OUT DEMON

A brother went one time to an old man and said, 'My brother leaves me and goes here and there, and I'm hurt because of it'.

The old man comforted him and said, 'Bear with him, brother, and God will see the suffering that you patiently endure and will bring him back to you. It's not easy to bring someone back to someone else with harshness—*demon cannot drive out demon.*[7] No, bring him back with kindness instead, for God brings people back to us by means of encouragement'.

Then he told him this story: 'There were two brothers in the Thebaid; one of them, influenced by the Devil to commit sin, said to the other, "I'm returning to the world", but the other one, weeping, said, "I won't let you leave, my brother, and waste all your effort and lose your virginity". He, however, would not be persuaded and said, "I won't stay except to leave; either come with me and I'll return to the world once again with you, or let me go and I will remain in the world".

'The one brother went and told a great old man and the old man said, "Go with him, and God, because of your efforts, will not allow him to fall". So he got up and went to the world, and when they came close to a village, God saw the effort he was making because of his love for his brother and he removed the warfare from the other brother. So the brother who left said to the brother who followed him into the world, "Let's return to the desert, brother. See, I imagined that I had sinned. What did I gain from that?" And they returned to their cells unharmed'.

[7] Mt 12:36.

233

June 6

SIMON THE STYLITE (CO)
NORBERT OF XANTEN, CANON, BISHOP, REFORMER (M)
INI KOPURIA, FOUNDER OF THE MELANESIAN BROTHERHOOD (A)

OUR LIFE AND OUR DEATH

Abba Antony said, 'Our life and our death is with our neighbor. If we gain our brother, we have gained God, but if we scandalize our brother, we have sinned against Christ'.

STOP BREATHING

A brother came to see Abba Poemen and said to him, 'Abba, I have many thoughts and they put me in danger'.

The old man led him outside and said to him, 'Expand your chest and do not breathe in'.

The brother said, 'I cannot do that'.

Then the old man said to him, 'If you cannot do that, no more can you prevent thoughts from arising, but you can resist them'.

ACCEPTABLE PRAYER

Question: How can a person know *that his prayer is acceptable to God*?[8]

Answer: When a person makes sure that *he does not wrong his neighbor in any way whatsoever*, then let him be sure that his prayer is acceptable to God. But if someone harms his neighbor in any way whatsoever, either physically or spiritually, his prayer is an

[8] 1 Pt 2:5.

234

abomination and is unacceptable. For the wailing of the one who is being wronged will never allow this person's prayer to come before the face of God. And if indeed he does not quickly reconcile with his neighbor, he will certainly not go unpunished his whole life by his own sins, for it is written that *whatever you bind on earth will be bound in heaven.*[9]

June 7

THε SCRIPTVRεS

The brothers came to Abba Antony and said to him, 'Speak a word; how are we to be saved?'
    'The Scriptures. They should teach you how.'

PεRSεVεRING IN THε ASCεTIC LIFε

One day Abba Antony went out and all the monks came to him and asked to hear him speak, and he spoke these words to them in the Egyptian language: 'The Scriptures are sufficient for us for instruction, but it is good for us to encourage one another in the faith and to train by means of words. You then, like children, bring what you know to your father and tell him about it while I, because I am your elder in years, will share with you what I know and have accomplished.

[9] Mt 18:18.

'Let everyone above all have this zeal in common so that having made a beginning they not hesitate or grow faint-hearted in their labors nor say, "We have spent a long time in ascetic discipline". Instead, as though we were beginning anew each day, let each of us increase in fervor. For the entire lifetime of a human being is very brief when measured against the age to come; accordingly, all our time here is nothing compared with life eternal.

'Everything in the world is sold according to its value and things of equal value are exchanged, but *the promise of eternal life*[10] is purchased for very little. For it is written: *The days of our life are seventy years or, if we are strong, perhaps eighty; more than this is pain and suffering.*[11] When we persevere in ascetic discipline for all eighty or even one hundred years, we will not reign for the equivalent of those one hundred years. Instead of a hundred years, we will reign forever and ever. And although we have contested on earth, we will not receive our inheritance here; we have promises in heaven instead. Once more: when we lay aside this perishable body we receive it back imperishable'.[12]

June 8
THOMAS KEN (A)[13]

HANDING OVER THE HOUSE KEYS

Abba Macarius said, 'Whoever fills himself with bread and water gives at the same time the key to his house to robbers'.

---

[10] 1 Tm 4:8.
[11] Ps 90:10.
[12] 1 Cor 15:42.
[13] English Church calendar. March 21 on the American Church calendar.

ANOINTED IN THE NAME OF CHRIST

One day our all-holy father came from the harvest field in the heat with the brothers and while he washed himself with water in order to rest a little from the labor, they brought him a young man who had a demon causing him great suffering. When our father saw the shamelessness of the unclean spirit and the manner in which he tortured the boy, he looked up towards heaven and groaned and took some of the water that he had washed in and anointed him in the name of Christ. When he poured the water on the young man, immediately the unclean spirit came out of him in the manner of a mongoose, and the young man was healed to the glory of God.

June 9
CYRIL, ARCHBISHOP OF ALEXANDRIA (O)
EPHREM OF EDESSA, DEACON, HYMNIST (RC,A)
COLUMBA, ABBOT OF IONA (O, A)

DO NOT LISTEN WHEN IT DOES NOT BENEFIT YOU

Do not give ear to anyone who speaks troubling things to you that cause you to be disturbed and forsake your cell.

REVEAL YOUR THOUGHTS

A brother was besieged by sexual sin and he got up at night and went to an old man and told him his thoughts. The old man comforted him and, having been profited, the brother returned to his cell. Once again, however, war broke out against him and again he went to the old man. He did this a number of times. The old man did not give him grief but told him profitable things and said to him, 'Do not give in but instead come here each time the demon bothers you and in doing so put him to shame. Shamed like this, he will stay away, for nothing so disgusts the demon of sexual sin as the revealing of his deeds and nothing gives him as much joy as when someone hides his thoughts'.

June 10
ЄPHRЄM OF ЄDЄSSA, DЄACON, TЄACHЄR OF THЄ FAITH (A)[14]

PRAISЄ, ЄNVY, AND HUMILITY

Abba Isaiah said, 'Whoever loves being praised by people cannot be without envy and whoever is envious cannot find humility. Such a person has handed over his soul to his enemies and these will drag his soul into numerous evils and destroy it'.

FAITH IN CHRIST HEALS

A young man possessed by a demon was brought to Abba Macarius. The old man placed one hand on his head and his other hand he placed over the young man's heart. His heart aflame, he prayed to God for an hour without ceasing so that the demon

[14] American Church calendar.

was suspended high in the air, crying out and saying, 'Have pity on me!' The young man became like a wineskin, so swollen was his body, and when he spoke in a loud voice, his eyes and ears and nose and mouth and all his lower members gushed like water pouring from a bottle and when he poured out all the water he returned to normal.

Then the old man held the young man in his arms as he prayed and said, 'Glory to you, Lord Jesus Christ, who saves those who have faith in you.' And he poured a pot of water over him and anointed him with holy oil, while he gave him a little water to drink. And he commanded him: '*Do not eat meat* for forty days *and do not drink wine*'.[15] And when the young man was well again, the old man gave him to his father, healed.

June 11
BARTHOLOMEW AND BARNABAS, APOSTLES (O)
BARNABAS, APOSTLE (RC,A)

THE MOTHER OF THE WISEST OF THOUGHTS

Abba Diadochus said, 'Just as the doors of the baths, when constantly left open, quickly expel heat to the outside, so it is with the soul: when it wishes to engage in numerous conversations, even if it sometimes talks about good things, it dissipates its own heat through the portal of speech. A seemly silence, therefore, is good, since such silence is nothing less than the mother of the wisest of thoughts'.

[15] Rom 14:21.

SHE CAN'T PLEASE EVERYBODY

Some old men came one day to Abba Arsenius and entreated him to say a word to them about those who live as hermits who do not see anyone.

The old man said to them, 'When a young virgin is still in her father's house, many young men wish to be married to her, but if she starts going outside the home, she is not pleasing to everyone. Some find her despicable, while others praise her, and so she no longer enjoys the esteem that she had formerly when she was sequestered. So it is with the soul, too: once it begins to open itself, it cannot satisfy everybody.'

June 12
ONNOPHRIUS THE GREAT, MONK (O)
ALICE (AEYDIS OF SCHAARBEEK), NUN (M)

SOUND ADVICE

Blessed Archbishop Theophilus, in the company of a certain provincial governor, once approached Abba Arsenius. The archbishop asked Arsenius a question, wanting to hear a word from him.

After remaining silent a short while, the old man answered them, 'If I speak to you, will you heed what I say?'

They promised to heed what he told them, so the old man said to them, 'Do not go near wherever you hear Arsenius is'.

DIDN'T I TELL YOU?

Now it happened that one day two Nubians were walking together on their way to Aswan. One of them had only one eye. His friend said to him, 'Come on, let's go get a blessing at the hands of this great man Abba Aaron'.

The one-eyed man said, 'He isn't a great man; if he really is, let him open my eye', and while the words were still in his mouth, his eye—which had been blind—regained its sight, but his good eye became blind!

When his friend saw what had happened, he was utterly amazed and said to him, 'Didn't I tell you that he is a *very* great man?'

The one-eyed man said, 'It's no great loss, for one eye has been shut while the other has been opened. However, let's go to him; perhaps he'll give light to the other eye'. So the two of them came to the holy man Abba Aaron.

My father said to the Nubian, who was not a believer, 'Since you think that it's no great loss, why are you here?' Immediately he became very fearful and worshiped him, saying, 'Open my eye!' and immediately he was able to see with the other eye. And the two believed, and went away joyful, and they proclaimed throughout the whole country the miracle that had taken place.

June 13
ANTHONY OF PADUA, DOCTOR OF THE CHURCH (RC)

GOD WILL GIVE YOU PEACE

A brother asked Abba Poemen, 'What shall I do? I get discouraged sitting in my cell'.

The old man said to him, 'Denigrate no one, condemn no one, nor slander anyone, and God will give you peace and you will sit in your cell undisturbed'.

TRUSTING TOO MUCH IN YOURSELF

'There was a monk', Abba John of Lycopolis said, 'who lived in a cave in the nearer desert and had given proof of the strongest ascetic discipline. He obtained his daily bread by the work of his own hands. But because he persevered with his prayers and made progress in the virtues, he came eventually to trust in himself, placing his reliance on his good way of life. Then the Tempter asked for him, as he did with Job, and in the evening presented him the image of a beautiful woman lost in the desert. Finding the door open, she darted into the cave, and throwing herself at the man's knees begged him to give her shelter since darkness had overtaken her. He took pity on her, which he should not have done, and received her as a guest in his cave. Moreover, he asked her about her journey. She told him how she had lost her way and sowed in him words of flattery and deceit. She kept on talking to him for some time, and somehow gently enticed him to fall in love with her. The conversation became much freer, and there was laughter and hilarity. With so much talking she led him astray. Then she began to touch his hand and beard and neck. And finally she made the ascetic her prisoner.

'As for him, his mind seethed with evil thoughts as he calculated that the matter was already within his grasp, and that he had the opportunity and the freedom to fulfill his pleasure. He then consented inwardly and in the end tried to unite himself with her sexually. He was frantic by now, like an excited stallion eager to mount a mare. But suddenly she gave a loud cry and vanished from his clutches, slipping away like a shadow. And the air resounded with a great peal of laughter. It was the demons who had led him astray with their deception rebuking him and calling out with a loud voice, "*All who exalt themselves will be*

242

humbled".[16] You once exalted yourself to the heavens but now you have been humiliated and brought down to the depths'.

June 14
BASIL THE GREAT (A)[17]

YOUR ENEMIES WANT TO STEAL YOUR POTS

Abba Macarius the Great said, 'If you pursue prayer, pay careful attention to yourself lest you place your pots in the hands of your enemies, for they desire to steal your pots, which are the thoughts of your soul. These are the precious pots with which you will serve God, for God does not look for you to glorify him only with your lips, while your thoughts wander to and fro and are scattered throughout the world, but requires that your soul and all its thoughts wait upon the sight of the Lord without distraction, for he is the great physician, the healer of souls and bodies, our Lord Jesus Christ. Let us beseech him to heal the illnesses of our souls and illumine our thoughts and the perceptions of our hearts that we may understand his great love for humanity and the suffering that he undertook in the world for us and the good things he has done for us day after day, although we are unworthy, for he is our master and savior, our Lord Jesus Christ'.

[16] Lk 14:11, 18:14.
[17] January 2 (RC).

THE SHEEP, ITS AILMENTS, AND HOW TO HEAL IT

It was said about Abba Macarius the Great that an old man paid him a visit along with a brother. They said to him, 'We wish to live together as one, our father'.

Abba Macarius said to the old man, 'First, be like a shepherd. If the ox-fly sows worms in the sheep, he gives it medicine until he kills the worms, but if the sheep shows an infestation he uses an unguent on it until he removes the infestation'.

The old man said to him, 'Tell me the meaning of this saying'.

Abba Macarius said to him, 'The ox-fly is like the Devil while the sheep is like the brother who lives with you. The worms are the passions and the pleasures of the demons who dwell in the soul and breed in the heart, like the worms that live in the wounds of the body; the medicine that wipes out the infestation is spiritual progress and abstinence and the saving teaching of God. These are the things that purify the soul, cleansing it of all passion and every evil of the wicked enemies that the demons send against us'.

June 15
BEGINNING OF THE FAST OF SS PETER AND PAUL (O)
EVELYN UNDERHILL, SPIRITUAL WRITER (A)

SPIRITUAL ACCOUNTABILITY AND FORMATION

Abba Antony would especially recommend that his disciples meditate without ceasing on what the Apostle said: *Do not let the sun go down on your anger.*[18] 'This saying', he said, 'governs every

---

[18] Eph 4:26.

commandment equally: not only should the sun not go down on anger, it should not go down on any other sin. For it is good and necessary for the sun not to condemn us for an evil done during the day, nor for the moon to pass judgement on us for a sin done at night, or for any kind of thought at all. In order for this practice to save us, then, it is good to listen to the Apostle and to observe what he says: *Examine yourselves, test yourselves.*[19]

'Each day, therefore, let each person take an accounting of the things he has done during the day and during the night and, if he has sinned, let him stop. If he has not sinned, let him not boast. Rather, let him continue doing what is good and not become negligent. Let him neither condemn his neighbor nor justify himself, as the blessed apostle Paul said, *until the Lord comes who searches out what is hidden.*[20]

'Often we ourselves are unaware of what we are doing. We do not know, but the Lord comprehends everything. When we judge one another, therefore, *let us suffer together and bear each other's burdens;*[21] let us examine ourselves and hasten to fill in what we are lacking. Let this system of observation assure us of not sinning: let each of us note and write down his deeds and the movements of his soul as though we were going to report them to each other. Be assured that if we are thoroughly ashamed to have others know these things, we will stop sinning and even stop thinking altogether about doing anything evil. What sinner wants to be seen? Who, after sinning, does not lie, wanting to escape undetected?

'Therefore, if we write down our thoughts as though we were going to report them to one another, we will keep ourselves very far away from filthy thoughts, ashamed as we are to have others know about them. So let this practice of writing things down take the place of our fellow ascetics' eyes so that, being as embarrassed to have our sins written down as seen, we will not think in our hearts about anything evil at all. If we form each other this way,

---

[19] 2 Cor 13:5.
[20] 1 Cor 4:5, Rom 2:16.
[21] See Gal 6:2.

we will be able to make a servant of the body and please the Lord while trampling on the Enemy's deceptions'.[22]

June 16
RICHARD OF CHICHESTER, BISHOP (A)
LUTGARDE, NUN (M)

HUMILITY AND PRAISE

It was said of Abba Poemen that he never wished to speak after another old man but that he preferred to praise him in everything he had said.

TRUE POSSESSIONS

'Therefore, children', Abba Antony said, *'let us not lose heart,*[23] and let us not think that what we are doing takes too much time or is too great an undertaking, for *the sufferings of the present time do not compare to the glory that is going to be revealed to us.*[24] Let us not look at the world and think that we have renounced great things, for even the whole world is very small when compared with all of heaven. If we were lords of all the earth and renounced the whole world, once again that would not compare with the kingdom of heaven. For just

[22] See 1 Cor 9:27, 7:32; Eph 6:11.
[23] See Gal 6:9.
[24] Rom 8:18.

as someone might sneer at a single copper drachma in order to gain a hundred gold drachmas, so the person who is lord of the whole world and renounces it gives up little *and receives a hundredfold*.[25] If the whole world is not equal in value to heaven, then the person who gives up a few acres forsakes nothing. Even if he gives up his house or great wealth, he has no reason to boast or be downhearted.

'We especially ought to consider that *if we do not give up these things for the sake of virtue, then later when we die we leave them behind, often to those to whom we do not wish to do so, as Ecclesiastes has reminded us*.[26] Why, then, do we not give them up for virtue's sake that we may inherit a kingdom? Let none of us, therefore, desire to acquire things for himself, for what profit is there in acquiring these things that we cannot take with us? Why do we not acquire instead those things that we *can* take with us: namely, clear thinking, prudence, righteousness, courage, understanding, godly love, love for the poor, faith in Christ, freedom from anger, hospitality? If we possess *these* things, we will find them going before us, *preparing lodging for us there in the land of the gentle*'.[27]

June 17

A CASK FULL OF HOLES

The person who stores up injuries and resentments and yet fancies that he prays might as well draw water from a well and pour it into a cask that is full of holes.

[25] See Mt 19:29.
[26] See Qo 2:18-19, 4:7-8, 6:1-2.
[27] See Ps 37:11, Mt 5:5, Mt 11:29.

IN THIS TIME OF FAMINE

God is limitless. A wise person in his cell is without measure. For his name is in heaven. His countenance casts forth rays of light from Jerusalem. The people behold him in this time of famine.

TWO IMAGES

A brother asked Abba Poemen, 'How can a person avoid speaking ill of his neighbor?'

The old man said to him, 'We and our brothers are two images: when a person is watchful about himself, and has to reproach himself, in his heart he thinks his brother better than he; but when he appears to himself to be good, then he thinks his brother evil compared to himself'.

June 18
ELISABETH OF SCHÖNAU, ABBESS (M)

DON'T INSTRUCT YOUR NEIGHBOR

Abba Poemen said, 'To instruct your neighbor is the same as reproving him'.

DO NOT DO YOUR OWN WILL

He also said, 'Do not do your own will; you need rather to humble yourself before your brother'.

248

A BIG HEAD

The demon of pride is the cause of the most damaging fall for the soul. For it induces the monk to deny that God is his helper and to consider that he himself is the cause of virtuous actions. Further, he gets a big head in regard to the brothers, considering them stupid because they do not all have this same opinion of him'.

June 19

DON'T FOOL YOURSELF

An old man said, 'If you are really fleeing, flee people; if you are really mocking people and the world, *make a fool of yourself*.[28]

BROTHER ASS

A brother asked an old man, 'What shall I do? My belly afflicts me, I eat a lot, I am unable to practice self-control, and little by little my body is losing the battle against wantonness'.

In reply the old man said to him, 'If you do not put fear and fasting above your belly, it will not go well with you'. And he told him this parable: 'A person had an ass, and when he was sitting

---

[28] See 1 Cor 4:10.

on it, it would wander here and there, so he took a stick and hit it. And the ass said to him, "Don't hit me and from now on I'll walk straight".

'After strolling about a little longer, the person got down from the ass and put the stick in the saddlebags on top of the animal. The ass did not know that he had saddlebags on him, but thinking that the person did not have the stick, he began to think contemptuously of the man and went into the fields. His owner came and took the stick and beat the ass until it went where it was supposed to go. You have to treat your belly the same way'.

June 20

THE THREE MOST HELPFUL THINGS

Abba Poemen said, 'These three things are the most helpful of all: fear of the Lord; prayer; and doing good to one's neighbor'.

A REPENTANT SINNER

Abba Sarmatas said, 'I prefer a sinful person who knows he has sinned and repents to a person who has not sinned and considers himself righteous'.

FINDING THE RIGHT PLACE

A brother questioned Abba Poemen, saying, 'I have found a place where peace is not disturbed by the brothers. Do you advise me to live there?'

The old man said to him, 'The place for you is where you will not harm your brother'.

June 21
ALOYSIUS GONZAGA, RELIGIOUS (RC)

DISCERNING GOOD AND EVIL EVENTS

One time when Abba Evagrius was in the desert, an old man who was fleeing from the priesthood came to see him. While he was on his way, walking on the road, his bread gave out. When his disciple was about to faint from hunger, he stopped on the road and an angel placed a pair of loaves before him and put them on the road that led into the mountain. When the old man arrived at Abba Evagrius', he said to him, 'When I was on my way to see you, I and my servant, we got hungry on the road. We did not find bread to eat. My servant was about to collapse from not eating and after we placed some skins down on the ground, we genuflected. While we were bent to the ground, the smell of hot bread came to us and when I got up I found two loaves of hot bread in front of me and when each of us had taken a loaf, we ate it, we recovered our strength, we started walking, and came to you. Tell me, therefore', he said, 'whether or not a demon has the power to do something like this'.

Abba Evagrius said to him, 'You and I have both had such events happen to us. A few days ago I too went to visit the brothers. As I was walking along, I found on the road a money purse with three solidi in it. I stopped and sat down beside it in case someone had dropped it and would be back to search for it. Although I spent a day sitting there, no one came to look for the money. I did not know where I could send the money because in truth I did not know who it belonged to. I sent my steward to the villages closest to me to ask whether or not someone had lost a money purse the past few days. When I didn't find anyone, I ordered my steward to distribute the money to strangers. Whether it was an angel or whether it was a demon that had left the purse, we distributed the money.

'As for you and me, whether what happened in our cases occurred on account of an angel or on account of a demon, let us give glory to God, for occurrences like these do not profit the soul at all except to purify it. Nevertheless, I give glory to you for having received food from an angel. Yes, it is possible for demons to steal some loaves of bread and bring them to someone, but such loaves will not nourish the body because things that belong to demons stink and if something comes from the demons the soul is confused when it sees it. If, however, it comes from the angels, the soul is not confused but remains steadfast and at peace at that time. Therefore, the person who is worthy to receive food from the angels first of all possesses discernment in thinking about the saying of the Apostle, who says, *Solid food is for the perfect, for those whose faculties have been trained by practice to distinguish evil from good*.[29]

[29] Heb 5:14.

INVISIBILITY

The measure of a wise person sitting in his cell is the Lord.
That person is like God because he is invisible.
The wise person in his cell will be hidden from the coming evils.

THE STUFF OF MARTYRS

Four monks of Scetis, clothed in skins, came one day to see the great Pambo. Each one revealed the virtue of his neighbor. The first fasted a great deal; the second was poor; the third had acquired great charity; and they said of the fourth that he had lived for twenty-two years in obedience to an old man.

Abba Pambo said to them, 'I tell you, the virtue of this last one is the greatest. Each of the others has obtained the virtue he wished to acquire; but the last one, restraining his own will, does the will of another. Now it is of such persons that the martyrs are made, if they persevere to the end.'

[30] July 6 on the Anglican calendar.

WATER FROM A ROCK, WINGS LIKE AN EAGLE'S

My name is Onnophrius, and for sixty years I have lived in this desert. I walk in the mountains like a wild beast and I never see anyone I recognize. Now I lived in a monastic community on the mountain of Shmoun in the Thebaid. We were all of one mind and lived in accord with one another, and peace dwelled in our midst. We lived together a life of quiet contemplation, glorifying God. Now I would spend the night in vigil with them, and I learned from them the rules of God. I heard them speaking about our father *Elijah the Tishbite*, saying that *in every way he was powerful in God*.[31] There lived in this desert also John the Baptist: *of those born of woman, none has arisen greater than he*.[32] He lived in desert places until the day of his manifestation to Israel.

I said to them, 'My fathers, aren't then those who live in the desert the elect—more so than we? Look, we see each other every day and we gather together for worship. When we're hungry we have the benefit of food prepared for us; when we're thirsty we have the benefit of water to drink. When we're weak the brothers help us and when we want a plate or a pot to eat with we serve each other out of love for God. Where will those who live in the desert on account of God find anyone if they run into trouble? Or if they are hungry where will they find food; if they are thirsty where will they find water to drink?'

They said to me, 'Indeed, when they begin their lives as anchorites they greatly rejoice on account of hunger and thirst and their agreeable manner of life. Therefore the Adversary, who fights against them to tempt them, does not want them to continue as

[31] See 1 Kgs 17-19.
[32] Mt 11:11.

254

anchorites because he knows that the reward is great which they will receive from God when they leave the body. Only when they endure do the mercies of God establish them. He causes the angels to serve them with food and *he brings them water from a rock.*[33] For it is written in Isaiah: *Those who wait for the Lord will renew their strength, they will spread their wings like the eagles. They will fly away and will not fall, they will journey and not be hungry.*[34] He says, *They will receive water from a rock.*[35] And again, *If they are hungry, he will make the grass in the field sweet in their mouths, as honey is sweet.*[36]

June 24
THE NATIVITY OF JOHN THE BAPTIST (O, RC, A)

THE MANY AND THE FEW

Abba Poemen said, 'Many of the Fathers have become very courageous in asceticism, but in fineness of perception there are very few'.

[33] Num 20:11.
[34] Is 40:31 (LXX).
[35] See Is 48:21.
[36] Ps 119:103, Ezek 3:3.

GAZING AT GOD

A wise person in his cell is the city of blessings; he is the dwelling place of the virtues and the Spirit is perfected within him.

You shall be a wise person in your cell, building up your soul as you sit in your cell, while glory is with you, while humility is with you, while the fear of God surrounds you day and night, while your cares are thrown down, while your soul and your thoughts watch God in astonishment, gazing at God all the days of your life.

June 25

A SHELF FULL OF BOOKS

A brother asked Abba Serapion, 'Tell me a word'.

The old man said, 'What can I tell you? You have taken what belongs to the widows and orphans and put it on this shelf'. (He saw that it was full of books.)

MOCKING THEIR THOUGHTS

It was said of Abba Theodore and Abba Lucius of Enaton that they spent fifty years mocking their thoughts, saying, 'After this winter, we will move away from here'. When summer came once again, they would say, 'After this summer, we will leave here'. They spent their whole lives this way, these fathers whose memories we should preserve always.

THE DISCIPLE'S SEVEN CROWNS

An old man was living in a cave in the Thebaid and had with him a reliable disciple. It was the old man's custom each evening to instruct his disciple in what was beneficial and after the instruction to offer a prayer and send him away to sleep. One evening, after the synaxis, as was his custom, the old man sat down to counsel the brother and while he was teaching him he was overcome by sleep. The brother waited for the old man to wake and make his customary prayer for him. He continued sitting a long time but the old man did not wake up; he was troubled at the thought of leaving and going to bed before being dismissed. Forcing himself to stay, he resisted the thought to leave and remained where he was. Again he was troubled but did not leave. He was troubled like this seven times but resisted the thought.

Later on, in the middle of the night, the old man woke up and found the disciple sitting beside him and he said, 'You haven't left yet?' and he said, 'No. You did not dismiss me, Abba'.

The old man said, 'So why didn't you wake me up?'

The brother said, 'I didn't dare wake you; I was afraid I'd annoy you'.

They stood up and said matins and after the synaxis the old man dismissed the brother. As the old man sat by himself, he had a mystical experience: someone was showing him a glorious place and a throne in it and upon the throne seven crowns. He asked the one who was showing him these things, 'Whose are these?' and he said to the old man, 'Your disciple's. This place and throne God has bestowed on him after he leaves the world. But the seven crowns he received last night'.

When the old man heard these things he was amazed and, becoming fearful, called the brother and said to him, 'Tell me, what did you do last night?' but the brother said, 'Forgive me, Abba, I didn't do anything'.

The old man, thinking that his disciple would not confess because he was being humble, said, 'I won't give up asking you unless you tell me what you did or what you thought about'.

But the brother, unaware that he had done anything, was at a loss what to say and said to the old man, 'Forgive me, Abba. I didn't do anything except this: I was troubled seven times by thoughts to leave without your dismissal but I didn't leave'.

When the old man heard this, he knew right away that each time his disciple fought against the thought he was given a crown by God.

June 27
CYRIL OF ALEXANDRIA, BISHOP, DOCTOR OF THE CHURCH (RC, A)

NO ONE WOULD WANT IT

Abba Pambo said, 'The monk should wear a garment of such a kind that he could throw it out of his cell and no one would steal it from him for three days'.

GOD, WE NO LONGER NEED YOU

A brother whom another brother had wronged came to see Abba Sisoës and said to him, 'My brother has hurt me and I want to avenge myself'.

The old man pleaded with him, saying, 'No, my child, leave vengeance to God'.

The brother said to him, 'I shall not rest until I have avenged myself'.

The old man said, 'Brother, let us pray'. Then the old man stood up and said, 'God, we no longer need you to care for us since we do justice for ourselves'.

Hearing these words, the brother fell at the old man's feet, saying, 'I will no longer seek justice from my brother. Forgive me, abba.'

June 28
IRENAEUS, BISHOP OF LYONS (RC, A)

WHAT IS FAITH?

A brother questioned Abba Poemen, saying, 'Give me a word'.

He said to him, 'The Fathers put compunction as the beginning of every action'.

The brother said again, 'Give me another word'.

The old man replied, 'As far as you can, do some manual work so as to be able to give alms, for it is written that alms and faith purify one of sin'.

The brother said, 'What is faith?'

The old man said, 'Faith is to live humbly and to give alms'.

ANTONY SEES AMOUN ENTER HEAVEN

Another time while he was sitting on the mountain, Antony looked up and saw someone being taken up into the air, and there was great rejoicing among those who met him. Then Antony marveled at and blessed so great a chorus and prayed to learn what this might be. Suddenly a voice came to him saying that this was the soul of Amoun, the monk who had lived in Nitria. He had practiced ascetic discipline until old age. (The distance from Nitria to the mountain where Antony lived was that of a thirteeen-day journey.) When those who were with Antony saw the old man's amazement, they asked to know what was causing it and they heard that Amoun had just now died.

The monks whom Antony told about the death of Amoun noted the date, and when the brothers from Nitria came thirty days later, they quizzed them and found out that Amoun had gone to his rest on that very day and hour in which the old man had seen his soul being borne aloft. They and the monks from Nitria were completely amazed at the purity of Antony's soul and at the manner in which he had learned about Amoun's death—at a distance of a thirteen-day journey!—and seen Amoun's soul ascending.

June 29
PETER AND PAUL, APOSTLES (O, RC, A)

PAY THEM OFF

A brother said to Abba Sisoës, 'How is it that the passions do not leave me?'

The old man said, 'Their tools are inside you; give them their pay and they will go'.

THOUGHTS NEED A PLACE TO REST

A brother asked an old man, 'How my thoughts afflict me! They often take me prisoner; I chastise them, yet they do not go away but stay where I put them'.

The old man answered him, 'You have to be hungry when you say to them, "Get away from me!" Otherwise they will not leave but will stay. As long as they have a place to rest, they will not leave'.

June 30
FIRST MARTYRS OF THE CHURCH OF ROME (RC)

WHEN WORDS AND LIFE CORRESPOND

Abba Isidore of Pelusia said, 'To live without speaking is better than to speak without living. For the former who lives right does good even by his silence but the latter does no good even when he speaks. When words and life correspond to one another, they are together the whole of philosophy'.

BRING ME MY STICK!

It was said of Abba Joseph of Panephysis that when he was at the point of death, while some old men were seated around him he looked towards the window and saw the Devil sitting close to it. Then calling his disciple he said to him, 'Bring me my stick, for there is one there who thinks I am getting old and have no more strength against him'. As he gripped his stick, the old man saw the Devil flee through the window like a dog and disappear from sight.

JULY

PENTECOST / ORDINARY TIME

THE INCENSE AND ALTAR OF GOD

Do not forsake God. Do not forsake your cell.
For the incense of God is a wise person in his cell.
The altar of God is a wise person in his cell.
For his cell is always filled with a sweet smell from the fruit of
    his good works.
The glory of God will appear to him there.

JUDGING ANOTHER

A brother at Scetis committed a fault. A council was called to
which Abba Moses was invited, but he refused to go to it. Then
the priest sent someone to say to him, 'Come, for everyone is
waiting for you'.

So he got up and went. He took a leaking jug, filled it with
water and carried it with him. The others came out to meet him
and said to him, 'What is this, Father?'

The old man said to them, 'My sins run out behind me, and I
do not see them, and today I am coming to judge the errors of
another'.

When they heard that, they said no more to the brother but forgave him.

MAINTAINING SILENCE

Another day when a council was being held in Scetis, the Fathers treated Moses with contempt in order to test him, saying, 'Why does this black man come among us?'

When he heard this he kept silence. When the council was dismissed, they said to him, 'Abba, did that not grieve you at all?'

He said to them, 'I was grieved, but I kept silence'.

July 2

DEPRIVING THE SOUL OF BREAD

Abba Poemen said, 'The soul humbles itself in nothing if it does not deprive itself of bread'.

ABBA MACARIUS AND THE DEAD MAN IN THE TOMB

It was said about Abba Macarius the Great that he spent three years living in a tomb in which there was a dead man. After the three years, when Abba Macarius wanted to leave the place, the dead man stood in front of the door and said, 'I will not let you leave, my father!'

The old man said, 'Why?'

The dead man said to him, 'Before you entered this tomb, I was consigned to great suffering and affliction, but when you came and lived here I found peace because of you. I am afraid, therefore, that if I allow you to leave, my suffering and affliction will come back again'.

As the dead man stood in front of the door to the tomb, there came a voice, 'Let the man of God leave, for if some small acts of righteousness had not been found in you so that because of them pity might be taken on you, God would not have sent his servant to spend these three years in this tomb in order that, because of him, pity might be taken on you'.

July 3
THOMAS THE APOSTLE (RC, A)[1]

A POT OF OLIVES AND A RECALCITRANT CAMEL

One time there was a famine over the whole earth and among the Libyans who lived on that mountain. As a result, some Libyan robbers came searching the desert. They came upon the cell of Abba Macarius of Alexandria with a camel in their possession, having loaded waterskins on it with water to drink in the desert. When they entered his cell, they found nothing of value in his cell. They

---

[1] December 21, the traditional date, on the American Episcopal Church calendar.

seized all the bodily necessities and his handiwork and a few palms and took them and loaded them on the camel.

Now it happened that when they had loaded the bags on the camel and wanted it to get up, the camel was unable to get up; it was bellowing but was unable to get up. Then morning came. All of a sudden the old man returned. He saw the men and the camel and thought they had brought him some bodily necessities from Egypt in order to receive his handiwork from him in return, as was his custom. But when he got closer, he recognized his baskets and his palms and his few bodily necessities. He kept quiet and said nothing.

When they saw the holy old man, they prostrated themselves and begged his forgiveness over and over. He, however, did not get angry nor did he beat them but walked right by them, went into his cell, and found that they had taken all his possessions except for a small pot, which had a few olives in it. (They had not seen it sitting behind the door.) The old man picked up the pot of olives and took it outside to them, and said to them, 'Do you want to know why the camel was not able to get up?'

They said, 'Yes'.

He said to them, 'Because you forgot these few olives; that's why'. And after he placed the pot on the camel and gave the animal a kick, it immediately got up. And he sent them away in peace and accompanied them off.

The next day some brothers came to see the old man. It was already time to eat and the brothers wanted to eat a little something. Therefore, when he knew their thoughts, he said to them, 'There's bread in your traveling skins; bring it here so we can eat a little something, for God has given the bodily necessities that were here in my dwelling to some men of the world who have wives because some poor folk needed them due to the severity of the famine'.

WHAT'S IN A NAME?

One day Abba Antony received a letter from Emperor Constantius asking him to come to Constantinople and he wondered whether he ought to go. So he said to Abba Paul, his disciple, 'Ought I to go?'

Paul replied, 'If you go, you will be called "Antony"; but if you stay here, you will be called "Abba Antony"'.

JUSTICE AND CONCERN FOR THE POOR

Antony's fame reached even the emperors. When Emperor Constantine and his sons, the emperors Constantius and Constans, learned about these things, they wrote to him as to a father and expressed their wish to receive letters from him in return. But Antony neither cared about the letters nor rejoiced over receiving them. He remained just as he was before the emperors wrote to him. When he received the letters, he summoned the monks and said, 'Why are you so amazed that the emperor writes to us? He is human, too. Instead, be more amazed that God has written the Law for human beings and has spoken to us through his own Son'.

So Antony did not want to accept the letters, saying that he did not know how to write letters to the emperors in return. Persuaded, however, by all the monks that the emperors were Christians and that he ought not to cause them offense by rejecting the letters, he allowed them to be read. So he replied, welcoming the emperors' letters because they worshipped Christ, advising them concerning salvation, and counseling them not to regard present things as important but to be mindful instead of the coming judgement and to know that Christ is the only, true, and eternal Emperor. He insisted that they be lovers of humanity and be concerned about justice and the poor. When the emperors received his letter, they rejoiced. So Antony was beloved of all, and everyone deemed him worthy to be their father.

SAVING A SHIPWRECKED BOAT

Temptation happened to come upon a brother one time in the cenobium of Abba Elit. Expelled from there, he left for the monastic community gathered around Abba Antony. After the brother stayed a while with Abba Antony, Antony sent him back to the monastery where he had come from.

When the brothers saw him, they expelled him once again and he returned to Abba Antony and said, 'They refuse to accept me, father'.

So the old man sent him back, saying, 'A boat was shipwrecked at sea and lost its cargo and was brought to shore with great effort'. When the monks heard that Abba Antony had sent him, they accepted him right away.

NAKED SLANDER

A brother asked Abba John the Little, 'How is it that my soul, which has its own wounds, is not ashamed to slander my neighbor?'

The old man told him a parable about slander: 'A certain person was poor and had a wife but he saw another woman, whom he was able to persuade, and took her as a wife also. Both of them were naked. Now because a festival was to take place somewhere, they begged him, saying, "Take us with you".

'So he took the two of them, put them in a large wine jar and, setting out in a ship, went where the festival was taking place. When it got hot and the people laid down to rest, one of the women looked out and when she didn't see anyone leapt out onto the rubbish pile; gathering old rags together, she made something to cover her and then went walking about quite freely. The other woman, sitting inside the jar naked, said, "Look! This whore isn't ashamed to walk around naked!"

'Angry with her, her husband said, "Amazing! She at least hides her shame while you, although completely naked, are not ashamed to say these things!"

'So it is with slander too'.

July 6

THOMAS MORE AND JOHN FISHER, REFORMATION MARTYRS (A)[2]

TRAFFICKING IN WORDS

A brother visited Abba Theodore of Pherme one time and spent three days begging to hear a word from him, but Abba Theodore did not answer him and he went away saddened. The old man's

---

[2] June 22 on the RC calendar.

disciple said, 'Abba, why didn't you say a word to him? Now look, he's gone away saddened'.

The old man said to him, 'You're right, I didn't say a word to him; he's a trafficker who wants to glorify himself with the words of others'.

STALKS OF CORN

Abba Poemen said, 'It is written, Bear *witness to what you have seen with your own eyes*,[3] *but I say to you*[4] that even if you have also touched with your hands, do not bear witness. For a brother was mocked in just such a way: he thought he saw his brother sinning with a woman; mad enough to go out and fight, he went and kicked them with his foot, so he thought, saying, "Stop this right now!" What do you know, they turned out to be stalks of corn! That is why I said to you "even if you have touched with your hands, do not reproach"'.

July 7

REBUKING A BAD-MOUTHING DEMON

There was a certain man whom a demon was wickedly tormenting. When his parents heard of Abba Aaron's fame, they bound their son hand and foot and set him on a donkey and took him

---

[3] See Prv 25:8 (LXX).
[4] See Mt 5:21-22, 27-28, 31-32, 38-39, 43-44.

to Abba Aaron. (Now it took four men to hold him.) And when they had brought him, they lifted him off the donkey and set him down by the door. Now the demon was speaking from inside the man, hurling out many disgusting words to my father, saying, 'Aren't you some soldier a long ways from the slaughter? Weren't your family noble folk who ate up people with oppressive loans? I remember one day when your father loaned some guy ten oboli and when the man, because of his poverty, could not come up with the money to pay your father back, he seized his house in lieu of payment. Wasn't what he did a sin? And you—you've come here saying, "I'm going to heal these sick people". You're no doctor!'

Now my father restrained himself until the demon had finished everything he had to say. He said to him, 'As for you, you don't deserve an answer. Now, therefore, I order you in the name of *the crucified Christ* to leave this man'.[5]

When the demon heard these words, he tried to take the man and flee. Then the holy man filled his hand with water and sprinkled it on his face three times, saying, 'In the name of the Holy Trinity, come out of him!' And the demon came out. The holy one said to him, 'Get yourself to Babylon of the Chaldeans, and stay there until the day of judgement when everyone shall receive according to what he has done. As for you, you will be thrown into the pit of Amente'.

When the demon heard these things, he left in a rage. Now when the man returned to his right state of mind, he glorified God, as did his parents and everyone accompanying them. Then they entreated the holy man to accept something, but he refused, saying that he had never accepted a gift of any kind since he had become a monk. (He was in the habit of telling me often, 'Do not set your gaze on the things of this world, which do not profit a person in any way, but as long as we have food and clothing, there will be enough for us. For indeed our Saviour said to his apostles, "*Do not acquire for yourselves gold or silver or copper in your belts*".[6] Therefore, it is

[5] See 1 Cor 1:23.
[6] Mt 10:9.

fitting for a monk to walk in this way and to lead a good life'.) As
a result, the parents renounced the world and followed the Lord.

WILD ANIMALS FLEE TO THEIR LAIRS

It was said about Abba Isidore the priest that whenever a brother
came to see him he would flee into his inner cell. The brothers
would say to him, 'Abba Isidore, what are you doing?'

He would say, 'When wild animals flee into their lairs they are
saved'.

BEFORE YOU ACCUSE ME,
TAKE A LOOK AT YOURSELF

A brother, tempted by a demon, went to an old man and said,
'Those two brothers are always together'.

But the old man understood that the brother was being mocked
by demons and he sent and called the two to him. When evening
came, he laid out a rush mat for those two brothers and covered
them with a single blanket, saying, 'These sons of God are saints'.
Conversely, he said to his disciple, 'Shut that other brother up in
a cell nearby, for he has in himself the very passion which he accused the others of having'.

WASH OFF THE FILTH

Abba Macarius said, 'If someone goes to the baths and does not strip off all his clothes, he is not able to bathe nor wash off all his filth; so it is with someone who makes progress as a monk: if he does not strip off all concerns of this world with all its desires filled with vain pleasures, he is not able to advance or make progress in virtue nor be victorious over all the arrows of the Enemy, which are filth'.

DO UNTO OTHERS

One of the old men used to say, 'If you hate something, don't do it to someone else. Do you hate it if someone slanders you? See to it that you do not slander anyone. Do you hate it if someone calumniates you? See to it that you do not calumniate anyone. Do you hate it if someone despises you or insults you or steals something that belongs to you, or does something similar to these? See to it that you do not do any of these to anyone. Whoever is able to keep this injunction will have done enough to save himself.'

CHOOSING TO REMAIN SILENT

Abba Poemen said, 'If a person remembered that it is written *By your words you will be justified and by your words you will be condemned*,[7] he would more readily choose to remain silent'.

IN THE PRESENCE OF THE LORD

John of Lycopolis said: 'So you, too, my children, should cultivate stillness and ceaselessly train yourselves for contemplation, that when you pray to God you may do so with a pure mind. For an ascetic is good if he is constantly training himself in the world, if he shows brotherly love and practices hospitality and charity, if he gives alms and is generous to visitors, if he helps the sick and does not give offense to anyone.

Such a person is good, he is exceedingly good, for he is a person who puts the commandments into practice and does them. But he is occupied with earthly things. Better and greater than he is the contemplative, who has risen from active works to the spiritual sphere and has left it to others to be anxious about earthly things. Since such a person has not only denied himself but even become forgetful of himself, he is concerned with the things of heaven. He stands unimpeded in the presence of God, without any anxiety holding him back. For such a person spends his life with God; he is occupied with God, and praises him with endless hymnody'.

[7] Mt 12:37.

THE SAME WORK

Abba Poemen said, 'If three people meet, of whom the first fully preserves interior peace, and the second gives thanks to God in illness, and the third serves with a pure mind, these three are doing the same work'.

WHAT WOULD JESUS DO?

Some heretics came to Abba Poemen one day and began to speak evil of the archbishop of Alexandria. The old man, who had remained silent till then, called his brother and said, 'Set the table, give them something to eat, and send them away in peace'.

THE ALPHABET OF A PEASANT

One day Abba Arsenius consulted an old Egyptian monk about his own thoughts. Someone noticed this and said to him, 'Abba Arsenius, how is it that you, with such a good Greek and Latin education, ask this peasant about your thoughts?'

He replied, 'I have indeed been taught Latin and Greek, but I do not know even the alphabet of this peasant'.

OPEN WARFARE

You shall not walk to your cell without learning about deceitfulness.

For the demons openly wage war against humans in the desert.

For they are stripped naked before God.

Therefore there is no pity in the demons towards the person who is sitting alone in peace.

A MOTH TO THE FLAME

Abba Macarius said, 'Woe to the soul that has not implored and entreated the Lord to rest in it and purify it from every blemish and every stain and keep it free from wild beasts and reptiles, which are the spirits of evil that take the form of small creatures and gnats that fly in the night: if they see a light at a distance or a burning wick, they come to it and fly into the flame and burn up in it. So it is with the monk who impels himself in all things by his own choice and free will: he will be found in the eternal fire'.

WEIGHING GOOD AND EVIL

One of the fathers said that beside the river near the village, there where blessed Silvanus lived in Palestine, dwelled a brother who pretended to be *a fool*:[8] whenever a brother met him, he would burst into laughter and as a result each person would get away from him and go away. Three fathers happened to visit Abba Silvanus and after offering a prayer they asked him to send someone with them so they might see the brothers in their cells, and so they said to him, 'Please do us the favor of asking a brother to take us to see everyone'. The old man said to a brother in their presence, 'Take them to all the brothers', but taking him aside, he instructed him, 'See that you don't take them to the half-witted brother or else they'll be scandalized'.

While they were touring the brothers' cells, the fathers asked their guide, 'Please, take us to everyone', and he said to them, 'Of course, of course', but in accordance with the old man's instructions, he did not take them to the half-wit's cell. When they returned to the old man, he said to them, 'Did you see the brothers?' and they said, 'Yes, and we give you our thanks, but we're sorry that we didn't visit everyone'. So, when the fathers were leaving, they once again said to the old man, 'We are truly thankful that we saw the brothers, but this one thing saddens us: we did not see everyone'. Then, taking the old man aside, the brother said to him, 'I did not take them to the half-witted brother'.

After the fathers had left, the old man pondered what had happened and went to that brother, the one who pretended to be a fool; without knocking, he quietly lifted the latch, came in on the brother suddenly, and found him sitting on a chair and holding two small baskets, one in his right hand and one in his left. When the brother saw the old man he began to laugh, as was his custom,

---

[8] See 1 Cor 4:10.

and the old man said to him, 'Stop that right now and tell me how you live in your cell'. Once again he started laughing. Abba Silvanus said to him, 'Do you know that except on Saturday and Sunday I do not leave my cell? But now I've come in the middle of the week, for God has sent me to you'.

Filled with fear because of this, the brother asked the old man's forgiveness and said to him, 'Forgive me, father. Each morning I sit holding these pebbles in front of me: if a good thought comes to me, I put a pebble in the basket on my right; if an evil thought, I put one in the one on the left. Each evening, then, I count the pebbles, and if there are more in the basket on the right, I eat, but if there are more on the left, I do not eat. And again the next day, if an evil thought comes to me, I say to myself, "Watch what you're doing; once again you're not going to eat"'.

When Abba Silvanus heard these things, he was amazed and said, 'Truly those fathers who visited were holy angels who wanted to make public the brother's virtue. Indeed, their coming has brought me great joy and spiritual gladness'

July 14
IGNATIUS OF ANTIOCH (CO)
KATERI TEKAKWITHA (RC)
JOHN KEBLE, PRIEST (A)

EVERYTHING WITH DISCERNMENT

An old man said, 'This is the life of the monk: work, obedience, meditation, not judging, not backbiting, not grumbling, for it is written, *Those who love the Lord hate evil.*[9] The life of the monk is to not indulge in what is wicked, to not let one's eyes look at evil, to not be a busybody, to not listen to what strangers say, to not use your hands for snatching but rather for giving, nor to have an arrogant heart, nor to act wickedly with your thoughts, nor to fill your belly, but rather to do everything with discernment. These things define the monk'.

A WORD FROM THE MOUTH OF GOD

Abba Ammon and Abba Theodore and Abba Jacob bore witness to us about Abba Pambo: If we asked for a word from Scripture or some other thing, he would not give us an answer right away but would say, 'I haven't figured out the meaning of this word yet; give me two or three days to ruminate on the word and I will give you an answer'.

It normally happened that he would spend two or three days or a whole week without giving us an answer, saying, 'If I do not know what sort of fruit this word will bear, whether it is a fruit of death or of life, I will not speak'. Therefore, the brothers received the word that he would speak as though it had come from the mouth of God.

[9] Ps 96:10.

FIVE TALENTS AND TWO

One day when the holy Bishoy had fasted for twenty-two days, Christ came to him and said, 'Bishoy, since you suffer so much on my behalf, I want you to be my chosen one'.

Bishoy said, 'What is my suffering, good master? Why, nothing at all. *Every perfect gift comes from you*, who give me strength.'[10]

The Saviour said, 'Every good work is acceptable to me and I will repay the worker full wages for his work. Come, then; follow me'.

Bishoy followed the Saviour into the desert until they came to a certain cave belonging to a desert-dweller. Then the Saviour said to Bishoy, 'Go inside and you will see a true champion'.

When Bishoy went in, he saw a man rolling on the ground, rubbing his mouth and face into the dirt. Perplexed at this man's excessive struggle, he immediately went outside to find out from the Saviour the reason for the man's wild struggle. The Saviour said, 'Did you see how many labors my suffering athlete endures for me?'

Bishoy said, 'I did see, Lord, and I was horrified at the pain and suffering caused by his labors, but since it is not clear to me why he is making these efforts, will Your Goodness explain it to me?'

The Saviour said, 'He has completed only two days of fasting yet look how he is overcome with hunger and parched with thirst'.

Then Bishoy said, 'Yes, it is obvious. And how can I have gone without eating for twenty-two days without suffering any of these terrible things?' he in turn inquired of the Saviour.

---

[10] See Jms 1:17.

Once again the Saviour answered him, 'Because you are strengthened by my grace, you fast with strength and perseverance. This fellow, however, like an athlete, fasts on his own; inflamed with desire, he allows himself to suffer beyond his ability to do so.'

Then Bishoy asked, 'What sort of reward will such a person receive from Your Goodness for his two days of fasting?'

The Saviour answered him, 'I will repay him with the same reward for two days as I will you for twenty-two, and that Gospel saying will apply to both of you: *Enter into the joy of your Lord*[11]—to you, who have received five talents, and to him, who has received two,[12] for both of you have been equally doing what is good and you have both been zealous to the best of your ability'. After the Saviour said these things, he left.

July 16

HEARING THE COCK CROW

One day Abba Isaac was sitting beside Abba Poemen when they heard a cock crow. Abba Isaac said to him, 'Is it possible to hear that here, abba?'

He replied, 'Isaac, why do you make me talk? You and those like you hear those noises, but the vigilant person does not trouble about them'.

[11] Mt 25:21, 23.
[12] See Mt 25:15-23.

THE HONOR OF THE POOR PERSON IN HIS CELL

Blessed is the person, poor and wretched, who withdraws from the distractions of the world; he is a friend of God just like Abraham, because *the Lord will not do anything that he has not revealed through his servants and his prophets.*[13]

Indeed, *God spoke with Abraham beside the tree of Mamre while he was sitting at the door of his tent at midday.*[14]

God *also spoke with Solomon in the house he had built.*[15] *Elijah, too, at the river Corath.*[16]

Now then, you who are poor, the honor of the poor person in his cell is very great.

July 17

PRACTICING PATIENCE

If you know how to practice patience you shall ever pray with joy.

A FOOL FOR CHRIST

There was an old man in Scetis by the name of Daniel and he had a disciple. One day, then, the old man took his disciple and went

---

[13] See 2 Kgs 17:23.
[14] See Gen 18:1.
[15] See 1 Kgs 9:1-2.
[16] See 1 Kgs 17:1-7.

up to Alexandria, because it is customary for the superior of Scetis to go up to see the pope for the Great Feast of Easter.

When they arrived at the city about five in the afternoon and as they were walking in the street, they saw a brother who was naked, wearing a loincloth around his loins. That brother was pretending to be half-witted and there were other imbeciles with him. The brother would go around like a half-wit and babble nonsensically and would snatch things from the stalls in the marketplace and give them to the other imbeciles.

His name was 'Mark of the Horse'. 'The Horse' is a public bath; there Mark the Fool worked and he would spend a hundred *noumia* a day and there he would sleep on the benches. From the hundred *noumia*, he would buy provisions for himself with ten *noumia* and give the rest to the other imbeciles. The whole city knew Mark of the Horse on account of his mad babbling.

The old man said to his disciple, 'Go and see where that half-wit is living', and he left and made inquiries and they told him, 'At the Horse; he's an imbecile'.

After the old man took leave of the pope the next day, in accordance with God's divine purpose he found Mark the Fool in the Great Tetrapylon, and the old man ran and took hold of him and began to cry out, saying, 'Men of Alexandria, help!'

The half-wit was mocking the old man and a large crowd gathered around them. The disciple, fearful, stood at a distance and everyone was saying to the old man, 'Do not take his insolence seriously; he's an imbecile!'

The old man said to them, '*You* are the imbeciles, for today I have not found a person in this city except for this fellow'.[17]

---

[17] Continues on 18 July.

A FOOL FOR CHRIST

Some clergy from the church, who knew the old man, also arrived and said to him, 'What has this half-wit ever done to you?'

The old man said to them, 'Take him to the pope for me', and they did so, and the old man said to the pope, 'Today in this city there is not such a vessel as this one'. The pope, knowing that the old man had been given confidence by God to speak about this fellow, threw himself at the imbecile's feet and began to adjure him to reveal to them who he was.

The imbecile came to himself and confessed, saying, 'I was a monk and was ruled by the demon of sexual sin for fifteen years. Coming to my senses, I said, "Mark, for fifteen years you've been a slave to the Enemy. Go and likewise be a slave to Christ". So I went to the Pempton and remained there eight years and after eight years I said to myself, "Come on, go to the City and make yourself a half-wit in order to be released from your sins". Today I have completed another eight years as an imbecile'. Those who heard wept and gave glory to God.

Mark slept in the episcopal residence along with the old man, and when dawn came the old man said to his disciple, 'Call Abba Mark for me to offer a prayer for us so we may leave for our cell'. So the disciple left and found Mark asleep in the Lord and he went and told the old man that Abba Mark had died. The old man told the pope and the pope told the general and he ordered everything to come to a stop in the city. The old man sent his disciple to Scetis, saying, 'Sound the signal and gather the fathers together and say to them, "Come to be blessed by the old man"'.

All of Scetis came wearing white and bearing olive branches and palms, and the Enaton and Kellia did likewise, and those in the monastic settlement of Nitria and all the lavras around Alexandria. As a result, the corpse was not buried for five days and they were forced to embalm blessed Mark's corpse. And so the whole city and the monks, with lighted candles and incense and tears, purified the center of the city and buried the precious corpse of blessed Mark the imbecile, glorifying and praising God, the lover of humanity, who gives such grace and glory to those who love him, both now and in the age to come.

July 19
MACRINA, DEACON, TEACHER OF THE FAITH (O, A)

BEGIN LIKE THIS

Amma Sarah said, 'It is good to give alms for people's sake. Even if it is done only to please people, through it one can begin to please God'.

A PENITENT AT THE DOOR, A PURE HEART

She also said, 'If I prayed God that everyone should approve of my conduct, I should find myself a penitent at the door of each one, but I shall rather pray that my heart may be pure towards all'.

MACRINA'S PRAYER

It is you, O Lord, who have freed us from the fear of death. You have made our life here the beginning of our true life. You grant our bodies to rest in sleep for a season and you rouse our bodies *again at the last trumpet*.[18]

You have given in trust to the earth our earthly bodies, which you have formed with your own hands, and you have restored what you have given, by transforming our mortality and ugliness by your immortality and your grace . . . .[19]

Eternal God, *for whom I was snatched from my mother's womb*,[20] whom my soul has loved with all its strength, *to whom I consecrated my flesh from my youth until now*,[21] entrust to me an angel of light, who will lead me by the hand to the place of refreshment, where the *water of repose* is, *in the bosom of the holy patriarchs* . . . .[22]

May you *who have power on earth to forgive sins*[23] forgive me, *that I may draw breath*[24] and that I be found in your presence, *having shed my body and without spot or wrinkle*[25] in the form of my soul, and that my soul may be innocent and spotless and may be received into your hands *like incense in your presence*.[26]

[18] 1 Cor 15:52.
[19] See 1 Cor 15:53.
[20] Ps 22 (21): 11.
[21] Song 1:7, *et passim*.
[22] Ps 23 (22):2; see Lk 16:26.
[23] Mt 9:6; Mk 2:10.
[24] Ps 39 (38):14.
[25] Col 2:11; Eph 5:27.
[26] Ps 141 (140):2.

PISENTIUS, BISHOP OF QIFT (CO)
HOLY PROPHET ELIJAH (O)
BARTOLOMÉ DE LAS CASAS, APOSTLE TO THE INDIES (RC, A)
MARGARET OF ANTIOCH, MARTYR (A)
ELIZABETH CADY STANTON, AMELIA BLOOMER,
SOJOURNER TRUTH, & HARRIET ROSS TUBMAN,
LIBERATORS AND PROPHETS (A)

PHYSICIAN, HEAL YOURSELF

Beware lest while appearing to heal another you do something to make yourself incurable and thus do serious damage to your prayer.

BREAD AND WINE

Amma Syncletica said, 'Do not fill yourself with bread and you will not desire wine'.

KINDLE THE DIVINE FIRE

Amma Syncletica said, 'In the beginning there are a great many battles and a good deal of suffering for those who are advancing towards God and afterwards, ineffable joy. It is like those who wish to light a fire; at first they are choked by the smoke and cry, and by this means obtain what they seek (as it is said, *Our God is a consuming fire*).[27] So we also must kindle the divine fire in ourselves through tears and hard work'.

[27] Heb 12:24.

A SINGLE NOD WILL DO IT

Abba Isaiah said, 'When someone wishes to render evil for evil, that person can injure his brother's soul even by a single nod of the head'.

THORNS

A brother said to Abba Poemen 'My body is getting sick, and yet my passions are not getting weaker'.

The old man said to him, 'The passions are like thorns'.

THE ADVANTAGES OF SOLITUDE

When under some provocation or other the irascible part of our soul is stirred up, it is just at that moment that the demons suggest to us the advantages of solitude so as to have us deliver ourselves from the disturbance rather than clear up the basic causes of the sadness.

THE FRUIT OF THE VINE

While yet a child, Abba Ephrem had a dream and then a vision. A branch of vine came out of his tongue, grew bigger, and filled everything under heaven. It was laden with beautiful fruit. All the birds of heaven came to eat of the fruit of the vine, and the more they ate the more the fruit increased.

ABBA EPHREM AND THE PROSTITUTE

One time, when Ephrem was on the road, a prostitute tried by her flatteries, if not to lead him to shameful intercourse, at least to make him angry, for no one had ever seen him angry. He said to her, 'Follow me'.

When they had reached a very crowded place, he said to her, 'Right here, come, do what you desire'.

But she, seeing the crowd, said to him, 'How can we do what we want to do in front of so great a crowd without being ashamed?'

He replied, 'If you blush before people, how much more should we blush before God, who *knows what is hidden in darkness*?'[28]

She was covered with shame and went away without having achieved anything.

---

[28] See Sir 42:20.

SATAN'S WORK

There was a communal meal one time at Abba Antony's community and there was a quantity of wine present. One of the old men took a small jar and a cup and took it to Abba Sisoës and gave it to him and he drank it. He likewise accepted a second cup and drank it. The brother also offered him a third cup but he did not take it, saying, 'Stop, brother, or don't you know that this is Satan's work?'

THE MEASURE OF WINE

A brother asked Abba Sisoës, 'What shall I do? I go to church and often there is an *agapē* and they make me stay for it'.

The old man said, 'You've asked a difficult question'.

So Abraham, his disciple, said, 'If the gathering takes place on Saturday or Sunday, and someone drinks three cups of wine, isn't that a lot?'

The old man said to him, 'If Satan is not in it, it isn't a lot'.

July 24

BORIS AND GLEB, MARTYRS (O)
THOMAS À KEMPIS (A)

I HAVE OFTEN REPENTED

Abba Arsenius used to say to himself, 'Arsenius, why have you left
the world? I have often repented of having spoken, but never of
having been silent'.

ANTONY'S VISION OF HEAVENLY ASCENT

A large number of monks have spoken unanimously about many
other such things that happened because of Antony. Yet these things
are not as marvelous as other even more marvelous events that were
manifested. One time when he was about to eat, he stood up to
pray close to the ninth hour when he perceived that he was being
carried off in thought and, amazing to relate, he stood there looking
at himself as if he were outside himself and were being led into the
air by certain beings. Then he saw standing in the air some terrible
and bitter beings who wanted to prevent him from passing by.

While those who were leading him fought against them,
these latter beings attempted to take an accounting of him to see
whether or not he was accountable to them. So, when these latter beings demanded an accounting of Antony from the day he
was born, those leading Antony stopped them, saying to them,
'The Lord has expunged the things pertaining to his birth, but
let an accounting be made from the day he became a monk and
consecrated himself to God'. When those who were going to
accuse him were unable to reproach him for anything, his path
immediately became clear and unobstructed, and immediately he
saw himself appear to come and stand before himself and Antony
was his normal self once again.

TO THE CELL FOR YOU!

You know your weakness. One person has one way, for another there is another way—to the cell for you!

ASCETICS, CHASTITY, ALMSGIVING

A person of devout life who was not a monk came to see Abba Poemen. Now it happened that there were other brothers with the old man, asking to hear a word from him. The old man said to the faithful secular, 'Say a word to the brothers'.

When he insisted, the secular said, 'Please excuse me, abba; I myself have come to learn'.

But he was urged on by the old man and so he said, 'I am a secular. I sell vegetables and do business; I take bundles to pieces and make smaller ones; I buy cheap and sell dear. What is more, I do not know how to speak of the Scriptures, so I will tell you a parable: A man said to his friends, "I want to go to see the emperor; come with me". One friend said to him, "I will go with you half the way". Then the man said to another friend, "Come and go with me to the emperor", and the friend said to him, "I will take you as far as the emperor's palace". The man said to a third friend, "Come with me to the emperor". The friend said, "I will come and take you to the palace and I will stay and speak and help you to have access to the emperor"'.

The brothers asked what the point of the parable was.

The secular answered them, 'The first friend is asceticism, which leads the way; the second is chastity, which takes us to heaven;

and the third is almsgiving, which with confidence presents us to God our King'.

The brothers withdrew, edified.

ME TOO

It was said about Abba Macarius the Great that when he lived in the interior desert he lived alone there as an anchorite. Further to the interior was another desert where some other brothers lived. The old man was watching the road one time when he saw Satan approaching, dressed like a traveler. He looked like he was wearing a linen tunic full of holes and from each hole there hung a pot.

Abba Macarius said to him, 'Old man, where are you going?' and he said, 'I'm on my way to stir up the brothers' thoughts'.

Abba Macarius said to him, 'What are you going to do with those pots?' and he said to him, 'I'm taking various kinds of food for the brothers to taste'.

Abba Macarius said to him, 'All of these?'

The Devil answered and said to the old man, 'If this one does not please one of the brothers, I offer him another; if that one does not please him, I offer him yet another. Certainly one of them has to please him!' After saying these things, he left.

The old man sat down and watched the road until the Devil returned. When the old man saw him, he said to him, 'Hello. How are you?'

The Devil said to him, 'Why do you care how I am?' and Abba Macarius said to him, 'What do you mean?'

295

The Devil said to him, 'The brothers were all rude to me and not one of them welcomed me'.

Abba Macarius replied and said, 'You didn't make a single friend there?' and the Devil replied and said, 'I did make one friend there and he obeys me. When he sees me, he comes running like the wind'.

The old man said to him, 'And what is his name?' and he said to Abba Macarius, 'His name is Theopemptus.' When he had said these things, he left.

Abba Macarius got up and went into the desert interior to his own and when the brothers heard about it *they brought palm branches and came out to greet him*.[29] What is more, each one got himself ready thinking that Abba Macarius would rest himself with him in his home. But the old man asked, 'Where does the brother called "Theopemptus" live in this settlement?' and when he found out, he went to his cell.

Theopemptus received him eagerly and with joy. The old man began to discuss the matter with him and said to him, 'Tell me about your thoughts, my child', and he said to Abba Macarius, 'Pray for me and I will prosper'.

The old man said to him, 'Don't your thoughts fight against you?' and he said to Abba Macarius, 'Up to now I have prospered', for he was ashamed to tell the truth.

The old man said to him, 'To this day I have practiced asceticism these many years and every one honors me. I am an old man and the spirit of fornication still troubles me'.

Theopemptus replied and said to him, 'Believe me, my father, I too have this trouble'.

The old man, giving himself permission to speak, spoke of other thoughts that fought against him until Theopemptus confessed. Then the old man said to him, 'How do you fast?' and he said to him, 'Until the ninth hour'.

[29] Jn 12:12-13.

The old man said to him, 'Fast until evening and keep your ascetic practices and recite by heart the Gospels and the rest of the Scriptures and if a thought comes to you do not look down to it but look upwards at all times and God will help you'.

When the old man had finished instructing the brother, he left for his own desert.

As the old man was watching the road, he saw that same demon and said to him, 'Where are you going?'

The demon said to Abba Macarius, 'I want to stir up the brothers' thoughts'.

When he returned, therefore, the saint said to him, 'How did it go with the brothers?' and he said to him, 'Badly'.

The old man said to him, 'Why?' and he said to Abba Macarius, 'They were all rude to me, and the worst one was that one who was my friend and who used to obey me. I don't know why he changed. Not only does he no longer obey me, but he has become the rudest of them all! I've sworn not to set foot there again, at least not for a while'.

When he had said these things, he departed and left the old man and the saint went inside his cell.

July 27

EVEN A NEW HEAVEN AND A NEW EARTH

Abba Poemen said, 'Even if a person were to make a new heaven and a new earth, he could not live free of care'.

FOURTEEN YEARS

Abba Ammonas said, 'I have spent fourteen years in Scetis, praying to God night and day to grant me victory over anger'.

ASK FOR WAR, NOT PEACE

Abba Poemen said of Abba John the Little that he had called on God and had his passions taken away by him and he was left untroubled. So John went to an old man and announced to him, 'I find myself at peace and am not at war about anything'.

The old man said to him, 'Go, entreat God to have the warfare return to you, for the soul makes progress through engaging in battles'.

When the warfare returned, he no longer prayed to have it taken away from him but would say, 'Lord, give me patience in battle'.

July 28

SINNERS NOT WELCOME

A brother questioned Abba Poemen, saying, 'If I see a brother whom I have heard is a sinner, I do not want to take him into my cell, but when I see a good brother I am happy to be with him'.

The old man said, 'If you do a little good to the good brother, do twice as much for the other. For he is sick. Now, there was an anchorite called Timothy in a cenobium. The abbot, having heard of a brother who was being tempted, asked Timothy about him, and the anchorite advised him to drive the brother away. Then when he had been driven away, the brother's temptation fell upon Timothy to the point where he was in danger. Then Timothy stood up before God and said, "I have sinned. Forgive me". Then a voice came which said to him, "Timothy, the only reason I have done this to you is because you despised your brother in the time of his temptation"'.

FORNICATION AND ALMSGIVING

Abba Timothy the priest said to Abba Poemen, 'There is a woman who commits fornication in Egypt and she gives her wages away in alms'.

Abba Poemen said, 'She will not go on committing fornication, for the fruit of faith is appearing in her'.

Now it happened that the mother of the priest Timothy came to see him and he asked her, 'Is that woman still living in fornication?'

She replied, 'Yes, and she has increased the number of her lovers. But also the amount of her alms'.

Abba Timothy told Abba Poemen. The latter said, 'She will not go on committing fornication'.

Abba Timothy's mother came again and said to him, 'You know that sinner? She wanted to come with me so that you might pray over her'.

When he heard this, he told Abba Poemen and Abba Poemen said to him, 'Go and meet her'.

When the woman saw him and heard the word of God from him, she was filled with compunction and said to him, weeping, 'From today forward I shall cling to God and resolve not to commit fornication any more'. She entered a monastery at once and was pleasing to God.

EXPERIENCE IN FELLING TREES

Abba Poemen said that Abba Ammonas said, 'A person can spend his whole time carrying an axe without succeeding in cutting down the tree, while another, with experience in tree-felling, brings the tree down with a few blows'. He said that the axe is discernment.

GO AWAY, TRAITOROUS HORSE!

One day, then, when Abba Macarius of Alexandria was an old man, I went to pay him a visit. I sat by the door so I could hear what he said. Abba Macarius had reached a hundred years. I heard him talking all by himself, saying, 'What do you want, Macarius, you wicked old man? Look now, you drink wine and use oil; what more do you want, you who have eaten your own gray hair?'

After this he spoke with the Devil, 'Have you nothing more to do with me? There's nothing for you here. Get away from me!'

He acted as though he despised his body, speaking like this: 'Go away, traitorous horse! You will never be well as long as I am with you!'

July 30

MY POOR ARE IN SCETIS

Now all our fathers, when they went to the harvest, would divide their harvest wage into two portions, a portion for charity and a portion for their own needs, and they would do likewise with the money from their handiwork. But our father Abba John would bring both portions to the desert, saying, 'My poor, my weak, my widows, and my orphans are in Scetis'.

GIVING TO OTHERS

Abba Pambo would also do this other thing: he gave nothing for the service of servants unless it was to an old man, poor and infirm, who was unable to acquire bread for himself. Moreover, with regard to the monks who lived there, he did not give them anything from the provisions he had at hand but instead chose for himself ten faithful brothers whom he sent to the islands and to Libya each year and to the lepers' colony in Alexandria; loading the boats with grain and bread, they would distribute them to those in need and also to the churches of villages that were in need and to the churches of the interior deserts in barbarian territory.

I tell you this so you (pl.) will understand why he did not give anything to the monks who lived there. Seek and you (sing.) will understand that he began a custom among the brothers who lived in Egypt and Pernouj: each one would give an *artaba* of grain per person each year and they would put them at the service of those in need, distributing them to the hospices *for lepers and to the widows and orphans.*[30] Each of the monks would have the responsibility each year to give the *artaba* of grain from his charitable labor, and this is their custom up to today.

A PIECE OF WOOD

Now it happened that on another day we were sitting with one another. A certain Nubian came out from the mountain with his son to drink water from the river. And when his young son put his hand into the river to scoop up some water to drink, a huge crocodile seized him and dragged him under and fled. Immediately his father threw himself to the ground and cried out and wept bitterly, for besides that son he had no other. Now as the man ran up the mountain crying out, he cut himself against the sharp edges of the rocks and severely injured himself. When I saw how heartbroken he was I told my father, Abba Aaron. He got up and came to the door and gestured to the Nubian with his hand to come to him. And when he had come, Abba Aaron saw the wounds on his body, and he wiped away the blood that had run over his body and took him and brought him inside his home. He brought him in by force and made him sit down.

Now when he had questioned him about what had happened (he could not understand what the Nubian was saying to him), my father said to me, "Rise, see if you can find anyone on the road.

---

[30] Dt 14:29; Is 1:17; Jm 1:27.

Call him. Perhaps you can find someone who knows how to speak with him. When I went out I found a man from Philae who was going to Aswan riding on a donkey. I called to him and said to him, 'Do you understand the language of the Nubians?' He said, 'Yes'. I took him to my father Abba Aaron. Now when that man saw the Nubian and the wounds all over his body, he was astonished and said to him, 'How were you wounded?' and the Nubian told him what had happened. The holy man Abba Aaron took a piece of wood and gave it to him, saying, 'Take it and throw it into the river where the crocodile seized your son'. And he went and did as Abba Aaron had told him.

Now it happened that when he threw the piece of wood into the water, a huge crocodile appeared and cast the little boy up on the shore—and he had not been injured in any way! And his father took him by the hand and brought him to the holy old man Abba Aaron. And when the Nubian saw this miracle, he shouted with joy and hugged Abba Aaron and kissed him. Now the interpreter went to Philae and did not go to Aswan that day; instead, he went about proclaiming the miracle that had taken place. And when the Nubian saw the miracle that had taken place, he went home glorifying God and proclaiming what had happened. And all those who heard glorified God and the holy man Abba Aaron until this very day.

AUGUST

PENTECOST / ORDINARY TIME

August 1

FLEE THIS

Abba Macarius the Great used to say to the brothers at Scetis when he dismissed the congregation, 'Flee, brothers'.

One of the fathers said to him, 'Where can we flee that's more desert than this?'

He put his finger to his lips and said, 'Flee this', and so he would go into his cell and shut the door and sit down.

A FAITHFUL FRIEND

A faithful friend is beyond price.[1]

If you keep a faithful friend by your side, he will remain faithful when you are afraid and will strengthen you and give you courage.

He will cause you to be a worker and will make you a citizen, and he will be a strong wall for you to lean against, and he will be a shade tree for you to rest under in all your troubles. He will be strength and power and consolation for you. He will find you

---

[1] Sir 6:15.

during your affliction. You will find him there when you are in distress; he will bear all your sufferings.

If you place all your sufferings on him, he will bear them.

August 2

SIN AND FIRE

Let the monk's life be one that imitates the angel of the Lord, consuming sin with fire, for a monk's life is a whole burnt-offering for those who sin.[2]

THE MIRACLE OF THE CHALICE

Yet again I heard another very amazing story from Abba Macarius of Alexandria: 'I was present on one of the feast days when the deacon was inside the sanctuary preparing the eucharistic offering. The chalice fell from his hand and broke into numerous pieces, for it was glass (truly, it was the desert and it was not possible for them to have silver). I myself heard the sound of the chalice breaking when it fell from the deacon's hand. I entered the sanctuary while all the people were seated saying the psalms. I said to the deacon, "Don't be upset and don't get discouraged, but gather up

[2] Jdg 6:19-24.

all the pieces and do not leave any behind. Put them on the altar, go, and leave them"'.

When Saint Abba Macarius left, he and the deacon, they sat a short while. Abba Macarius said to the deacon, 'Go to the altar. Tell no one what you are going to see there.' The deacon went inside and found the chalice in perfect condition: it was put back together. The signs of the broken fragments were visible, but it no longer looked dropped. That chalice still exists today.

'When I heard about this miracle' Abba Macarius continued, 'I went to the deacon, who had become a priest. He showed me that chalice. I saw it with my own eyes. I kissed it and glorified God. When the father of the monastery of Tashenthosh of the village of Jani came, he paid a visit to the monastic community. He brought a large supply of money and distributed it to the old men of the desert places. He asked the priest there for that chalice and the priest gave it to him as a token of remembrance. Indeed, that chalice resides in the monastery of Tashenthosh to this very day'.

August 3

GOING BACK AND FORTH

A brother asked Abba Theodore, 'Abba, do you want me not to eat bread for a few days?'

The old man said to him, 'What you're doing is good; I've done the same thing'.

The brother said to him, 'I want therefore to take my chick-peas to the bakery and have them make flour from them'.

309

Abba Theodore spoke to him again, 'If you're going to the bakery, make yourself bread. What's the need for all this going back and forth?'

LAMP OIL AND HONEY

One of the old men was sick and, since he was unable to take any food for days, his disciple begged him to let him bring him a little cream soup made from white flour. He left and made the dish and brought it to the old man to eat. There was sitting there a jar containing a small amount of honey and another jar containing linseed oil that stank and was used only as oil for lamps. The brother was not paying attention and put some of this oil into the old man's food. When the old man tasted it, he did not say anything but ate it without saying a word. The disciple insisted that the old man eat a second helping and forced him to eat. Then he gave him a third serving, but the old man refused to eat, saying, 'Really, child, I can't'.

The disciple, however, encouraged him to eat and said, 'It's good, abba. Look, I'll eat with you'. When he tasted the food and realized what he had done, he fell on his face and said, 'God help me, Abba! I almost killed you and you put the sin on my shoulders by not saying anything!'

The old man said to him, 'Child, don't blame yourself; if God had wanted me to eat honey, you would have used honey'.

August 4

MARY MAGDALENE (CO)
SEVEN SLEEPERS OF EPHESUS (O)
JEAN-MARIE VIANNEY, PRIEST (RC)

USEFUL AND DESTRUCTIVE GRIEF

Amma Syncletica said, 'There is grief that is useful, and there is grief that is destructive. The first sort consists in weeping over one's own faults and weeping over the weakness of one's neighbors in order not to destroy one's purpose, so as to attach oneself to the perfect good. But there is also a grief that comes from the Enemy, full of mockery, which some call *accidie*. This spirit must be cast out, mainly by prayer and psalmody'.

TURNING PROBLEMS INTO PROFITS

Amma Theodora asked Archbishop Theophilus about some words of the Apostle, saying, 'What does this mean: *Knowing how to profit by difficult circumstances?*'[3]

He said to her, 'This saying shows us how to profit at all times. For example, is it a time of excess for you? By humility and patience buy up the time of excess, and draw profit from it. Is it a time of shame? Buy it up by means of resignation and win it. So everything that goes against us can, if we wish, become profitable to us'.

[3] Col 4:5.

311

GREED, MERCY, AND COMPASSION

There was a man from the surrounding countryside there who
had a noble son whom he had raised to adulthood from a child.
There was a woman named Flavia who entrusted a document to
the parents of that youth, which they gave to their son to protect.
When the youth died suddenly, his parents did not know where
the document was. That woman, Flaviana, went to recover her deposit, that is, the document that she had entrusted to them. When
they were at a loss regarding it and could not find it because they
did not know where the young man had put it, with great anger
she threatened that she would make them her slaves if they did
not restore her document to her.

Then the parents of the youth, when they continued to be
hounded by that woman, left their beloved child unburied and
hurried to where the saints were living, with a great crowd following them, that is, their relatives and neighbors. They prostrated themselves at the feet of Abba Lucius and Abba Longinus,
imploring them, 'Ask the Lord Christ, whose servants you are, to
reveal the soul of our child who has died so we may learn from
him where he placed the document that the wife of the rich man
entrusted to us, because she is now threatening to make us slaves
if we do not find the document and give it to her!'

When the blessed ones heard this story from the young man's
parents, they felt pity for them on account of the love and compassion of Christ that was in them; they immediately arose and
followed them without hesitation or being bothered at all. When
they reached the house where the dead youth was, they went inside
to where the deceased lay and knelt down and prayed that God
might wish to manifest a miracle through blessed Abba Longinus
who was filled with virtues. Suddenly he was *filled with the Holy*

Spirit.[4] He seized the child's hand in front of the crowd and spoke thus: 'God, *who raised Lazarus,*[5] will also on this occasion now restore your spirit to you so you may tell us where you put the document belonging to the rich man's wife so she will not take your parents as slaves'.

Immediately the spirit returned to the young man; he rose up and sat and opened his mouth. With everyone standing there listening, he told them where the document had been placed in the house. And his parents asked him other things that they did not know and he gave them an account of everything they asked him, and so he immediately lay down again. When the people of Lycia saw this miracle that had taken place through the saints, they glorified God, who alone works such wonders.

August 6
THE TRANSFIGURATION OF THE LORD (O, RC, A)

THE INNER AND THE OUTER

A brother questioned Abba Arsenius to hear a word from him and the old man said to him, 'Strive with all your might to bring your interior activity into accord with God, and you will overcome exterior passions'.

[4] See Acts 2:4.
[5] See Jn 11:1-12:19.

I SAW THE GLORY OF GOD

One time Abba Silvanus' disciple Zacharias entered and found him in ecstasy with his hands stretched towards heaven. Closing the door, he went away. Coming at the sixth and ninth hours, he found him in the same place. At the tenth hour he knocked, entered, and found him at peace and said to him, 'What has happened today, Father?'

Abba Silvanus replied, 'I was ill today, my child'.

But the disciple seized his feet and said to him, 'I will not let you go until you have told me what you have seen'.

The old man said, 'I was taken up to heaven and I saw the glory of God and I stayed there till now and now I have been sent away'.

August 7

DISCERNING THE SPIRIT(S)

Abba Antony said, 'But the attacks and apparitions of the evil ones are disturbing, with crashing and roaring noises and shouts, similar to the commotion that juvenile delinquents and robbers make. From these immediately arise terror in the soul, confusion, and disordered thoughts, dejection, hatred for other ascetics, listlessness, sadness, homesickness, and fear of death; and later, the desire for evil, the neglect of virtue, and disorder in one's character. When, therefore, you see some apparitions, you become fearful, but if the fear is immediately taken away and in its place comes unutterable joy, along with tranquility and confidence and renewed spirits and calm thoughts and all the other things I have mentioned earlier, both courage and love for God, be of good courage and pray. For the soul's joy and its orderly condition demonstrate the holiness of each person. So *Abraham rejoiced when he saw the Lord*,[6] and John *leapt for joy* when the voice of Mary, the Mother of God, reached him.[7]But if the appearance of certain spirits is accompanied by disturbances and knockings outside and worldly apparitions and the threat of death and the other things I have spoken about earlier, know that this is an assault of the evil ones'.

Antony continued, 'In addition, let there be this other sign for you: when the soul of certain people remains fearful, enemies are present, for the demons do not remove fearfulness from such persons *as the great archangel did for Mary and Zacharias and as the angel did who appeared to the women at the tomb*.[8] On the contrary, when the demons see people who are fearful, they make the apparitions even stronger to make them cower even more. Afterwards, setting on them, the demons mock them and say, "*Prostrate yourselves and worship us!*"[9] They deceived the polytheists this way, for this is how the polytheists were convinced by the demons that the demons were so-called "gods". But as for us, the Lord did not allow us to be deceived by the Devil. Whenever such apparitions came to him, the Lord rebuked them and said, "*Get behind me, Satan!*"[10] For it is written, *The Lord your God shall you worship and him only shall you serve*.[11]On this account, then, let the Deceitful One be more and more despised by us, for what the Lord said, this he has done for us so that when the demons hear such words from us, they are turned away by the Lord, who rebuked them with such words as these'.

[6] See Jn 8:56.
[7] Lk 1:41.
[8] See Lk 1:30, 3:13; Mt 28:5.
[9] See Mt 4:9.
[10] Mt 4:19, 16:23.
[11] Mt 4:10; see Dt 6:13.

WHAT'S NEEDED TO CROSS THE SEA

Abba Mark said, 'The person who wishes to cross the spiritual sea is patient, humble, vigilant, and abstinent. If he rushes to enter the water without these four he only troubles his heart and is unable to cross'.

SERVING THE FLESH

There was an old man and each day he would eat three biscuits. A brother came to visit the old man and when they had sat down to eat, the old man set three biscuits before the brother. When the old man saw that the brother was still hungry, he brought him three more. When they had their fill and stood up, the old man condemned the brother and said to him, 'It is not fitting, brother, to serve the flesh'. The brother asked the old man's forgiveness and left.

The next day, when it was time for the old man to eat, he placed before himself, as was his custom, the three biscuits; after eating them he was still hungry but restrained himself. The following day the same thing happened to him. As a result, the old man began to lose his willpower and thought that he had been forsaken by God. Throwing himself before God, with tears he was imploring God for the reason why he had been forsaken and he saw an angel speaking to him, 'This has happened to you because you condemned the brother. Know, therefore, that when someone is able to exercise self-control or do any other good thing, he is able to do it not on his own power but because it is the grace of God that empowers each person'.

GO IN OR PASS ON BY

An old man said, 'Be like someone who, passing by a tavern in the marketplace, catches the scent of cooking meat or something roasting. Whoever wishes to, goes inside and eats; whoever does not wish to, simply smells what is cooking, passes on by, and goes his way. It is the same with you: shake off what smells bad; get up and pray, saying, "Son of God, help me!" Do this also for other thoughts, for our job is not to yank out thoughts by the roots but to struggle against them'.

PERSEVERE LIKE THE KICK-BOXER

With regard to the thought of sexual sin, an old hermit said, 'You want to save yourself by lying in bed? Go work; go toil; *go seek, and you will find*;[12] *be vigilant*;[13] *knock and it will be opened to you.*[14] In the world there are kick-boxers; after being hit often and persevering and enduring, they receive a crown. Many times one athlete will even be hit by two others, endures the blows, and defeats those hitting him. You have seen how, on account of their persistence, they persevere with such great endurance; you too, therefore, stand firm and persevere, and God will fight the Enemy on your behalf'.

[12] Mt 7:7//Lk 11:9.
[13] See Mt 24:42.
[14] Mt 7:7//Lk 11:10.

WATCH YOUR STEP

When a monk met some consecrated virgins on the road, he avoided them by stepping off the road. The superior of the virgins said to him, 'If you were a perfect monk, you would not have noticed that we are women'.

GIVE TO CAESAR . . . .

One time the governor of the district wanted to see Abba Poemen but the old man would not agree to meet him. The governor, therefore, under the pretext that the son of Poemen's sister was a criminal, seized him and threw him into prison. 'If the old man comes and intercedes on his behalf, I will let him go'.

Poemen's sister went weeping to Poemen's door but he would not give her any kind of response. She reproached him, saying, 'You hard-hearted thing, have mercy on me! He's my only son!' But he sent someone out to say to her, 'Poemen has not fathered any children'. So she went away.

When the governor heard this, he said, 'If you ask me to release him with just one word, I'll let him go'.

The old man stated in turn, 'Judge him according to your laws and if he deserves to die, let him be put to death; if not, do as you wish'.

August 11

THE DEMON WHO ATE HIS NEIGHBORS

An old woman came to Abba Macarius one time bringing him her son bound in iron fetters, detained by two men, for this young man was possessed by a madly raging demon. His mother was walking behind him, weeping. This was what that demon was doing: after eating three measures of bread and drinking a jug of water each day, he would vomit and all the food would disintegrate like smoke and the food would be consumed like a fire devouring stubble. And the food that he ate each day was not enough for him but he would turn even to his excrement: he would eat it and also drink his urine.

His mother threw herself at the feet of Saint Abba Macarius, weeping and pleading with him, saying, 'Help me in my widowhood and my feebleness! This is my only child and this evil demon has taken control of him'.

He said to her, 'Be patient, old woman. I believe that God will take pity on you and your little one. Therefore be patient a few days'.

The saint ordered them to lay him in a cell inside the hospital and there cover his mouth so he could not eat and drink. I myself saw the place where the sick lay; the place lay about seventy yards from the church.

After twenty days he opened the door of the young man's cell, brought him out, and undid his fetters because in truth the demon had left him, and the man of God spoke to the young man's mother, 'How many loaves of bread would you have your son eat each day?'

She said to him, 'I would have him eat eight pounds of bread a day'.

The old man grew angry and rebuked her, saying, 'The amount you're saying is too much, but if you have more than you need, give five pounds each day to the helpless widows and give the other three pounds to your son every day. Listen, and I will also tell you how this demon got power over your son. His father died and left you a few necessities, more than you needed to live, and there were old women, widows—poor, powerless, and infirm—who were your neighbors and were in need of alms and you gave them nothing. Because of this, God allowed this demon to enter your son so he would eat your goods and dissipate them through his insatiable appetite so you yourselves would become poor because you would not give alms to the infirm'.

And in this way he taught them to give alms, having given the young man back to his mother, healed, praying to God and giving thanks to Christ.

August 12
BESA, DISCIPLE OF SHENUTE (CO)

PRAYER

Prayer is an ascent of the spirit to God.

FAST TO GIVE

An old man said, 'It is also good to fast in order to give food to a poor person'.

THE FAINTING DONKEY

Now there was also in Philae a man who owned a donkey that he worked in the mill. When he was getting ready to go home, the donkey fell down right there at his feet and died. But he, because of his great faith in the righteous man Abba Aaron, left the donkey lying there dead and ran to him and told him about it.

Now the righteous one said to him, 'He has not died, my son, but has fainted'. He gave him a staff and said to him, 'Go and strike him with it three times and he will stand up'.

The man took the staff and left and struck the donkey with it three times and it got up on its feet as it usually did. The man came to my father and said to him, 'Thank you, my father, for the favor which God has shown me'.

Now my father admonished him not to tell anyone what had happened, saying, 'Do not allow anyone to disbelieve our words. For indeed our Saviour said, "*Truly, truly, I say to you, whoever believes in me, the works which I do he shall do also, and he shall do things greater than these*"'.[15]

August 13
MAXIMOS THE CONFESSOR (GO)
TIKHON OF ZADONSK, MONK (RO)

MY SON AND HEIR

Our father Bishoy from that time added even greater spiritual struggles, always importuning God to rise above the need for food.

[15] Jn 14:12.

Food for him was partaking each Sunday of the body and blood of our Lord Jesus Christ. The Saviour once again in his compassion appeared to his servant and said to him, 'Why are you still making requests about food when you do not eat anyway? You should use this time to ask for other things'.

Bishoy said, 'Lord, when I leave the desert here to go visit the brothers, I want to return as quickly as possible. I cannot bear to be gone long, even for the sake of others'.

He said, 'Do not be sad about this. When you are away from the desert here, I have not left you'.

Then Bishoy said, 'Free me from anger, Christ'.

'If you want to defeat anger and rage', he said, 'do not rebuke anyone or hate anyone or denigrate anyone. If you guard yourself against doing these, you will not get angry'.

Bishoy said, 'Compassionate Master and patient Lord, if someone walks according to your commandments and visits those who love you in order to care for them, will he gain or lose because of his zeal?'

The Saviour said, '*Just as the worker who goes out to the field to work will be paid by the landowner without delay* so too will I reward those who do good or teach or assist me.[16] I will repay such persons as these with resplendent rewards in the heavenly Jerusalem'.

Then Bishoy again asked, 'If someone struggles safe and sound and ministers to others, while another person struggles and does not minister to others, how does the reward differ for each person?'

The Saviour said, 'The person who spiritually struggles alone is my disciple, but the person who spiritually struggles and ministers to others is my son and heir'.

Bishoy again said, 'If someone is serious about ministering to others and spiritually struggles as much as possible but does not find himself at all the equal of those who only spiritually struggle because his care for others prevents him from taking on more exacting spiritual struggles, will he receive equal payment?'

'Yes', the Saviour said, 'he will ascend to heaven'.

[16] Mt 20; see Dt 24:15 (LXX).

TIT FOR TAT

Abba Or said, 'If you see that I am thinking adversely about someone, know that that person is thinking the same way about me'.

A PART OF JUSTICE

It is a part of justice that you should pray not only for your own purification but also for that of every person. In doing this you will imitate the practice of the angels.

NO NEED TO SEE ME

In Abba Or's neighborhood there was a villager named Longinus who gave a great deal away in alms. He asked one of the Fathers who came to see him to take him to Abba Or. The monk went to the old man and praised the villager, saying that he was good and gave many alms. The old man thought about this and then said, 'Yes, he is good'.

Then the monk began to beg him, saying, 'Abba, let him come and see you'.

But the old man answered, 'Truly, there is no need for him to cross this valley in order to see me'.

---

[17] American Church calendar.

August 15
DORMITION OF THE THEOTOKOS (GO)
ASSUMPTION OF THE VIRGIN MARY (RC)
THE BLESSED VIRGIN MARY (A)

EXAMINING YOUR THOUGHTS

It was said of Abba Poemen that every time he prepared to go to the *synaxis*, he sat alone and examined his thoughts for about an hour, and then he set off.

THE FIRST LIGHT OF MORNING

Whenever a brother came to our father Abba John at dusk to ask him about what is profitable for a soul, they spoke about virtue until they noticed the first light of morning. As morning came, our father came out from his cell accompanying the brother, and once again our father began speaking with the brother from morning again until the ninth hour of the day concerning spiritual things. Finally he brought the brother in and, after they ate in love, the brother departed in peace.

SATAN, HIS FOUR DEMONS, AND A FALLEN MONK

One of the old men from Thebes used to say: I was the child of a priest who served idols. When I was little, therefore, I used to sit in the temple and watch my father come in and offer sacrifices to the idol. One time, then, I came in secretly after him and I saw Satan sitting on his throne with his army standing around him and suddenly one of his leaders came and made obeisance to him. In response the Devil said to him, 'Where have you come from?' and he said, 'I was in this certain village and I stirred up warfare and great unrest and caused blood to be spilled and have come to report to you'. And the Devil said to him, 'How long did it take you to do this?' and he answered 'Thirty days'. The Devil ordered him to be flogged and said, 'Why did it take you so long!'

Suddenly another one was there making obeisance to him and the Devil said to him, 'Where have you come from?' and in reply the demon said, 'I was in the sea and I stirred up storms and caused ships to sink and, having killed large numbers of people, have come to report to you'. The Devil said to him, 'How long did it take you to do this?' and the demon answered and said, 'Twenty days'. So the Devil ordered this one to be flogged too, saying, 'Why did it take you so long to do this simple task?'

Suddenly a third one came and made obeisance to the Devil and the Devil also said to him, 'And you, where have you come from?' and in reply he said to him, 'I was in such-and-such a city where a wedding took place and I stirred up warfare and caused a great deal of blood to be spilled—even between the bride and groom!—and have come to report to you'. The Devil said, 'How many days did it take you to do this?' and he said, 'Ten'. The Devil ordered this one also to be beaten for having taken so long.

A fourth one also came to pay him obeisance and the Devil said to him, 'Where have you come from?' and he said, 'I was in the desert. Look what I've done! I've been waging war against a certain monk for forty years and now this very night I caused him to fall into sin!'

When the Devil heard this he rose and kissed him and, taking off the crown he was wearing, he placed it upon the demon's head and sat him on the throne with him, saying, 'You have done a great thing!'

August 17

TENDING THE SOUL, EATING GOOD FRUIT

A monk's field is a good soul that bears gospel fruit; by tending the soul, the monk will eat its good fruit, for *its fruit*, the reward for his labors, *is sweet in the monk's mouth.*[18]

HE'S DOING EXACTLY WHAT WE WANT

Abba Daniel of Scetis related that a brother who was living in Egypt was walking along the road one time and, when evening overtook him, on account of the cold, he went inside a tomb to sleep. Two demons were passing by and the one said to the other,

---

[18] Song 2:3.

326

'Do you see how courageous this monk is, sleeping in a tomb? Come on, let's harass him'.

The other one replied, 'Why should we harass him? This guy's doing exactly what we want, eating and drinking and slandering and disregarding the monastic assembly. Let's ignore him and instead go afflict those who afflict us and who night and day wage war against us with their prayers'.

August 18
JANE FRANCES DE CHANTAL, RELIGIOUS (RC)

WE WORK FOR WHAT WE EAT AND WEAR

Abba Pambo gloried in the Lord while telling us numerous times, 'Neither I nor my servants are aware of eating a single piece of bread given to us by someone else without working for it with our hands, nor have we clothed ourselves through the labor of strangers without working for it ourselves'.

SINS FRONT AND BACK

A council was convened one time in Scetis and the fathers were talking about a brother who had done something wrong, but Abba Pior remained silent.

Later he got up, went outside and, taking a sack, filled it with sand, and was hauling it behind him; he also filled a small basket with sand and was pushing it along in front of him. When he was asked by the fathers what this might mean, he said, 'This sack, which is filled with sand, represents my offences because they are numerous and I have put them behind me; therefore I do not trouble myself weeping over them. Now take a look at this little basket in front of me: it represents my brother's sins, and I spend all my time judging my brother for them. It shouldn't be done this way. No, instead I should carry my sins in front of me and concern myself with them and implore God to forgive me them'.

When they heard this, the fathers said, 'Truly this is the way of salvation'.

───────────

August 19
TRANSFIGURATION OF CHRIST (CO)
BLESSED GUERRIC OF IGNY (M)

IT'S NOT THE NAME

Again it was said about Abba Macarius that one time when he was praying in his cell a voice came to him, saying, 'Macarius, you have not yet reached the level of two women who live in such-and-such a village'.

When the old man got up early in the morning, he took his palm-tree staff and set out on his journey. When he reached the village, an angel walked with him, guiding him to the house. When he knocked at the door, the women opened it to him. When they realized it was Abba Macarius, they did obeisance to him on the ground and received him with joy. The old man said to them, 'On account of you I have patiently endured the hardships of this journey through the desert and have come here. Tell me, therefore, what is your way of life?'

They, however, wanting to conceal their way of life, said to him, 'Why do you inquire about the way of life of those who are defiled?'

After the old man had asked their forgiveness, he said to them, 'Do not hide anything from me, for it is God who has sent me'.

They became fearful and revealed everything to him, saying, 'Forgive us, our father. The two of us are strangers to each other according to the world, but by mutual agreement, we have been made two sisters according to the flesh. Look, it has been fifteen years today that we have lived in this house and we do not recall that we have ever quarreled with one another or that one of us has ever said an idle word to her companion. On the contrary, we are always at peace and of one mind. We agreed to leave our husbands and to exchange married life for the life of virginity. But when we implored our husbands over and over concerning what we wanted, they did not agree to let us go. When we could not accomplish our goal, we drew up a covenant between ourselves and God that to the day of our death our mouths would not speak a worldly utterance but that we would direct our thoughts to God and his saints at all times and would devote ourselves unceasingly to prayers and fastings and acts of charity.'

When Abba Macarius heard these things, he said, 'Truly, it is not the name of "monk" or "lay person" or "virgin" or "wife and husband" but an upright disposition that God seeks, and he gives his Holy Spirit to all of these people'.

And after the old man had profited from meeting the two women, he returned to his cell, clapping his hands and saying, 'I have not been at peace with my brothers like these lay women have with one another'.

SILENCE BEYOND COMPARE

Abba Poemen said that a brother who lived with some other brothers asked Abba Bessarion, 'What should I do?'

The old man said to him, 'Keep silence and do not always be comparing yourself with others'.

KEEP IT TO YOURSELF, SATAN

It was said of a brother that he had to fight against blasphemy and he was ashamed to admit it. He went where he heard some great old men lived to see them in order to open his heart to them, but when he got there he was ashamed to admit his temptation. So he kept going to see Abba Poemen. The old man saw he was worried, and he was sorry the young man did not tell him what was wrong. So one day he forestalled him and said, 'For a long time you have been coming here to tell me what is troubling you, and when you are here you will not tell me about it, but each time you go away unhappy, keeping your thoughts to yourself. Now tell me, my child, what it is all about'.

The brother said to him, 'The demon wars against me to make me blaspheme God and I am ashamed to say so'. So he told him all about it and immediately he was relieved.

The old man said to him, 'Do not be unhappy, my child, but every time this thought comes to you, say, "It is no affair of mine; may your blasphemy remain upon you, Satan, for my soul does not want it!" Now everything that the soul does not desire does not long remain', and the brother went away healed.

HOME IMPROVEMENT

Abba Poemen said, 'Instructing one's neighbor is for the person who is whole and without passions; for what is the use of building the house of another while destroying one's own?'

LEARNING A TRADE

He also said, 'What is the good of giving oneself to a trade without seeking to learn it?'

DIFFERENT SORTS OF MATERIALS

He also said, 'When a person prepares to build a house, he gathers together all he needs to be able to construct it, and he collects different sorts of materials. So it is with us: let us acquire a little of the virtues'.

THE EMPTY CHURCH

Abba Daniel of Scetis related that there was a monk by the name of Doulas who was counted among the greatest of the fathers: At that time the Enemy, unable to bear the vitality of this fellow's patient endurance, insinuated himself to one of the brothers who were living as hermits; going into the church, the brother stripped it of all the priestly vessels and left the cenobium without being noticed.

When it came time for the celebration of the synaxis, the precentor came in to cense the church and found everything stolen. He left and reported it to the abbot and struck the signal and all the brothers assembled and began to get agitated, saying, 'No one could have taken them except brother you-know-who, and that is why he has not come to the synaxis. If he had not done it he would have been the first one here, as always'.

They sent for him and found him standing in prayer and, knocking on the door, they went inside and violently dragged him out. He entreated them, saying, 'What's the matter, fathers?'

They, however, heaped abuse and reproaches on him as they dragged him out: 'You sacrilegious thief, you don't deserve to live! Hasn't it been enough for you that you've bothered us all these years? Now you've even gone and struck at our very souls!'

He said, 'Forgive me. I've done wrong', and they took him to the abbot and said to him, 'Abba, this is the person who from the beginning has been turning the cenobium upside down!' and one by one they began to say 'I know that he secretly ate vegetables!' 'He stole bread and gave it to those outside!' 'I found him drinking the best wine!'

All of them lied and were believed, while he told the truth and was not listened to. So the abbot took off the monk's habit, saying, 'These are not things that a Christian does!' Clapping him into irons, they handed him over to the steward of the lavra and he stripped him and beat him with an ox-hide whip to find out if what they were saying about him was true. But Doulas laughed and said, 'Forgive me. I've done wrong'.

Enraged at what he said, the steward ordered him to be thrown into the jail cell; securing his feet in the stocks, he wrote the duke with details about the matter. Immediately civil servants came, and they took him and put him on an unsaddled beast, with heavy irons clapped around his neck, and dragged him through the middle of the city.[19]

August 23
IRENAEUS OF LYONS, BISHOP (O)

Led before the magistrate, the monk was asked who he was and where he was from and why he had become a monk, but he said nothing more than 'I have sinned. Forgive me'. Enraged, the duke ordered him to be stretched out on the rack and to have his back flayed to pieces with rawhide whips. With all four limbs stretched out, and flogged unmercifully by the cords, with a smile on his face he said to the duke, 'Beat me, beat me, you are making my money shine even more brightly!'

The duke said, 'I'll show you that your idiotic behavior will melt faster than snow!' and he ordered fiery coals spread out under the monk's belly and dazzling white salt to be mixed and poured on his wounds. Those standing there were marveling at his incredible

---

[19] Continues on August 23 and 24.

endurance and were saying to him, 'Tell us where you put the priestly vessels and you can go', but he kept saying, 'I don't know anything about it'.

Scarcely had the duke ordered him to be removed from the torture when he commanded the monk to be led away to prison and held without food and with complete neglect. The next day he sent someone to the lavra and ordered the monks of the cenobium and the abbot to be brought and when they came the duke said to them, 'After making every effort and subjecting him to numerous punishments, I have been unable to find out anything more than you did'.

The brothers said to him, 'Master, he has done many other wicked things and for God's sake we put up with him, expecting to reform him, and look what's happened! He's gone from bad to worse!'

He said to them, 'So what shall I do with him?'

They said to him, 'Whatever seems legally best'.

He said to them, 'The law calls for executing those who commit acts of sacrilege'.

They said, 'Let him be put to death'.

The duke dismissed them and brought the brother in and, sitting on the judgement seat, said to him, 'Confess, you wretch, and escape death'.

The brother said, 'If you order me to say what isn't true, I'll say it'.

The duke said, 'I don't want you to bear false witness against yourself'.

The brother said, 'I didn't do any of the things I'm being questioned about'. When the duke saw that the monk had nothing to say, he ordered him to be beheaded. [20]

---

[20] Continues on August 24.

August 24

Filled with compunction, the hermit who had taken the sacred vessels came to himself and said, 'Sooner or later this matter is going to be found out. Even if you escape detection here, what will you do on the day of judgement? How will you defend yourself with regard to these wicked acts?' So he went to the abbot and said to him, 'Hurry, send word so the brother doesn't die; the sacred vessels have been found!'

So the abbot sent someone who reported to the duke and the brother was set free and they brought him to the cenobium. Everyone began to fall at his feet in supplication, saying, 'We have sinned against you. Forgive us'.

He began to weep and said, 'Forgive *me*! I owe all of you a great debt of thanks: on account of these great sufferings I am considered worthy of so many good things!'

The brother lived for three days, then went to the Lord. When one of the brothers came to see how he was doing, he found him on his knees lying on the ground, for he had been praying and making an act of prostration and in this way gave up his spirit while his body remained lying in an act of prostration.

The brother went and told the abbot and he ordered the brother's body to be carried into the church in order to be buried there. When, therefore, they had placed him in front of the altar, the abbot ordered the signal to be given in order that the entire lavra might be assembled, and the body was interred with many honors. When they were gathered together, each monk wished to receive a blessing from him. When the abbot saw this, therefore, he placed the brother's body in the sanctuary and, having secured the bolts, awaited the abba of the lavra in order to inter the brother together.

When, therefore, the father of the lavra came with the clergy and offered prayer, they said to the abbot, 'Open the door and bring out the body so it may be buried, for indeed it is time to say the prayers appointed for the ninth hour'. When they opened the

doors, *they found nothing except his clothes and sandals*[21] and everyone
was amazed and began to glorify God with tears, saying, 'Look,
brothers, at what sort of things forbearance and humility procure
for us, as you can see with your own eyes!'

August 25
APOSTLE BARTHOLOMEW (O)

WEAVING A SPIDER'S WEB

The monk who keeps vigil with *psalms and hymns and spiritual
songs*[22] drives away the phantasms of the night, but the monk
who prides himself on his achievements and goes to sleep weaves
a spider's web.

WHAT HAVE WE GOT TO WORRY ABOUT?

A brother asked Abba Poemen, 'What should I do?'
      The old man said to him, 'When God is watching over us, what
have we got to worry about?'
      The brother said to him, 'Our sins'.
      Then the old man said, 'Let us enter into our cell and, sitting
there, remember our sins, and the Lord will come and help us in
everything'.

---

[21] See Lk 24:12.
[22] Eph 5:19, Col 3:16.

A FEW SMALL POTS

A brother who lived in a monastery, who had another brother living in the monastery with him, stole some small pots from the storeroom of the steward of the monastery. The thief put the pots in a sack and deposited them with the brother who did not know that they were stolen but who thought they belonged to the thief. A little later the pots turned up missing and the monks searched each of the brothers' cells. When they found them in the possession of the brother with whom the pots had been deposited, he threw himself down and asked for forgiveness.

The brother who had stolen the pots and deposited them with the second brother heaped scorn on the brother in whose cell the pots were discovered and slapped him on the face, wishing to cast him out of the monastery, and in all these things the accused did not deny anything but even humbled himself before the first brother, saying, 'I have sinned. Forgive me'.

The brother in whose cell the pots were found became the object of hatred of the priest and of all the brothers in the monastery; the brother who stole the pots especially hated him and reproached him every hour of the day, calling him a thief in front of the brothers.

After the accused had spent two years in the monastery, enduring this great reproach, God revealed the matter to Abba Macarius in Scetis and Abba Macarius went to Egypt in order to see the brother.

When he drew near the monastery, all the brothers *gathered together with palm branches* in order to stand before Abba Macarius.[23] The accused brother said, 'I am disgraced. I did not take a palm branch nor did I go to meet the old man, for I am filled with shame, as you yourselves can see'.

[23] See Jn 12:12-13.

When the brothers went out and stood before the old man, he greeted them one by one. When he did not see the brother who had been accused of theft, he asked where he was and the brothers explained to Abba Macarius why the thief was ashamed to come greet him. When Abba Macarius heard this, he laughed and entered the monastery.

The accused brother came humbly to meet him and asked the old man's forgiveness just as Abba Macarius asked forgiveness of the brother, and they accepted forgiveness from each other. Abba Macarius said to the brothers, 'Neither I nor you are as honorable as this fellow: not only has he endured great reproach but he has taken upon his head even the sin of the brother who stole the pots'. And Abba Macarius restored him to his place. The other brother, however, took up his sheepskin mantle and left that monastery and did not return to it.

August 27
POEMEN THE GREAT, MONK (O)
MONICA, MOTHER OF AUGUSTINE OF HIPPO (RC, A)

THE MANY AND THE FEW

Abba Poemen said, 'Many become powerful, but few eminent'.

WATCH OUT

Abba Poemen said, 'If you have visions or hear voices, do not tell your neighbor about it, for it is a delusion in the battle'.

A HOUSE LACKING ONE VIRTUE

He also said, groaning, 'All the virtues come to this house except one and without that virtue it is hard for a person to stand'.

Then they asked him what this virtue was, and he said, 'For a person to blame himself'.

August 28
MOSES THE ETHIOPIAN, MONK (O)
AUGUSTINE, BISHOP OF HIPPO (RC, A)

THAT DANGEROUS SOLITUDE

A brother came to Scetis to visit Abba Moses and asked him for a word.

The old man said to him, 'Go, sit in your cell, and your cell will teach you everything'.

ABBA MOSES WINS AN ARGUMENT

It was said of Abba Moses at Scetis that when he had arranged to go to Petra, he grew tired in the course of the journey and said to himself, 'How can I find the water I need there?'

Then a voice said to him, 'Go, and do not be anxious about anything'. So he went.

Some Fathers came to see him and he had only a bottle of water. He used it all up in cooking lentils for them. The old man was worried, so he went in and came out of his cell, and he prayed to God, and a cloud of rain came to Petra and filled all the cisterns.

After this, the visitors said to the old man, 'Tell us why you went in and out'.

The old man said to them, 'I was arguing with God, saying, "You brought me here and now I have no water for your servants". That is why I was going in and out; I was going on at God till he sent us some water'.

August 29

BEHEADING OF JOHN THE BAPTIST (O, RC, A)

EATING, SLEEPING, AND SPEAKING

An old man said, 'Do not eat unless you are hungry and do not sleep until you are sleepy and do not speak before asked something'.

WATCH YOURSELF

When you arrive at the blessing of the cell, watch yourself on the right because the demons wage war against you with compassion to save someone so they may take away the blessing of the cell from you.

MORE THAN HABIT

Whether you pray along with the brothers or alone, strive to make your prayer more than a mere habit. Make it a true inner experience.

ZEALOUSLY SEEK GENTLENESS

Moreover, my son, zealously seek gentleness, for it is written concerning our father Moses: *He was more gentle than everyone on earth.*[24]

And it is written: *The gentle will inherit the earth,*[25] and again, *Guard your heart with all vigilance.*[26] Indeed, the ways of life come from these precepts.

A CAMEL LOADED WITH BREAD

An old man said, 'If temptation comes upon a person, from all sides afflictions multiply against him in order to discourage him and make him grumble'. And the old man recounted the following story: There was a certain brother at Kellia and temptation came upon him, and if someone saw him, that person wanted neither to greet the brother nor invite him into his cell; if he lacked bread, no one supplied him with any; no one called him in from the harvest when it was time for the agape meal, as is the custom.

One time, therefore, when he returned from the harvest, he did not have any bread in his cell—and for all these things he gave thanks to God. When God saw his patient endurance, he removed from him the warfare brought on by the temptation—and suddenly someone was knocking on his door, having come from Egypt with a camel loaded with bread! And the brother began to cry out, 'Lord, am I not worthy to have a little affliction?' When the temptation passed by, the brothers prevailed upon him to rest himself in their cells and in the church.

[24] Num 12:3.
[25] Mt 5:4.
[26] Prv 4:23.

A LOVER OF SOULS

Amma Theodora said that a teacher ought to be a stranger to the desire for domination, vainglory, and pride; one should not be able to fool him by flattery, nor blind him by gifts, nor conquer him by means of the stomach, nor dominate him by anger; but he should be patient, gentle, and humble as far as possible; he must be tested and without partisanship, full of concern, and a lover of souls.

TELL THE TRUTH

A brother asked one of the fathers, 'If I'm somewhere and affliction overtakes me and I don't have anyone with whom I can talk about it in confidence, what shall I do?'

The old man said, 'I believe that God himself will send you his grace and reassure you if you tell him the truth when you make your request. I heard a story in Scetis relating to this: There was a fellow who was doing battle and because he didn't have confidence about going to anyone, he got his sheepskin cloak ready one night in order to go away. Suddenly that night the grace of God appeared to him in the form of a virgin who comforted him, saying, "Don't go anywhere. Stay here a while with me. Contrary to what you have heard, no evil will happen to you". Persuaded by her, he remained, and right away his heart was healed'.

SEPTEMBER

PENTECOST / ORDINARY TIME

SAND INTO CEREAL

They also said about Saint Abba Macarius the Alexandrian that when he was a young man living in Alexandria he was a mime by trade and was world-famous. When he had become a monk, exalted in virtue in the desert places, his fellow mimes heard that *he had become exalted in God's work.*[1] They came to see him in the desert, seven in number, and when they had greeted him they sat beside him. They were full of admiration for him and his way of life. When it came time for them to eat, he put water in the pot and carried it to the oven, wanting to cook some cereal for them. While he heated the water to bring it to a boil, before he poured the meal into the pot he sat and chatted with them as he had when he had been a mime living in the world.

When they saw how he was behaving, they said to one another, 'Weren't we told that he had become a man of God? Now look—he's the same as he was when he was in the world with us. We don't see any change from the way he behaved when he was with us in Alexandria'.

When Abba Macarius saw them speaking with one another about the great freedom of speech he used with them, he brought in an empty dish, gave it to the greatest among them, and said to

---

[1] Jn 6:29; 1 Cor 15:58.

him, 'Fill this dish with sand and pour it into the pot so we can cook the cereal and eat'.

When they heard 'sand', they joked among themselves, saying, 'Truly Macarius has become more of a mime now than when he was with us in the world!'

Once again he said to them, 'Do what I told him'.

They obeyed him: they filled the plate with sand and poured it into the pot. He made the cereal and it turned out like a cereal made from tasty wheat. When the seven mimes saw the miracle that had taken place through the holy old man Abba Macarius, they did not return to Egypt but renounced the world. They became monks and adopted the practices of the holy old man Abba Macarius.

September 2
THE MARTYRS OF NEW GUINEA (RC, A)

EAT WHAT IS SENT BY GOD

An old man said, 'The Devil prefers to attack through the use of a monk's weakness, for a habit established over a long period of time assumes a natural propensity, especially among those who are the most negligent. Therefore, do not desire to give yourself every food that you want but when you eat what is sent to you by God, give thanks to him at all times'.

TRAINING REQUIRED

Question: How can a person live in solitude?

Answer: If the athlete does not practice with other athletes he cannot learn how to be victorious and so be able to compete alone with his opponent. It's the same with the monk: if he is not first trained with brothers and learns to master his thoughts, he cannot live in solitude and do battle with thoughts.

September 3
GREGORY THE GREAT, BISHOP OF ROME (RC, A)[2]

REACHING PORT TOO SOON

A brother came to Abba Theodore of Pherme and began to talk and enumerate things that he had not yet put into practice.

The old man said to him, 'You haven't found a ship yet, nor have you put your cargo aboard, and before setting sail you've already arrived at your port of destination. First, do the work; then you'll come to the things you're talking about now'.

THE DEMON OF PROFIT

It was said about Abba Macarius that he happened to be in the wadi gathering palm branches, and when he had finished collecting them and they had all been gathered so he could tie them together, a demon came upon him in the form of a monk who

---

[2] See also March 12.

seemed to be harsh and angry. He said to him, 'Macarius, do not tie the palm leaves together until you give me my share'.

The old man said to him, 'Come, take what you want'.

The demon said to him, 'Divide them. Give me part and take part for yourself too'.

The old man divided them and made one part larger than the other and said to the demon, 'Take whichever of these two you want'.

The demon said to him, 'No, you did all the work. You go first; take whichever pile you want'.

The old man took the smaller portion and immediately the demon cried out, 'You are powerful, Macarius! I have defeated numbers of people, but you have defeated me!'

The old man said to him, 'Who are you, then?' and the demon said to him, 'I am the demon of profit'.

And when the old man said a prayer, the demon disappeared.

September 4

THOSE WHO TAKE UP THE SWORD

One day, when the brothers were sitting beside him, Abba Moses said, 'Look, the barbarians are coming to Scetis today. Get up and flee!'

They said to him, 'Abba, won't you flee too?'

He said to them, 'As for me, I have been waiting for this day for many years, that the word of the Lord Christ may be fulfilled which says, *All who take up the sword will perish by the sword*'.[3]

[3] Mt 26:52.

They said to him, 'We will not flee either, but we will die with you'.

He said to them, 'That is nothing to do with me; let everyone decide for himself whether he stays or not'.

Now there were seven brothers there and he said to them, 'Look, the barbarians are drawing near to the door'.

The barbarians then came in and slew them. But one monk fled and hid under the cover of a pile of rope and he saw seven crowns descending and crowning the others.

MUD WRESTLING

A certain old man was living in Kellia, and this thought came to him: 'Go and take a wife for yourself', so he got up, made some mud, and fashioned a wife for himself. And the old man said, 'Here's your wife: now you have to work hard to feed her', and he worked, toiling mightily.

The next day he once again got up, made some mud, fashioned a daughter for himself, and said to his thought, 'Look, your wife has given birth: now you have to work even harder to be able to feed and clothe her child'.

So he toiled even harder and wore out his body and said to his thought, 'I can't bear such toil any longer', and he said, 'If, then, you're unable to toil, don't seek a wife'.

When God saw his toil, he took away the thought from him and he was at peace.

WHAT DO YOU WANT WITH THAT GUY?

A woman who had a disease in her breast called 'cancer' by physicians heard about Abba Longinus the Great, that the Lord worked cures through him. She arose in faith and went to him. (*She had told the doctors all her symptoms and none of them had cured her*.)[4] When she went to the seashore, she came upon Saint Abba Longinus gathering wood on the shore of the sea as was his custom. She asked him, 'Where is the servant of God, Abba Longinus?'

He said, 'What do you want with him?'

She told him about her illness. But he said to her, 'What do you want with that guy? He is nothing'. Then he made the sign of the cross where she was ill, saying, 'May my Lord Jesus Christ do with you *according to your faith*'.[5]

The woman believed and turned to go home. When she had gone just a little ways, she was healed of her illness. When she entered the city, she told everyone about the cure that had happened to her through the saint. When they told her it was Abba Longinus who had healed her, the woman gave glory to God.

A FOOL AND A HERETIC

A provincial governor heard one time about Abba Moses and went to Scetis to see him and when some of the brothers told the old man about it he got up and fled into the marsh. The governor ran into him and said, 'Tell us, old man, where is Abba Moses' cell?'

[4] See Mk 5:26.
[5] See Lk 7:50, 8:48.

and he said to them, 'What do you want from him? He's a fool and a heretic'.

The governor went to the church and told the clergy, 'Hearing people talk about Abba Moses, I went to see him. An old man going to Egypt ran into us and we said to him, "Where is Abba Moses' cell?" and he said to us, "What do you want from him? He's a fool and a heretic"'.

When the clergy heard this, they were aggrieved and said to the governor, 'What sort of old man was this who said these things against the saint?' and he said, 'A big black man, wearing old clothes'.

The clergy said, 'That was Abba Moses himself and because he did not want to meet you he said these things against himself'.

September 6

TEACH YOUR HEART

Abba Poemen said, 'Teach your heart to keep what your tongue teaches'.

PRACTICE MAKES PERFECT

Again he said, 'People speak perfectly—and don't put even the least little bit of it into practice'.

MODERATING THE PASSIONS

Abba Nilus said, 'The person who loves contemplative quiet remains invulnerable to the Enemy's arrows, but the person who mixes with crowds of people continuously receives blows. When the irascible part of the soul is at peace it becomes gentle, and when desire has been stilled by contemplative quiet it is inclined to be more lenient, in accordance with reason, and becomes accustomed to being gentle. Simply put, every passion that is not aroused becomes progressively moderated and eventually is stilled altogether, in time having forgotten how to function. Finally, when all that remains is the passion's bare memories of its actions, the part of the soul that is disposed to the passions withdraws altogether'.

September 7

A HYPOTHETICAL CASE

A brother asked an old man to decide a hypothetical case for him. 'Suppose', he said, 'I see someone doing something and I tell someone else about it. I myself', he said, 'do not judge him; we just talk about him. Therefore it isn't slander, even in thought'.

The old man said, 'If you have a movement subject to the passions, it is slander, but if you are free of the passions, it is not slander. But in order not to multiply evils, it is best to keep silent'.

I MYSELF AM A SLOB

So another brother said to the old man, 'If I go to one of the fathers and ask him, "I want to live with such-and-such a person,"

352

and he sees that this is not good for me, what will he say to me in response? If he says to me "Do not go", doesn't he condemn the other person by what he is thinking?'

The old man said, 'Not many people have this sort of subtlety. If the movement is subject to the passions it harms itself and the word does not have power. What, then? Whoever says 'I do not know' frees himself and if he is freed from the passions, he does not condemn anyone but accuses himself, saying, "In truth, I myself am slovenly and perhaps it is not good for me". And if that fellow is wise, he won't go, for the father did not speak in order to cause evil but rather in order that evil not increase'.

September 8
RAPHAEL, ARCHANGEL (CO)
NATIVITY OF THE THEOTOKOS (O)
BIRTH OF THE VIRGIN MARY (RC, A)[6]

DO NOT LOSE YOURSELF

Abba Macarius said, 'If you reprove someone, you yourself get carried away by anger and you are satisfying your own passion. Do not lose yourself, therefore, in order to save another'.

THE DEVIL, WITH A SCYTHE

When Abba Macarius was returning from the marsh to his cell one day carrying some palm leaves, he met the Devil on the road

---

[6] Not on the Episcopal Church calendar.

with a scythe. The latter struck at him as much as he pleased, but in vain, and he said to Abba Macarius, 'What is your power, Macarius, that makes me powerless against you? All that you do, I do, too: you fast, so do I; you keep vigil, and I do not sleep at all. In one thing only do you beat me'.

Abba Macarius asked what that was.

The Devil said, 'Your humility. Because of that I can do nothing against you'.

September 9
POEMEN, HERMIT (CO)
JOACHIM AND ANNA, PARENTS OF THE VIRGIN MARY (O)
PETER CLAVER, PRIEST (RC)

YOUR HEART

Abba Poemen said, 'Do not give your heart to that which does not satisfy your heart'.

IT'S NONE OF MY BUSINESS

A brother asked Abba Poemen, 'An inheritance has been left me; what should I do?'

The old man said to him, 'Go, come back in three days and I will tell you'.

So the brother returned as it had been decided. Then the old man said, 'What shall I say to you, brother? If I tell you to give it to the church, they will make banquets with it; if I tell you to give it to your relations, you will not receive any profit from it; if I tell you to give it to the poor, you will not do it. Do as you like, it's none of my business'.

September 10
BLESSED OGIER OF LOCEDIO (M)

BACKBITING

Question: With what kind of thought can a person put an end to backbiting?

Answer: Just as the person who allows fire to be placed on his chest is injured, so also the person who agrees to meet with people will never entirely get away from backbiting.

JUSTIFIABLE ANGER

A brother questioned Abba Poemen, saying, 'What does it mean to be angry with your brother without cause?'

He said, 'If your brother hurts you by his arrogance and you are angry with him because of it, that is getting angry without cause. If he plucks out your right eye and cuts off your right hand, and you get angry with him, you are angry without cause. But if he separates you from God, then be angry with him'.

MY FATHER IS IMMORTAL!

A monk said, 'One of the monks was informed of his father's death. He told the person who had informed him, "Stop blaspheming! My father is immortal!"'

RICH MAN, POOR MAN

Abba Macarius the Great, passing through a village one time with some brothers, heard a young boy say to his mother, 'My mother, a rich man loves me and cherishes me, but I detest him. A poor man detests me, but I cherish him'.

When Saint Abba Macarius heard these words, he was utterly astonished. The brothers said to him, 'What is it about these words, my father, that astonishes you so completely like this?'

The old man struck his chest and said, 'What a great mystery there is in these words!'

They begged him, 'Tell us!'

He said to them, 'Truly, my children, the Lord is the rich man: he loves us, but we do not want to obey him. Our enemy, the Devil, is the poor man: he detests us, but we love his filthy acts and abominable practices and vain desires and the rest of his pleasures'.

A PREGNANT WIFE, POTS SMEARED WITH SOOT

[*A young woman becomes pregnant with a young man in her village. When they find out, they decide to blame Abba Macarius. Egged on by her parents, a mob finds Macarius.*]

The crowd brought Abba Macarius out and beat him badly enough to kill him. Finally they bound to his back some pots smeared with soot and dragged him through the middle of the village, with a crowd of children walking with him, beating him and pulling him this way and that like they do to those who are crazy, all of them crying, 'He stuck the girl!'

After Abba Macarius was badly humiliated with blows and mocking words, some of the faithful came from a distance and, when they saw him near death, asked him what had happened. And when they understood they said, 'What you people are saying is not true. We know from our previous experience with him that this man is faithful and righteous'. And they stood around him and loosened the bonds and also broke the pots smeared with soot that had been placed around his neck. And the young man's father said, 'Impossible! You can't do that until he guarantees that when the young girl gives birth he will pay the cost of her delivery and provide for the raising of her child'. Then the man who served him said to him, 'Please, make me the surety'. And he became surety for Abba Macarius and so they released him. He returned to his cell half dead.

When he entered his cell, he said to himself, 'Macarius, look! You have found yourself a wife. Now the situation requires you to work night and day so you can provide for yourself and for her and her child'. And so he diligently got to work and he gave the baskets that he made to his servant in order to sell them and give the money he made to the woman so that when she gave birth she could use it for herself and her child. When the time came for that wretched young girl to give birth, the labor pains were severe and difficult. She was in danger of dying for four days and four nights and was not able to give birth. She said, 'Truly I deserve to die; not only have I sinned but I have also falsely accused God's servant the anchorite. That holy man did not touch me at all; no, it was such and such young man who got me pregnant'.

When that wretched girl gave birth after confessing the truth, the servant of Saint Abba Macarius ran to him with great rejoicing and pride and said to him, 'That young girl who falsely accused you was not able to give birth until she confessed!' Everyone who heard what had happened wanted to come see Abba Macarius— all of them—glorifying him and greatly praising him. But Abba Macarius, fearful that the people would disturb him, got up and fled to Scetis.

September 13
FOUNDING OF THE CHURCH OF THE HOLY SEPULCHRE (O)
CYPRIAN, BISHOP AND MARTYR OF CARTHAGE (A)[7]
JOHN CHRYSOSTOM, BISHOP AND DOCTOR (RC, A)

BEHIND THEIR BACKS

Abba Poemen said, 'People's wickedness is hidden behind their backs'.

[7] Episcopal Church calendar. See also September 15.

OTHERS

Do not look toward others.
Also, do not let others look toward you.
Allow yourself only one out of a thousand as an advisor
and you will be at peace all the days of your life.

A FEW DRIED FIGS

The old men used to tell how one day someone handed round a few dried figs in Scetis. Because they were not worth anything, no one took any to Abba Arsenius in order not to offend him.

Learning of it, the old man did not come to the synaxis, saying, 'You have cast me out by not giving me a share of the blessing that God had given the brothers and which I was not worthy to receive'.

Everyone heard of this and was edified at the old man's humility. Then the priest went to take him the small dried figs and brought him to the synaxis with joy.

September 14
EXALTATION OF THE HOLY CROSS (O)
JOHN CHRYSOSTOM, ARCHBISHOP (O)
TRIUMPH OF THE HOLY CROSS (RC)
HOLY CROSS DAY (A)

FIRE AND WATER

Abba Evagrius asked Abba Macarius while he was sitting beside him with some other brothers, 'How does Satan find all these evil thoughts to throw at the brothers?'

Abba Macarius said to him, 'Whoever kindles a fire in an oven holds a lot of kindling in his hands and does not hesitate to throw it into the fire. So too the Devil: he kindles fires and does not hesitate to throw into everyone's heart all kinds of evil kindling, that is, defilements. We see moreover that water extinguishes and is victorious over the power of the fire. So it is with the help of the Protector, our Lord Jesus Christ, and the invincible power of the cross: if we throw our weaknesses at his feet, all of Satan's evil branches are extinguished in us and our Lord Jesus Christ causes our hearts to burn and boil in the Spirit with celestial fire and be filled with rejoicing'.

ASCENDING THE CROSS

Again Abba Isaiah said: If our Lord Jesus Christ had not first healed all the passions of humanity for which he came into the world, he would not have ascended the cross, for before the Lord came in flesh, humanity was blind, dumb, paralyzed, deaf, leprous, lame, and dead on account of everything that was contrary to nature. When, however, God had mercy on us and came into the world, he raised the dead, made the lame walk, the blind see, the dumb speak, the deaf hear, and resurrected a new person, free of all illness. Then he ascended the cross. They hung two thieves beside

360

him; the one on the right glorified him and appealed to him, saying, *"Remember me, Lord, in your kingdom"*, *but the one on the left blasphemed him.*[8] This means that before the intellect comes to its senses from carelessness, it is with the Enemy, and if our Lord Jesus Christ resurrects it from its carelessness, granting it to see and discern all things, it will be able to ascend the cross.

September 15
OUR LADY OF SORROWS (RC)
CYPRIAN, BISHOP OF CARTHAGE (A)[9]

EVEN THOSE WITH SWORDS IN THEIR HANDS

A brother said to Abba Poemen, 'I see that wherever I go I find support'.

The old man said to him, 'Even those who hold a sword in their hands have God who takes pity on them in the present time. If we are courageous, he will have mercy on us'.

PLEASE GIVE THEM MY WALKING STICK

Abba Euprepius helped some thieves when they were stealing from him. When they had taken away what was inside his cell, Abba Euprepius saw that they had left his stick and he was sorry. So he

[8] Lk 22:42.
[9] English Church calendar.

361

took it and ran after them to give it to them. But the thieves did not want to take it, fearing that something would happen to them if they did. So he asked someone he met who was going the same way to give the stick to them.

September 16
CYPRIAN, BISHOP AND MARTYR (RC)
CORNELIUS, POPE AND MARTYR (RC)
NINIAN, MONK, BISHOP, APOSTLE TO THE SCOTS (A)

DON'T LET THE DEVIL SNEAK UP ON YOU

You will know God in your cell. Keep him with you and the Devil will depart from you, which will allow you to tame him.

Therefore, my beloved, do not allow the Devil behind you in the contest lest he mock you and give you trouble.

NOCTURNAL TEMPTATIONS

Question: What shall a person do with regard to the temptation that comes upon him to deride the flesh during sleep?

Answer: If someone finds his adversary asleep and strikes him, the one who does the striking cannot deride the one whom he has struck as though he had defeated him (for there is no victory for him but rather condemnation). In the same way, temptation that comes while we're asleep is ineffectual.

YOU CAN'T BUILD A SHIP WITHOUT NAILS

Amma Syncletica said, 'Just as one cannot build a ship unless one has some nails, so it is impossible to be saved without humility'.

THE SOUL IS LIKE A SHIP

Amma Syncletica said, 'We must arm ourselves in every way against the demons. For they attack us from outside and they also stir us up from within. The soul is, then, like a ship when great waves break over it and at the same time it sinks because the hold is too full. We are just like that: we lose as much by the exterior faults we commit as by the thoughts inside us. So we must watch for people's attacks that come from outside us, and also repel the interior onslaughts of our thoughts'.

WAR IS WAGED ON THE FIELD OF THOUGHT

The demons strive against persons of the world chiefly through their deeds, but in the case of monks for the most part by means of thoughts, since the desert deprives them of such affairs. Just as it is easier to sin by thought than by deed, so also is the war fought on the field of thought more severe than that which is conducted in the area of things and events. For the mind is easily moved indeed, and hard to control in the presence of sinful fantasies.

September 18

SOMETHING AS SMALL AS A CUP OF WATER

Now on another occasion a man from the city of Aswan came
to Abba Aaron one day. He continuously wept before him and
said, 'There is a certain rich man in my city to whom I owe ten
obeli, and I can't get the money to pay him. I have begged him,
"Be patient with me and I will repay you". But he would not
agree to this and has seized me for what I owe him. He wants
to take my vineyard from me which I inherited from my parents and from which I make a small profit, enough for my poor
children and me to live on. I *am* paying him the interest I owe
him. I beg you, your Holiness, to send a message to him to ease
up on me, for someone from his household told me, "He's going
to press you for the principal and haul you into court so he can
take away your vineyard". But I believe that if you were to send
a message he would not refuse to listen to you'. As he said these
things, he wept.

Now evening had come and the man rose to go on home,
but Abba Aaron saw his distress and said to him, 'Stay here until
morning, for it's late now', and he stayed in the outer court. Now
the holy man Abba Aaron rose and went to the upper room. He
spent the whole night petitioning God and praying on behalf of
that man. When morning came, the man tried to return home
but the holy man Abba Aaron said to him, 'Stay here a little longer
and you will go home with your mind at ease'.

While these words were still in his mouth, the rich man came
riding on a donkey which was being led, and two other men
were following him in order to guide him to the righteous one.
His eyes were open but he could not see. He threw himself down
at my father's feet and worshiped him. Abba Aaron took hold of
him and raised him to his feet. Then the holy one said to him,
'Have you not heard the Law which says, *You shall not covet any
of your neighbor's possessions: not his house or his field or his livestock*

or his vineyard or his olive trees?[10] It says also *Woe to those who join house to house and field to field and take away their neighbors' possessions.*[11] Again the Saviour cried out, "*Blessed are the merciful, for to them shall mercy be shown*".[12] Then again, "*Mercy shall make a person triumph over judgement*"[13]

September 19
JANUARIUS, BISHOP, MARTYR (RC)
THEODORE OF TARSUS, ARCHBISHOP OF CANTERBURY (A)

AS SMALL AS A CUP OF WATER

Now when the holy man Abba Aaron had said these words to the rich man, the latter answered, saying, 'Have mercy on me, righteous and honorable one! Please ask Christ on my behalf that this darkness over my eyes cease, and I will never disobey you in anything'. The holy one said to him, 'Do you believe that I am able to do this?' The rich man answered, 'Oh yes, I do, my holy father! What is more, listen to me and I will relate to your Charity what happened to me. Now it happened that when the man about whom you have spoken with me had left yesterday, I went up to my house and went to bed. I woke up at night and sensed this great darkness over my eyes. And when morning came I said to my household, "I cannot see today". Now they said to me,

---

[10] Ex 20:17; Dt. 5:21.
[11] Is 5:8; Micah 2:2.
[12] Mt 5:7, 6:14.
[13] Jm 2:13. Continues on September 19.

365

"Clearly this has happened to you through the holy man Abba Aaron. We saw the man with whom you were talking yesterday about money go to him". As soon as I heard that he had gone to your Holiness, I knew that this had happened to me because of him. I myself have come to you because this I believe: that you have the power to heal me'.

The holy man said to him, 'If you show mercy to the poor man, Christ himself will heal you'. The rich man called one of those who had come with him, and he took the loan agreement from him and gave it to the righteous man Abba Aaron. The holy man Abba Aaron said to him, 'If you give wages to the poor man in this world, God will give you your wages in the world to come'. Then he made the sign of the cross over the rich man's eyes. Abba Aaron said to him, 'Wash your face in faith'. Now as soon as he had washed his face, he was able to see. Those who had accompanied him were amazed and glorified God.

The rich man rose and prostrated himself before the holy man Abba Aaron, giving thanks both to God and to Abba Aaron because he could see. The holy one gave the loan agreement to the poor man and commanded him, saying, 'You too are to be merciful to your neighbor, as mercy has been shown to you. Do not ever say, "I am a poor man, I'm not able to keep the commandment in the Gospel". The Gospel will never accept any excuse from you that you make, poor man. But *even for something as small as a cup of cold water, God will reward you!*[14] *Do not be like that worthless servant whose lord forgave a debt of many talents. He went and squeezed his fellow-servant for the little bit he owed him.*[15] *No, be like the wise servant who doubled his talent'.*[16]

The poor man answered, 'Pray for me, my holy father, and I will keep everything which you require of me'. And in this way both men profited, and they left Abba Aaron, glorifying God.

[14] Mk 9:41.
[15] Mt 18:28.
[16] Mt 25:14-23.

WEAKNESS IS FERTILE

Do not cling to weakness, for weakness begets weakness.

THE NATURE OF VIRTUE

Abba Antony said, 'Having begun, therefore, and having already set out on the path to virtue, *let us press ahead even harder to reach our goal.*[17] And let no one turn back, *like Lot's wife,*[18] because the Lord has pointedly said, *"No one who puts his hand to the plough and turns back is fit for the kingdom of heaven".*[19] Now "turning back" is nothing but feeling regret and thinking once more about worldly things. Do not be afraid to hear about virtue and do not be surprised at the term. *For virtue is not far from us,*[20] nor does it stand outside us; it works within us, and the task is easy if only we want it to be. *The Greeks leave home and cross the sea*[21] in order to be educated, but we have no need to leave home for the kingdom of heaven or to cross the sea for virtue. The Lord has already said, *"The kingdom of God is within you".*[22]

'All virtue needs, then, is for us to will it, because it is within us and has its origins from us. Virtue comes into being because the soul naturally possesses the rational faculty of understanding. Virtue maintains its nature when it remains as it came into being, and it came into being good and perfectly upright. Therefore, Joshua the

---

[17] See Phil 3:13.
[18] See Gen 19:26.
[19] Lk 9:62, 7:32.
[20] See Dt 30:11.
[21] See Dt 30:13.
[22] Lk 17:21.

son of Nun commanded the people, saying, *"Incline your hearts to the Lord God of Israel"*,[23] and John said, *"Make your paths straight"*.[24] The soul is "straight" when its rational faculty of understanding is as it was created according to nature. On the other hand, when it bends and becomes twisted contrary to its nature, then we speak of the soul's evil. Therefore, the task is not difficult: if we remain as we came into being, then virtue is with us, but if we think about bad things, we are judged as evil. If this matter could be inferred from something external to us, something that had to be acquired from outside ourselves, it would be truly difficult; but since it lies within us, let us protect ourselves from filthy thoughts. And since we have received the soul as a trust, *let us protect it for the Lord*[25] that he may acknowledge his work—that is, the soul—as being the same as when he created it.

September 21
MATTHEW, APOSTLE AND EVANGELIST (RC, A)

HOW TO LOVE GOD

Question: How can a person receive the gift of loving God?

Answer: When someone sees his brother in difficulty and cries out to God to help him, then he receives knowledge of how one ought to love God.

[23] Jos 24:23.
[24] Mt 3:3; see Is 40:3.
[25] See 2 Tm 1:14.

PERISHING BY THE SWORD

Abba Paphnutius said, 'When I was walking along the road one time, on account of the fog I wandered off the road and found myself near a village and I saw some people talking shamefully. I turned around, threw myself down, and condemned myself before God. Suddenly an angel came, holding a sword, and he said to me, "Paphnutius, everyone who judges their brothers perishes by this sword, but you have done well because you have not condemned but have instead humbled yourself before God as though it were you who had sinned. Therefore *your name is inscribed in the book of life*"'.[26]

September 22

A HUNDRED YEARS OF SOLITUDE

Abba Poemen said that Abba Ammonas said, 'A person may remain for a hundred years in his cell without learning how to live in the cell'.

THREE FINE BOOKS

Abba Theodore of Pherme possessed three fine books, and he went to see Abba Macarius and said to him, 'I have three fine books from which I benefit, and the brothers also make use of them and benefit from them. Tell me, therefore, what I should do'.

[26] See Phil 4:3.

The old man answered and said, 'Your actions are good, but poverty is better than everything'.

When he heard this, he went and sold the books and gave the money they brought him to those who could use it.

COMPREHENSION

Abba Amoun of Raïthou asked Abba Sisoës, 'When I read Scripture, my thoughts want to nurse each word so I will have something to say if asked a question'.

The old man said to him, 'There is no need to do that; it is better to get control of yourself through purity of spirit and then comprehend what you are reading and talk about it'.

RIPPING OPEN THE DEVIL'S BELLY

Our holy father Abba John became more and more humble, like wheat: when it matures and it is time for the harvest, it places itself below the whole creation. However, when it was revealed to him that someone had fallen into sin or another person was troubled by passions, as a good and compassionate father, especially with good and benevolent discernment, he taught and instructed them. He wisely worked with each of them, protecting them with counsel appropriate to them so that they would be saved: he eagerly helped one lift the light yoke of repentance and with his richness healed him and reconciled him peacefully with God in purity and watchfulness hereafter. This other one Abba John would likewise teach to do battle according to the law in order to destroy the darkness and all its powers through self-control and perseverance in God. Our all-holy father, acting this way like a skillful doctor of souls, ripped open the belly of the Devil and his evil demons so that as a result Satan gnashed his teeth and cried out in the air, saying, 'Jesus, you and your companions disturb me!'

September 24
ALL SAINTS OF ALASKA (RO)

EARS FILLED WITH ARGUMENT

It was said of Abba John that when he went to church at Scetis, he heard some brothers arguing, so he returned to his cell. He went around it three times and then went in.

Some brothers who had seen him wondered why he had done this, and they went to ask him. He said to them, 'My ears were full of that argument, so I circled around in order to purify them, and thus I entered my cell with my mind at rest'.

STANDING NAKED IN THE ARENA

An old man said, 'Just as an opponent in a boxing match fights with his fists, so should the opponent—that is, the monk—repulse thoughts, stretching out his hands to heaven and calling on God for help. The opponent stands naked in the stadium, contending, naked and unhindered, anointing himself with oil and being instructed by his trainer how he ought to fight. Then the other opponent comes from the opposite corner; he sprinkles sand— that is, earth—over himself in order to more easily get hold of his opponent. Contemplate this mystically for yourself, monk. The trainer is God, who brings us victory. We are the wrestlers; our rival is the Adversary. The sand is the things of this world. Observe the Enemy's skill. Stand unhindered, therefore, and you will win, for when the spirit is weighed down by material things it does not receive the immaterial and holy word'.

September 25
SERGEI OF RADONEZH, MONASTIC REFORMER (RO, A)

THE KEY TO YOUR HOUSE

Abba Macarius said, 'The person who will fill himself with bread and water has given the key to his house to thieves'.

LANDSCAPE GARDENING

If your spirit still looks around at the time of prayer, then it does not yet pray as a monk. You are no better than a person of affairs engaged in a kind of landscape gardening.

DIFFICULTIES

Saint Gregory said, 'If you do not hope for difficulties as you propose to advance in philosophy, such a beginning is not philosophical and you bring reproach on those who form you. If someone expects difficulties without actually encountering them, that is given by grace; and if someone does encounter them, either he suffers them patiently or you know that he gives the lie to the profession he has made'.

September 26
REPOSE OF JOHN THE THEOLOGIAN (O)
COSMAS AND DAMIAN, MARTYRS (RC)
LANCELOT ANDREWES, BISHOP OF WINCHESTER (A)[27]

BREAKFAST

One of the old men paid a visit to another old man and the latter said to his disciple, 'Make us a small dish of lentils'. So he made the lentils and moistened some bread. And they continued talking about spiritual matters until noon the next day.

Once again the old man said to his disciple, 'Make us a small dish of lentils, child', and the disciple said to him, 'I made it yesterday'. So they stood up and tasted the food.

---

[27] American Church calendar. September 25 on other Anglican calendars.

ANOTHER KIND OF BREAKFAST

Another old man paid a visit to one of the old men. The latter boiled some lentils and said to him, 'Let's pray a short office'. So the one completed the entire Psalter while the other recited the two great prophets by heart. When morning came, the old man who had made the visit left and forgot about the food.

September 27
EXALTATION OF THE HOLY CROSS (CO)
VINCENT DE PAUL, PRIEST (RC, A)

THIS DOWNPOUR IS ENOUGH!

They also told this concerning the righteous Abba Macarius the Alexandrian: One time the sky would not rain on the earth and multitudes of worms and pests appeared in the people's fields. Abba Timothy, archbishop of Alexandria, sent some envoys to Abba Macarius to beseech him: 'Come to Alexandria. Entreat God to cause it to rain and kill the worms and pests'.

When they persuaded him with great entreaties, he went with them to Alexandria. When he drew near the city, *a great crowd came out to meet him with palm branches.*[28] When he reached the Tetrapylōn, which is in the middle of the city, he prayed to God with all his heart. When he came to the Gate of the Sun, the sky began to pour forth drops. When he entered the church, it rained heavily for two days and two nights without interruption; as a

[28] Jn 12:13.

result, the people thought that the earth would be inundated and overwhelmed by the large amount of rain in the air.

The old man said to the archbishop, 'For what purpose have you sent for me? Why have you caused me to forsake my cell and come here?'

The crowds answered him, 'We brought you here to have you pray for it to rain—and now look, you have taken pity on us! This downpour is enough! Pray, therefore, for the rain to depart from us, lest it destroy all of us and we all die, we and our children and our livestock and everything that we own!'

The holy old man Abba Macarius prayed, and immediately the rain slackened; at the same time, the sky cleared through the grace of God and the prayers of Saint Abba Macarius. Then the non-Christians of Alexandria cried out, saying, 'A magician enters the Gate of the Sun and the judge did not know about it!'

Abba Macarius spent three days there. He healed a multitude of people with illnesses there, some of them paralytics, and a multitude of other kinds of illnesses in the three days that he spent in Alexandria when he came there from the desert.

September 28
CHARITON, MONK, CONFESSOR (O)
WENCESLAU, MARTYR (RC)

NO ANCHORITES HERE

A governor once came to see Abba Simon. When Abba Simon heard about it, he got his belt and climbed a palm tree to prune it. The visitors called out, 'Old man, where is the anchorite?' He said to them, 'There isn't any anchorite here'. When he said this, they left.

FIRST IMPRESSIONS

Another time another governor came to see him and the clergy came on ahead and said, 'Abba, get yourself ready. The governor has heard about you and is coming to be blessed by you'.

He said, 'Yes, I will get myself ready'. So he put on his old patched-up habit, took some bread and cheese in his hands, went outside, and sat in the gateway eating. When the governor arrived with his body of troops and saw him, they thought nothing of him, saying, 'Is this the anchorite about whom we heard so much?' And they turned around and left in a hurry.

September 29
CYRIACUS, HERMIT OF PALESTINE (O)
MICHAEL, GABRIEL, AND RAPHAEL, ARCHANGELS (RC)
MICHAEL AND ALL ANGELS (A)

WILES AND MAD LIES

Do not welcome vainglory, for you will not be able to bear its wiles and mad lies as it plants lying thoughts within you.

If you give your heart to it in lying dreams, it makes progress, persisting in vain thoughts; as a result, it leads some astray among those who welcome the spirit that loves the saying written thus: 'When the liar speaks, he speaks according to his own nature, for *he is a liar and also its father*.[29]

[29] See Jn 8:44.

GREAT PEACE OF SOUL

While Abba Macarius was in Egypt, he discovered a man who owned a beast of burden engaged in plundering Macarius' goods. So he came up to the thief as if he had been a stranger and he helped him to load the animal. He saw him off in great peace of soul, saying, *'We have brought nothing into this world and we cannot take anything out of the world.*[30] *The Lord gave and the Lord has taken away; blessed be the name of the Lord'.*[31]

September 30
JEROME, PRIEST, MONK OF BETHLEHEM,
DOCTOR OF THE CHURCH (RC,A)
GREGORY THE ILLUMINATOR (GO)

THERE ARE MANY NEEDY IN THE VILLAGES OF EGYPT

The Father of Envy and Misanthropic Enemy, seeing Abba Bishoy safely avoiding his ambushes, invincible against his wiles and victorious against his plots, gnashed his teeth in anger. Unable to approach him because of the divine power Bishoy had received from God, he treacherously contrived to overcome him by other means. He thought Bishoy could be easily defeated through greed for material possessions and hastened to put forward the pretext of almsgiving so that if by this means Bishoy lapsed from his life of poverty, a way might be found to commit terrible deeds against him.

[30] 1 Tim 6:7.
[31] Job 1:21.

On account of this, the chameleon-like Enemy approached one of the rulers of Egypt, a proud and rich man, and in the form of an angel the Treacherous One appeared and said to him, 'You, depart; go to the desert, and you will find a poor man by the name of Bishoy. Although poor, his way of life is rich; he is resplendently adorned with the virtues, and is a chosen vessel of God's grace. When you find him, kindly lavish all your money and praise on him'.

That ruler, not suspecting the demonic scheme but instead believing that the power appearing to him was angelic, took cargo consisting of all kinds of goods and went to see the holy man. The divine power surrounding Bishoy revealed the plan, however, telling him in detail how the Enemy was using the ruler's gifts to plot against him. The divine man immediately arose and went to meet the ruler. When he met him, he was asked by him, 'Who might this Bishoy be, and where does he live?'

Bishoy responded, 'And why are you looking for him?'

The ruler said, 'I have brought goods, and gold. I want to give them to him to distribute to the monks'.

Bishoy said, 'Forgive me, my Christ-loving friend. If we want to live in this desert, gold or silver is of no use to us. Come now, no one living here will accept anything from you. So go, and do not be sad: God has accepted your gift, if you distribute what you have brought to the poor and needy, for there are many needy in the villages of Egypt, both orphans and widows. If you provide for them in God's name, you will have your reward'.

Persuaded by the words of the holy man, the ruler returned home.

OCTOBER

PENTECOST / ORDINARY TIME

October 1
CYPRIAN, BISHOP OF CARTHAGE (CO)
PROTECTION OF THE MOST HOLY THEOTOKOS (O)
THÉRÈSE OF THE CHILD JESUS, DOCTOR OF THE CHURCH (RC)
REMIGIUS, BISHOP OF RHEIMS (A)

THE LIVING AND THE DEAD

Do not give rest to your thoughts until rest comes to you without rest. Let them be dead while you live with God.

THE MAT IN THE OVEN

It was said of Abba Macarius the Great that he was in a monastery one time. If the brothers handed in a mat each day, he would himself hand in three every day. When the brothers saw this, they said to the abbot, 'Unless this foreign brother hands in one mat every day, we will not allow him to live with us'.

When the abbot went to Abba Macarius' cell, wishing to speak with him, he stopped outside the cell. He heard that with every slap of his foot that he made he stood up and prayed and offered three acts of repentance. The abbot immediately returned and said, 'Bring me one of Abba Macarius' mats'.

When they brought it, he took it and threw it into the bakery oven and after a long time, when they were stoking the oven, he ordered the fire to be put out. He saw that the mat had not burned at all and was lying in the fire, and the abbot said to the brothers, 'Manual work without ascetic practice is nothing'.

KINDS OF GIVING

Abba Isaiah said, 'If you give someone something that he desires and let him keep it, you have imitated the nature of Jesus. If, on the other hand, you ask for it back, you have imitated the nature of Adam. If you accept interest, however, you have contravened even Adam's nature'.

WAX MELTING BEFORE A FIRE

Saint Syncletica said, 'Just as treasure that is brought to light is soon dispersed, a virtue that is made known and publicized is obliterated. Just as wax melts before a fire, so too is the soul dissipated by praise and loses its strength'.

BEARING HEAVENLY FRUIT

Again she said, 'Just as it is not possible to be a plant and a seed at one and the same time, so it is impossible for us to be surrounded by worldly honor and bear heavenly fruit'.

BOTH INSIDE AND OUTSIDE THE CELL

One day Abba Daniel and Abba Ammoës went on a journey together. Abba Ammoës said, 'When shall we, too, settle down, in a cell, Father?'

Abba Daniel replied, '*Who shall separate us henceforth from God?*[2] God is in the cell, and, on the other hand, he is outside also'.

THE FIRE AND THE PHANTASM

Abba Macarius of Alexandria also told us this other story: Every ascetic practice that I had undertaken I had successfully completed, but the desire also entered my heart to do this: I wanted to spend five days with my heart focused on God at all times without paying any attention at all to the ways of this age. Having made this promise in my heart, I entered my cell in the interior desert so no one could find me, and I stood on the mat in my cell. I fought with my thought, speaking thus: 'Watch yourself. Do not come down from heaven: there you have the patriarchs and prophets and apostles; there you have the angels and archangels and the powers on high and the cherubim and seraphim. Cleave to God: the Father and the only-begotten Son and the Holy Spirit, the consubstantial Trinity. Climb high upon the cross of the Son who is in heaven. Do not come down from that mighty place'.

And when I had finished two days, he said, and two nights, the demons became so demented that they changed themselves into a

---

[1] October 9 on the western calendar.
[2] See Rom 8:35.

crowd of phantasms. Sometimes they took on the appearance of lions scratching my feet with their claws; sometimes serpents entwining themselves around my feet. Finally, they took on the appearance of fiery flames in order to burn up everything inside the cell; they burned up everything except for the soles of my feet so that I thought I too was going to be burned up. Finally, the fire and the phantasms fled. On the fifth day I was unable to master my thought without distraction but I returned to worldly worries and human ways of seeing. I understood that if I was going to succeed in completing this commandment, I would destroy my understanding and become insanely arrogant. For this reason I was at peace allowing the cares of this world into my heart so I would not fall into arrogance.

October 4
FRANCIS OF ASSISI, FRIAR, DEACON (RC, A)

REMAIN WHERE YOU ARE

My son, obey God and keep his commandments, and be wise and remain in your dwelling, which is your delight, and your cell will remain with you in your heart as you seek its blessing, and the labor of your cell will go with you to God.

TAKE THIS WINE TO OUR BROTHER

When Abba Poemen went one time into Egypt to live, he happened to have as his neighbor a brother who had a wife. The old man knew about it and never reproached him. One night the woman happened to give birth and when the old man learned about it he summoned his youngest brother and said, 'Take with you a flask of wine and give it to our neighbor; he has need of it today'. (The brothers did not know why he was doing this.)

The brother did as the old man had ordered him and the married brother benefitted from this action and was moved to compunction. A few days later he left his wife, having provided her with whatever she might need, and went and spoke to the old man, 'From today on I am a penitent, father'. And he went and lived by himself in a cell near the old man and went to see him very frequently and the old man illuminated for him the way to God and gained him for the Lord.

October 5

WAVES AND ROCK

Question: Can a person sin because of an idea?

Answer: Waves will never injure rock; in the same way an unsuccessful assault will never harm a person, for it is written that any sin not brought to completion is not a sin.

VAGRANTS AND TRUE VAGRANCY

It was said about Abba Agathon that he spent quite a long time building a cell with his disciples and, when they finished it, they came to live there from that time on. During the first week he saw something that displeased him and said to his disciples, 'Get up, let's leave this place'.

But his disciples were very upset and said, 'If you had already decided to move, why did we go to all the trouble of building the cell? People are going to be scandalized and will say, "Look, they've moved again, those vagrants!"

When he saw how weak-spirited they were, he said to them, 'If some are indeed scandalized, others, on the contrary, will be edified and will say, "Blessed are people like these! They have moved on account of God and have despised everything". But whoever wants to leave may go; as for me, I am going'.

So they threw themselves to the ground, begging him until he allowed them to travel with him.

October 6
APOSTLE THOMAS (O)
INNOCENT OF ALASKA, BISHOP (RO)
BRUNO THE CARTHUSIAN (RC)
WILLIAM TYNDALE, PRIEST (A)

ROCK AND WHEAT

A brother asked Abba Macarius, 'Tell me what it is to live in obedience, my father'.

Abba Macarius said to him, 'It is like rock: if you use the rock to crush the wheat and extract all the filth from it, the wheat becomes pure bread. It is the same with you, my child: the rock is your father; you are the wheat. If you obey your father, he will intercede with the Lord on your behalf. He will extract all the filth of Satan from you and, instead of pure bread, you too will be a godly son'.

THE SWEET NAME

A brother fell on account of a transgression and went to Abba Macarius in tears, saying, 'Pray for me, my father, because *I have fallen into the sickness of Sodom*;[3] I have stumbled doing that which you already know about'.

Abba Macarius said to him, 'Have courage, my child. Take hold of that which is outside of time, that which is without beginning, that which will endure forever, which has no end, the help of those who have no hope except in him alone, the sweet name on every person's lips, the sole sweetness, the perfect life, who possesses numerous treasuries of compassion, our Lord Jesus Christ, our true God. May he be your consolation and helper and the one who forgives you. My child, I say to you, if a virgin falls on account of a transgression and preserves herself as she was originally created, I say to you that if she is joyful on account of the shame on her face and the scorn heaped on her, Christ rejoices over her as though over a virgin. It is the same with you, my child, since you have revealed your shame, as Holy Scripture says, *Confess your sins to one another so that entreaty may be made for you and you may be forgiven and be saved*,[4] for Peter said to the Lord, "*How many times shall I forgive my brother? Up to seven times?*" The good God said to him, "*I do not say to you seven times but seven times seventy times*".[5]

[3] See Gen 19:1-24.
[4] Jm 5:16.
[5] Mt 18:21.

THE CAMEL WITH A BROKEN LEG

Now it happened that when the bishop was sitting in his dwelling reading the holy gospels, certain Nubians came with their camels. One of the strong camels had knocked down a weak one and broken its leg. When the Nubians saw what had happened, they began to fight among themselves. The owner of the camel whose leg had been broken said to the owner of the other one, 'I'm going to take your camel to replace my own', and a great argument arose between the two of them. When Mark the priest saw them fighting with each other, he went and told the bishop. He decided not to go down to them, but when he came to the place in the lectionary where it is written, *Blessed are the peacemakers, for they shall be called children of God*,[6] immediately he tied up the book and went down to them.

Now when the Nubians saw him, the one who had suffered the loss ran to him and said, 'Come and sit down, my father, and hear our case'. So the bishop sat down. The Nubian said to him, 'I tied up my camel, but my friend, he didn't tie his. His camel came and knocked mine to the ground and broke its leg'. When this one had finished speaking, the other one said, 'It's true, I did tie up my camel, but he broke loose, and I didn't know it'.

The bishop had been sitting quietly until they finished all they had to say. Then the holy bishop said to them, 'Was there any other argument between you before today, or is this matter of the camel all there is?' One of them said, 'I will tell you the truth, my holy father. See, we've traveled together for thirty years and we haven't fought with each other even a single day'. The holy bishop said, 'Bring me the camel whose leg is broken', and they brought it to him. It was true, the leg bone was broken and was being held

[6] Mt 5:9.

together only by the hide, and the camel was walking with great difficulty, dragging its leg. When the holy bishop saw the animal, he said to Isaiah the deacon, 'Go and bring me a little water in a dish', and he went and got it for him. He said, 'Sprinkle some on its leg, saying, "In the name of the Father and of the Son and of the Holy Spirit"'. And Isaiah made the sign of the cross over the camel as the bishop had told him, and its leg was healed as though it had never been broken at all.

When the Nubians saw what had happened, they were amazed, for they did not know God. Certain men, inhabitants of Philae, were passing by. When they saw what had happened, they glorified God and went to their town and spread the fame of the holy bishop concerning what they had seen.

October 8
PELAGIA THE PENITENT (O)

EMBRACE GOD

Now then, my beloved, whom God has taken to himself, embrace him in patient endurance. Do not lose heart. Do not neglect God's grace until with joy and certainty you ascend to God.

THE TWO KINDS OF ARROGANCE

Abba John of Lycopolis said, 'The vice of arrogance is a serious one and most dangerous and overthrows even souls at the height of perfection; therefore I want you above all to beware of this. There is a species of this evil which is two-fold. It happens to some that in the first stages of their conversion, when either they have performed some small act of abstinence, or spent some money piously on the poor, then, just when they ought to take care to reject any such feeling, they behave as if they were superior to those on whom they have bestowed something. There is, however, another kind of arrogance, when anyone who is approaching the highest virtue does not ascribe it wholly to God but to his own labors and zeal, and both seeks glory from others and loses it from God. Therefore, my little children, let us flee the vice of arrogance in any form, lest we fall into the trap the Devil has put in our way'.

October 9
ANDRONICUS AND ATHANASIA (GO)
JAMES, SON OF ALPHAEUS, APOSTLE (O)
TIKHON, METROPOLITAN OF MOSCOW (RO)
DENYS AND COMPANIONS, MARTYRS (RC, A)
ROBERT GROSSETESTE, BISHOP OF LINCOLN (A)

WARRING MONASTERIES

[*In the* Life of Daniel of Scetis, *Andronicus and Athanasia are a wealthy Christian couple in Antioch. After their two young children die, they leave everything and go to the deserts of Egypt, where they live separately as monks. They meet one day, but Andronicus does not recognize Athanasia, now named Athanasius, and they travel and live together as monastic brethren. Athanasia/Athanasius soon dies.*]

With olive branches and palm branches, they carried out the precious corpse of Athanasia, giving glory to God, who had provided the woman with such great endurance. And the old man Abba Daniel remained during the week of mourning for Athanasia. Afterwards, the old man wanted to take Abba Andronicus with him, but he refused, saying, 'I will die with my lady'.

So the old man once again said goodbye but before he could reach the shrine of Saint Menas a brother said, 'Abba Andronicus follows Abba Athanasius'. Hearing this, the old man sent word to Scetis, saying, 'Abba Andronicus is following Brother Athanasius'. When they heard, they went up and found him alive and after they received his blessing he went to sleep in the Lord. War broke out between the fathers of Oktokaidekaton and those of Scetis; the latter were saying, 'The brother is ours and we are going to take him to Scetis and keep him there so his prayers may help us'. Those from Oktokaidekaton were saying, 'We are going to bury him with his sister'. Abba Daniel as well was also saying that he should be buried there. Those from Scetis did not listen to him and said, 'The old man belongs to heaven and no longer fears bodily conflict; we, however, are younger and want the brother so his prayers may help us'.

When the old man saw that a great disturbance was taking place, he said to the brothers, 'Truly, if you do not listen to me, I too will remain here and will be buried with my children'. Then they were at peace and they brought out the corpse of brother Andronicus. They said to the old man, 'Let us go to Scetis'. The old man said to them, 'Allow me to observe the week of mourning for the brother', but they did not allow him to remain there.

391

DON'T BREAK THE LAW

An old man said, 'Do not judge the person who commits sexual sin, even if you yourself are chaste; if you do, you likewise break the law yourself, for he who said, "*Do not commit sexual sin*"[7] also said, "*Do not judge*"'.[8]

THE MOTHER OF ALL EVILS

Abba Isaiah said, 'I think it is a great and honorable thing to defeat vainglory and make progress in the knowledge of God, for whoever falls into the hands of this wicked passion of vainglory alienates himself from peace and hardens his heart against the saints, and the end of all his evil ways is to fall into haughtiness, which is arrogance, the mother of all evils. As for you, faithful servant of Christ, keep your practices hidden, and with your heart's toil take care that you do not lose the reward that your practices will bring you because you are trying to please people. *Whoever does something to show off for people will receive his reward in full*, as the Lord said'.[9]

[7] Mt 5:27.
[8] Mt 7:1.
[9] Mt 6:5.

THE REAL THEOLOGIAN

If you are a theologian you truly pray. If you truly pray, you are a theologian.

GIVE GLORY TO GOD

Abba Sisoës said: When I was in Scetis with Abba Macarius, we went up with him, seven of us, to work the harvest. Listen here: a widow was gleaning behind us and she would not stop weeping. So the old man called to the owner of the field and said to him, 'What's the matter with this old woman who weeps all the time?'

He said to him, 'Her husband received a deposit from someone and he died suddenly and hadn't told her where he had put it, and the owner of the deposit wants to seize her and her children as slaves.'

The old man said to him, 'Tell her to come to us where we are resting during the heat.'

When she came, the old man said to her, 'Why are you weeping all the time?'

She said to him, 'My husband received a deposit from someone and he didn't tell me where he put it.'

The old man said to her, 'Come, show me where you buried him.' He took the brothers with him and left with her and when they came to the place the old man said to her, 'Go home.' While they prayed, the old man called to the dead man, saying, 'So and so, where did you put the other man's deposit?'

He replied and said, 'It's in my house, beneath the foot of the bed.'

The old man said to him, 'Now you can rest until the day of resurrection.'

When the brothers saw this, they fell at his feet in fear. The old man said to them, 'It was not on account of me that this happened, for I am nothing, but it was for the sake of this widow and her orphans that God has done this. This is what is great: that God wants the soul to be without sin'. And they went and told the widow where the deposit was and she took it and gave it to its owner and freed her children. Those who heard about this gave glory to God.

October 12

ASK YOUR FATHER

Abba Antony said, 'Nine monks fell away after many labors and were obsessed with spiritual pride, for they put their trust in their own works and, being deceived, did not give due heed to the commandment that says, *Ask your father and he will tell you*'.[10]

IF MOSES HADN'T ENTERED THE DARKNESS

It was said concerning Abba Macarius that a brother came to see him one time and told him, 'My father, my thoughts say to me, "Go, visit the sick", for this, it is said, is a great commandment'.

---

[10] Dt 32:7.

Abba Macarius said to him a prophetic word: It was the mouth without lie, our Lord Jesus Christ, who said, *'I was sick and you visited me'.*[11] *He took on human flesh and made it one with himself and he took on humanity in everything except sin alone,*[12] but I say to you, my child, sitting in your cell is better for you than visiting, for afterwards a time will come when they will mock those who remain in their cells and the word of Abba Antony will be fulfilled: 'If they see someone who is not mad, they will rise up against him and say, "You are mad!" because he is not like them.' I say to you, my child, *if Moses had not entered the darkness, he would not have been given the tablets of the covenant written by the finger of God.*[13]

October 13
EDWARD THE CONFESSOR (A)

OUR MOUTHS AND OUR STOMACHS

A brother asked Abba Tithoës, 'How should I guard my heart?'

The old man said to him, 'How can we guard our hearts when our mouths and our stomachs are open?'

GOING TO WORK

A certain great old man, having gone down to the Nile, found a still bed of rushes; he sat down there and was peeling off the outer layers

[11] Mt 25:36.
[12] Heb 4:15.
[13] Ex 19-23.

of reeds that he found in the river, plaiting a rope, and throwing it into the Nile. He continued to do this until some people came and saw him. Finally they left. He was not working because he had to but worked in order to toil and to have contemplative quiet.

I WAS DEAD LONG BEFORE THIS

Abba David related this about Abba Arsenius. One day a magistrate came, bringing him the will of a senator, a member of his family who had left him a very large inheritance. Arsenius took it and was about to destroy it. But the magistrate threw himself at his feet, saying, 'I beg you, do not destroy it or they will cut off my head'.

Abba Arsenius said to him, 'But I was dead long before this senator who has just died', and he returned the will to the magistrate without accepting anything.

October 14
CALLISTUS, POPE (RC)

THE BROTHER AND THE MURDERER

Abba Poemen said, 'If a person has attained to that which the Apostle speaks of, *to the pure, everything is pure*,[14] he sees himself to be less than all creatures'.

[14] Titus 1:15.

The brother said, 'How can I deem myself less than a murderer?'

The old man said, 'When a person has really comprehended this saying, if he sees a person committing a murder he says, "He has committed only this one sin but I commit sins every day"'.

STAYING PUT AND KEEPING SILENT

Question: Is it good to live in the desert?

Answer: When the children of Israel put an end to the distraction of Egypt and lived in tents, at that time it was made known to them how they ought to fear God. Indeed, boats driven about by storm in the middle of the sea accomplish nothing; but when they come to harbor, then they engage in business. In the same way, if a person is not steadfast in one place he will never receive the knowledge of truth. Indeed, above all the virtues God has chosen silence, for it is written, *Upon whom shall I look except upon the humble and quiet and him who trembles at my words?*[15]

October 15
TERESA OF ÁVILA, DOCTOR OF THE CHURCH (RC, A)

THOSE WHO ARE GREAT ATHLETES

Amma Syncletica said, 'Those who are great athletes must contend against stronger enemies'.

[15] Is 66:2 (LXX).

HOLD ON TO THE CROSS

She also said, 'If you have begun to do well, do not turn back through constraint of the Enemy, for through your endurance, the Enemy is destroyed. Those who put out to sea at first sail with favorable wind; then the sails spread, but later the winds become adverse. Then the ship is tossed by the waves and is no longer controlled by the rudder. But when in a little while there is a calm, and the tempest dies down, then the ship sails on again. So it is with us when we are driven by the spirits who are against us: we hold to the cross as our sail so we can set a safe course'.

October 16
HEDWIG, RELIGIOUS (RC)
MARGARET MARY ALOCOQUE, VIRGIN (RC)
HUGH LATIMER AND NICHOLAS RIDLEY, BISHOPS;
THOMAS CRANMER, ARCHBISHOP OF CANTERBURY, MARTYRS (A)

TRUE WEALTH

Know that you are wealthy on account of *the depths of the wisdom that will be yours in love.*[16]

---

[16] See Rom 11:33.

RULE WITH GOD

Hold on to teaching with all humility and in addition say to yourself: *O the depths of the riches and wisdom and knowledge of God!* and rule with God.[17]

REMEMBER THIS

When you pray, keep your memory under close custody. Do not let it suggest your own fancies to you, but rather have it convey the awareness of your reaching out to God. Remember this—the memory has a powerful proclivity for causing detriments to the spirit at the time of prayer.

When you are at prayer the memory activates fantasies of either past happenings or fresh concerns or else of persons you have previously injured.

October 17
PAUL OF TAMMA (CO)
MARTYRS COSMAS AND DAMIAN OF ARABIA (GO)
IGNATIUS OF ANTIOCH (RC, A)

ABBA PAUL DEFEATS THE DEVIL

A man suddenly came to the entrance of my dwelling; he called to me, and I went out to see who it was. That man said to me, 'Are you Ezekiel?'

[17] Rom 11:33.

I said to him, 'Yes, I am.'

He said to me, 'Let me enter your dwelling so I can have a word with you; I do not want the brothers to hear what I am saying and become afraid'.

I welcomed him inside because of his fine manner of speaking.

He said to me, 'My brother Ezekiel, do you know what has happened?'

I said, 'No'.

He said to me, 'I have come, walking in the desert for seven hours since yesterday, I with some other men, looking for rocks from which we could make bath powder. We found highwaymen in the mountain; we took up our implements in our hands and were barely able to escape their clutches alive. And when we fled their hands, we came upon a great man who had been bound and thrown down into the valley and we released him. He said to us, "Leave me here, but if you go to the mountain, you will find this certain dwelling; call inside: 'Ezekiel, your father says, "Come to me in the desert, for thieves have robbed me; they have tied me up, wishing to kill me, but God has rescued my soul from their hands"'"' We asked him, "What is your name?" He said to us, "My name is Paul, and I am from Tamma in the nome of Koeis".

I, Ezekiel, when I heard these words, I was troubled because he had spoken the name of my father and his village.

That man spoke to me again, 'Get up, follow me so I can take you to him, for I see that you are afraid'.

I walked with him in the middle of the desert. We walked, completing the first day and the second. I said to him, 'Aren't we there yet?'

He said, 'No'.

We spent a third day walking in the desert. I said to him again, 'Haven't we reached him yet?'

He said, 'Look, we're approaching him now'.

While he was speaking to me he changed shape and became a huge Ethiopian; his eyes were filled with blood, his whole body bristled with spines, and he gave off a foul odor like a billy goat. He said to me, 'Don't you know who I am, Ezekiel?'

I said to him, 'No'.

He said to me, 'I was the one who dried up the well that time. Your father beat me until I filled it up like it was before. I suffered putting up with you and your father. You two have not gotten very smart'.

I said to him, 'Why, you're the Devil, whom the Lord punishes for all the evil you've done to the servants of Christ!'

But he rushed at me like a ferocious lion, wanting to kill me, and I cried out, 'Father, help me!'

Immediately my father heard my voice as though he were right by me. He got up immediately and came to me through the grace of God. When my father drew near to him, the Devil suddenly changed and took on the form of a monk wearing a skin and carrying some small sheaves of palm branches. He went up to my father and prostrated himself at his feet according to the rule of our fellow monks. Immediately my father traced a line around him so he would not be able to move this way or that, for he knew that it was the Devil. He grabbed him and bound him hand and foot and rolled him down into the valley. We left him and went our way.

I said to my father, 'What was it that you did to that shameless creature?'

My father said to me, 'God delivered him to me so I could punish him as I saw fit since he dared to tempt us'.

After my father said these things, we rose and went to our dwelling, glorifying God.

THE LION LEAVES THE DESERT

Truly, the lion leaves the desert and erases his paw prints with his tail. If he prevails over the person who has come out after him, he goes up in complete confidence.

LEST GRIEF SWALLOW HIM AT A GULP

The brothers would gather around Evagrius on Saturday and Sunday, discussing their thoughts with him throughout the night, listening to his words of encouragement until sunrise. And thus they would leave rejoicing and glorifying God, for Evagrius' teaching was very sweet. When they came to see him, he encouraged them, saying to them, 'My brothers, if one of you has either a profound or a troubled thought, let him be silent until the brothers depart and let him reflect on it alone with me. Let us not make him speak in front of the brothers lest a little one perish on account of his thoughts and grief swallow him at a gulp'.

October 19
JEAN DE BRÉBEUF AND ISAAC JOGUES,
MISSIONARIES, MARTYRS (RC)[18]
PAUL OF THE CROSS, PRIEST (RC)
HENRY MARTYN, PRIEST, TRANSLATOR OF SCRIPTURE (A)

DON'T TAKE AWAY MY FOSTER FATHER!

Someone brought an old man money, saying, 'Keep this for your expenses. You've gotten old and you're ill' (for he was a leper), but in response the old man said, 'For sixty years God has fed me, and now you've come to take away my foster father? Look, I've been ill all these years and I haven't needed a thing: God has supplied me with what I've needed and has kept me fed.' And he refused to accept it.

THE SHE-ASS AND HER FOAL

A brother asked an old man, 'My thoughts wander and I'm troubled by them'.

The old man said to him, 'Go on sitting in your cell and they will come back again. If a she-ass is tethered, her foal gambols here and there but wherever he goes he comes back to his mother again. It's the same with the thoughts of someone who for God's sake perseveres in staying in his cell: even if his thoughts wander a little, they nevertheless return to him again'.

[18] Also known as the Canadian, or North American, martyrs.

NO FESTIVAL LIKE IT

There is no festival like the worship of God in your dwelling.

CAN A PERSON BE DEAD?

A brother asked Abba Poemen, 'Can a person be dead?'

He replied, 'The person who is inclined to sin starts to die, but the person who applies himself to good will live and will put it into practice'.

THE PASSIONS WORK IN FOUR STAGES

Another brother questioned Abba Poemen in these words: 'What does "See that none of you repays evil for evil" mean?'

The old man said to him, 'Passions work in four stages—first, in the heart; second, in the face; third, in words; and fourth, it is essential not to render evil for evil in deeds. If you can purify your heart, passion will not come into your expression; but if it comes into your face, take care not to speak; but if you do speak, cut the conversation short in case you render evil for evil'.[19]

[19] 1 Thes 5:15.

A NEW BEGINNING

Abba Poemen said concerning Abba Pior that every day he made a new beginning.

FOUR THOUSAND SOLIDI, ONE SOLIDUS

Jacob, the servant of Abba Pambo, who resembled him in every ascetic practice except in language alone, bore witness to me: One time Anatolius the Spaniard came to see him; he had been a secretary, a relative of Albinus, who was from Rome, and he had renounced the world. He filled a purse with gold which contained four thousand *solidi* and placed it before the feet of Abba Pambo, thinking that the old man would glorify him or be proud of him or exalt him on account of the money. But Abba Pambo did his handiwork in silence. He did not pay the money any attention nor did he say a word to him, and Anatolius said to him, 'My father, I have brought these necessities to provide for the poor'.

The old man said to him, 'I already know that, my son'.

Anatolius said to him, 'But I want you to know how much it is'.

The old man said, 'That which you have brought has no need for you to recount its number'.

Therefore Anatolius placed the money before him and left. He spoke to the priests, 'My soul has not profited from this large amount of money I brought as much as it has from the disposition and self-possession of the old man. He treated me as though I'd brought him *one* solidus!'

BE SQUARE, NOT ROUND

A brother questioned Abba Matoës, saying, 'What am I to do?
My tongue makes me suffer, and every time I go among people,
I cannot control it, but I condemn them in all the good they are
doing and I reproach them with it. What am I to do?'

The old man replied, 'If you cannot contain yourself, flee into
solitude. For this is a sickness. The person who dwells with brothers
must not be square, but round, so as to turn himself towards all'.

He went on, 'It is not through virtue that I live in solitude, but
through weakness; those who live in the midst of people are the
strong ones'.

ABUSE THE DEAD, PRAISE THE DEAD

A brother paid a visit to Abba Macarius the Great and said to him,
'My father, tell me a word how I may be saved'.

The old man said to him, 'Go to the tombs, abuse the dead, and
throw stones at them'.

So the brother went and abused them and came and told the
old man. The old man said to him, 'Didn't they say anything to
you?'

He said, 'No'.

The old man said to him, 'Go tomorrow and praise them, saying,
"You are apostles and saints and righteous people"'.

He returned to the old man and said, 'I praised them', and the
old man said to him, 'Didn't they say anything in reply?'

He said, 'No'.

The old man said to him, 'You saw how you abused them and
they did not say anything to you and how you praised them and
they said nothing in reply; it's the same with you: if you wish to

be saved, go, be dead, take no account of people's scorn or their compliments, like the dead themselves, and you can be saved'.

THE CREATIVE POWER OF GOD

When Abba Bishoy returned to his cave, the Devil appeared to him and said, 'What violence you do me, Bishoy! Why do none of the plans I contrive against you work? You ward them all off! I am leaving, then, to wage war against others. I have been beaten; I am never coming back to attack you!'

The divine man rebuked him, 'Be quiet!' he said. 'You are full of evil'.

Put to shame and chased off, the Devil no longer dared to come near him. Bishoy returned to the inner desert: there he dwelled in the flesh but in the spirit he lived side by side with the heavenly beings and conversed with their Lord and Master, devoting himself to difficult spiritual practices that differed in no way from those of the incorporeal beings. So the Holy Spirit, who dwelled in him, was pleased to make Bishoy a witness to heavenly treasures and to the joy that the righteous share in heaven.

While he was praying, he soared to heaven. Filled with joy, he first saw the delights of paradise, then he observed the Church of the First-born in heaven. Partaking of the immaterial food provided by the spiritual teaching above, he was deemed worthy to receive the gift of fasting and abstinence. Once a week he shared in the Holy Communion on the Lord's Day and would fast until the following Sunday, and this grace stayed with him because he was so enriched by the nature of God of which he partook.

Let no one who obeys the divine law doubt that I bear witness to the truth, for everything is subject to divine command. I will tell the truth: after the fear-instilling partaking of Holy Communion, he went without eating for seventy days—and this is not at all remarkable if one considers the unimaginable might possessed by divine power. The partaking of foods completes the natural cycle; it is a force that empties the body which then needs these foods to effect growth and change. But the creative power of God, which is not subject at all to natural law, fully and unstintingly gives to those of the highest spiritual qualities the ability to transcend nature. We know that on earth the creative power of God preserved life for ill-fed children in Ephesus for three hundred years and more and will maintain Elijah in heaven until the last days. But these examples will have to suffice.

October 24
BLESSED ELESBAAN, KING OF ETHIOPIA (O)
ANTHONY CLARET, BISHOP (RC)

YOU WHO ARE POOR

You,[20] who are poor, if you cling to the Lord alone, the Lord will also remain with you and have you rule with him.

[20] Singular.

ACT A LITTLE VIOLENTLY

Abba Macarius said, 'The rank of monk is like that of the angels. Just as the angels stand in the Lord's presence at all times and no earthly thing hinders them from standing in his presence, so too it is with the monk: it is fitting that he should be like the angels his whole life. In doing this he will fulfill the word of our Savior who commands each of us *to deny himself and take up his cross and follow him*.[21] In the same way, act a little violently, my beloved children, in order that you may acquire virtue for yourselves, and virtue alone, for it is written, *The kingdom of heaven belongs to those who take it by force*'.[22]

October 25
CRISPIN & CRISPINIAN, MARTYRS AT ROME (A)

AN ARROGANT TONGUE

Do not walk with someone whose strength comes from an arrogant tongue.

IMAGELESS PRAYER

The spirit that possesses health is the one which has no images of the things of this world at the time of prayer.

[21] Mt 10:38//Lk 14:27.
[22] Mt 11:12.

UNDERSTANDING SCRIPTURE

Now Matthew for his part nurtured this ascetic practice: He could never be persuaded to speak about any saying from Scripture, and if anyone asked him about a reading from the Scriptures, he would answer them in this way: 'Forgive me, I do not understand it', even though he was very learned and had been instructed in the writings of the Holy Scriptures.

October 26
CEDD, ABBOT OF LASTINGHAM (A)

JUDGE NO ONE ELSE

Abba Macarius of Alexandria went one day to Abba Pachomius of Tabennisi. Pachomius asked him, 'When brothers do not submit to the Rule, is it right to correct them?'

Abba Macarius said to him, 'Correct and judge justly those who are subject to you, but judge no one else. *For truly it is written, Is it not those inside the Church whom you are to judge? God judges those outside*'.[23]

A MONK OUGHT TO ASK HIMSELF

Abba Nisterus said that a monk ought to ask himself every night and every morning, 'What have we done that is as God wills and

---

[23] 1 Cor 5:12-13.

410

what have we left undone of that which he does not will? He must do this throughout his whole life. Every day strive to come before God without sin. Pray to God in his presence, for he is really present. Do not impose rules on yourself; do not judge anyone.'

October 27
GREGORY OF NYSSA (CO)

YOU'VE SEEN ONLY THE SIN

An old man said, 'Even if someone sins in some way in your presence, do not judge him but consider yourself more of a sinner than he is, for you have seen the sin but you have not seen the repentance'.

BRING ME SOME WATER

There was also a certain laborer who lived a little to the south of us and worked in a vineyard. Now it happened that when he had climbed up a date palm tree to gather dates, the belt holding him broke. He fell backwards to the ground and seemed to be dead. Now his son was sitting under the palm tree and when he saw what had happened, he wept bitterly. And when the men who were nearby [heard him crying out], they went to see what had happened. When they saw their friend lying on the ground as though dead, they said to his son, 'Go to the holy man Abba Aaron, and get a small bowl of water from him in faith and throw it on your father. Maybe he will wake up'.

The young boy went weeping to the holy one. Now the holy one was sitting by the door because he had a fever and was exhausted. The young man threw himself down before him and told him what had happened. Now when the righteous and compassionate one heard what had happened, his heart was heavy and he said to me, 'Bring me a little water, and let the young man take it and throw it on his father in the name of Christ'. So I brought the water to him. He made the sign of the cross over it and gave it to the young man to take and throw it on his father. As soon as he threw it on him, he immediately got up. He came with his son and worshiped at the feet of the holy man Abba Aaron. The holy one raised him up, saying, 'Worship God, for I am the least of God's servants'. When he rose, his son told him what had happened, saying, 'When I threw the water on you, you trembled and then stood as though you'd just woken from sleep'. And so they went away from him in peace.

October 28
SIMON AND JUDE, APOSTLES (RC, A)

JUDGING YOUR NEIGHBOR

Abba Isaiah said, 'If the thought comes to you to judge your neighbor for some sin, first think to yourself that you are more of a sinner than he is, and do not believe that your good deeds are pleasing to God; thus you will not dare to judge your neighbor'.

NEITHER THE APPEARANCE NOR THE FINERY
OF A PROSTITUTE

They also said concerning Abba Pambo that Abba Athanasius sent for him one time and had him brought to Alexandria. When he entered the city he saw a woman of the theater adorned with finery. Immediately his eyes filled with tears. Therefore, when the brothers who were with him saw him, they said to him, 'Our father, we beg you, tell us what caused these tears'.

He said to them, 'Two things move me at this moment: one is the destruction of this soul that I see now; the other is my own ungrateful soul which, in adorning itself with the virtues and in pleasing the Lord and his angels, does not even have the appearance or the finery of this prostitute'.

October 29
JAMES HANNINGTON, BISHOP, MARTYR (A)

THE SLAVE OF GLORY

Abba Isidore of Pelusia said, 'Prize the virtues and do not be the slave of glory. The former are immortal, while the latter soon fades'.

WHEN DID YOU COME HERE?

One of the fathers was living in a place and was leading a good monastic life. He had a brother who was the superior of a lavra so he said to himself, 'Why do I stay here and toil? I'll go to my brother and he'll supply me with what I need'. He got up and went to his brother and when his brother saw him he rejoiced. And the father said to his brother, 'I want to stay here, but give me a cell so I can be by myself, and he gave it to him. And from that hour he forgot that his brother was there.

When the monks of the lavra saw that he was the superior's brother, thinking that his brother would supply him with his needs, they did not bring him anything nor did they call him to a cell in order for him to be given some bread.

Because he was pious, however, he did not trouble anyone about this. Then he was thinking to himself, 'Perhaps it isn't God's will that I stay here'. So he got the key to his cell and took it to his brother and said to him, 'Forgive me. I'm unable to stay here'.

His brother the superior was amazed and said, 'When did you come here?'

He said to the superior, 'Wasn't it you who gave me the key to my cell?'

His brother the superior said, 'Believe me, I don't remember that you even came here. But for the Lord's sake tell me what thinking brought you here'.

The father said to him, 'I was hoping that I would have things easy with you'.

His brother the superior said to him, 'God has rightly, then, hidden your coming from me because you weren't placing your hope in him but rather in me'. And the father got up and went to his original place.

THE GROUND CANNOT FALL

Our fathers have somewhere told a story about our father Abba John, saying, 'Just as the ground cannot fall, in the same way our father Abba John the Little is incapable of falling at all because of his great humility'. Abba John, the disciple of Abba Amoi the Upper Egyptian, completed great obedience, patiently submitting to his spiritual father, *boiling with the fire of the Holy Spirit*.[24]

THE TREE OF OBEDIENCE

Now one day Abba Amoi took a dry piece of wood and went with it on a path far from his cell into the desert (the distance was about twelve miles), and he planted it there. Abba Amoi called to Abba John his disciple and said to him, 'John, my son, give a basin of water to this wood daily until it bears fruit'.

Now the water was a long way from the place where the tree was planted, but Abba John would leave with the basin of at night and would return in the morning. He did this for three years and the tree lived, blossomed, and brought forth fruit. The elder Abba Amoi took the fruit of the tree and brought it to the church and gave it to the elders, saying, '*Take, eat from the fruit of obedience*'.[25]

When the elders saw this wondrous thing, they marveled, giving glory to God, saying, 'Our God, if the blessed life were not in this brother, this mystery would not have taken place through him! Blessed be Jesus Christ, God the Logos, he who performs wonders

[24] See Mt 3:11; Acts 2:3-4.
[25] Mt 26:26 and see Gen 3.

through his saints, for he himself said, "*If one does my bidding, we, I and my father, will come and dwell within him, and everything that he asks in my name will be given to him*"'.[26] And that tree still exists among us today as a faithful proof of the virtue of our all-holy father shining through these great achievements.

October 31

WANTING A WIFE

Abba Olympius of the Cells was tempted to fornication. His thoughts said to him, 'Go, and take a wife'. He got up, found some mud, made a woman, and said to himself, 'Here is your wife. Now you must work hard in order to feed her'. So he worked, giving himself a great deal of trouble.

The next day, making some mud again, he formed it into a girl and said to his thoughts, 'Your wife has had a child. You must work harder so you can feed her and clothe your child'.

So he wore himself out doing this, and said to his thoughts, 'I cannot bear this weariness, stop wanting a wife!' God, seeing his efforts, took away the conflicts from him and he was at peace.

LIGHT FROM LIGHT

There was an old man at Scetis, very austere of body, but not very clear in his thoughts. He went to see Abba John to ask him about

[26] Jn 14:13, 21, 23.

forgetfulness. Having received a word from him, he returned to his cell and forgot what Abba John had said to him. He went off again to ask him and having heard the same word from him he returned with it. As he got near his cell, he forgot again. This he did many times; he went to see Abba John, but while he was returning he was overcome by forgetfulness. Later, meeting the old man, he said to him, 'Do you know, abba, that I have forgotten again what you said to me? But I did not want to overburden you, so I did not come back'.

Abba John said to him, 'Go and light a lamp'. He lit it. Abba John said to him, 'Bring some more lamps, and light them from the first'. He did so. Then Abba John said to the old man, 'Has that lamp suffered any loss from the fact that other lamps have been lit from it'.

The old man said, 'No'.

Abba John continued, 'So it is with John; even if the whole of Scetis came to see me, *they would not separate me from the love of Christ*.[27] Consequently, whenever you want to, come to me without hesitation'.

[27] See Rom 8:35.

NOVEMBER

PENTECOST / ORDINARY TIME

November 1

ALL SAINTS' DAY (RC, A)
LUKE THE EVANGELIST (CO)
COSMOS AND DAMIEN (O)

THE TREES OF PARADISE

Our father Abba John said, 'The saints resemble the trees of paradise laden with the fruits of life which, in their glory and the blessings they give, are of many kinds, through the saving spring of the Holy Spirit, which waters them all'.

OBSERVE ALL THE SAINTS

Now then, my son, observe all the saints, see how they are one with God.

For it is they who walked in estrangement and poverty and want, rejected by everyone, until they defeated the Adversary, *wandering in deserts and mountains and caves and holes in the ground, in need, afflicted, suffering, those of whom the world was not worthy.*[1]

Remember, then, that our Saviour came in poverty; he laid down the ways for us so that we might follow in his footsteps and become imitators of him, as it is written: *Be imitators of me as I am of Christ,*[2] and also imitate his other apostles.

[1] Heb 11:38.
[2] 1 Cor 11:1.

421

For when Christ was about to send them forth, he did not give them a multitude of commandments to follow but gave them only the commandment of poverty.

As it is written in the Gospel according to Matthew: *When you go forth to preach, do not acquire for yourselves gold or silver or copper in your belts, nor two tunics, nor sandals.*[3] These are all words he spoke concerning poverty.

November 2
COMMEMORATION OF ALL FAITHFUL DEPARTED (ALL SOULS) (RC, A)

ABBA MAXIMUS BECOMES ILL; HIS DEATH

Then after these events, it pleased God's loving kindness for humanity to grant rest to Saints Maximus and Domitius and remove them from this perishable world and its passing afflictions and take them where they would have easeful and heavenly rest filled with eternal joy and happiness, where grief and sorrow and lamentation are absent.

Then, on the holy feast day of the Epiphany, blessed Abba Maximus was the first to lie down ill, seized with a high fever. When the illness grew worse, he said, 'Please summon our father Abba Macarius for me'. Then, after the sun had set, he said to us, 'What time is it?' We told him it was the close of day. He said, 'In a little while I will go to my place of eternal rest'.

When night arrived, our father Abba Macarius told us, 'Light the lamp so it will give us light,', so we lit it. Then the spirit of

---

[3] Mt 9:9-10.

blessed Abba Maximus was taken up to heaven and he spoke thus: '*Send your light and your truth, my God, and guide my heart on your path, for I believe that you will make straight my path.*'[4] Deliver me from the power of the evil spirits, the demons of the air. Make ready my feet on your paths, my God, that I may come to you without impediment. Be my powerful hope, Jesus my God, *for you are my light and my salvation. Whom shall I fear?*'[5] After this he was silent for a while.

Then he spoke again, 'Arise, let us leave. Look! Look! The apostles and prophets have come to take me away from here'. Then he became silent. A few minutes later, Saint Abba Macarius saw the choir of saints coming for Abba Maximus. Abba Macarius quickly rose and stood staring while remaining silent. When I saw that the lamp had almost gone out, I said to the old man, Abba Macarius, 'Do you want me to light the lamp, my father?'

But he responded, 'Be quiet, my son. This is not the time to talk'.

Then blessed Maximus spoke to one of the saints, asking him the names of the saints gathered around him. We did not hear what he said but Abba Macarius the Spiritbearer told us that they told him the names of the saints around Abba Maximus. And when Abba Maximus' soul enjoyed the presence of the saints, it immediately left his body with joy. In this way the blessed one died in peace. He went to his rest with all the saints on January 22nd.

[4] See Pr 3:6, Mt 3:3, Jn 1:23.
[5] Ps 27:1.

WITHDRAW, FLEE

Do not be afraid of the demons. They are powerless before God.

Instead be afraid for the person whom you will save, *fleeing inward in the knowledge that it is the time for withdrawal.*[6]

For David withdrew and was saved.[7] Withdraw earnestly on your own behalf.

For the saints and our Lord died at the hands of others, and I have suffered more on account of the war with others than the war with the desert.

So, therefore, flee to yourself alone.

For Andrew was found walking alone in the city of the cannibals.

THE UNTETHERED ASS

Some brothers went from Scetis to see Abba Antony. When they got into the boat to go see him, they found another old man on board who also wanted to go there. The brothers did not know him. They sat in the boat, talking about the words of the fathers and passages from Scripture and in turn talking about the work they did with their hands. But the old man kept silent concerning all these things.

When they arrived at the dock, it turned out that the old man was also going to see Abba Antony. When they came to Antony,

---

[6] See Rom 13:11, 1 Cor 7:29.
[7] See 1 Sam 19:18.

he said to them, 'Did you find this old man to be a good traveling companion?'

He also spoke to the old man: 'You have found good brothers to accompany you, Abba'.

The old man said to him, 'They are good people, but their courtyard does not have a door; whoever wants to can enter the stable, untether the ass and set it loose'.

November 4

RELYING ON THE NAME OF CHRIST

Abba Macarius the Great said, 'Concentrate on this name of our Lord Jesus Christ with a contrite heart, the words welling up from your lips and drawing you to them. And do not depict him with an image in your mind but concentrate on calling to him: "Our Lord Jesus, have mercy on me"'. Do these things in peace and you will see the peace of his divinity within you; he will run off the darkness of the passions that dwell within you and *he will purify the inner person* just as Adam was pure in paradise.[9] This is the blessed name that John the Evangelist pronounced: *Light of the world and unending sweetness, the food of life and the true food*.[10]

---

[8] Episcopal Church calendar; November 6 in the Church of England.
[9] 2 Cor 4:16; Eph 3:16.
[10] Jn 6:48, 6:55, 8:12.

Abba Evagrius said: I visited Abba Macarius, distressed by my thoughts and the passions of the body. I said to him, 'My father, tell me a word so I may live'.

Abba Macarius said to me, 'Bind the ship's cable to the mooring anvil and through the grace of our Lord Jesus Christ the ship will pass through the diabolical waves and tumults of this murky sea and the deep darkness of this vain world'.

I said to him, 'What is the ship? What is the ship's cable? What is the mooring anvil?'

Abba Macarius said to me, 'The ship is your heart. Guard it. The ship's cable is your spirit; bind it to our Lord Jesus Christ, who is the mooring anvil that prevails over all the tumults and diabolical waves that fight against the saints. For it is not easy to say with each breath, "Lord Jesus, have mercy on me. I bless you, my Lord Jesus". If you are distressed by people and the misfortunes of this world, say "My Lord Jesus, help me." The fish swallows the waves and will be ensnared in them and will not know it. But when we persevere in the saving name of our Lord Jesus Christ, he, through the things he does for us, *will ensnare the Devil by his nostrils*[11] and we will know our weakness, because *our help is in our Lord* Jesus Christ"'.[12]

---

[11] Job 40:26.
[12] Ps 124:8.

REMEMBERING THE POOR

Pachomius and Palamon practiced the ascesis together and gave time to prayers. Their work consisted of spinning and weaving hair sacks. In their work *they toiled not for themselves but they remembered the poor*, as the Apostle says.[13]

HOSPITALITY

One brother, an ascetic who was not eating bread, went to visit a great old man. Some other foreigners were also there and the old man made a little cooked food for their benefit. When they sat down to eat, the ascetic brother set before himself a single soaked chickpea and ate.

When they got up, the old man took the brother aside and said to him, 'Brother, if you visit someone, do not exhibit your way of life. If you want to keep to your own way of life, stay in your cell and never come out'.

Persuaded by what the old man had said, he became more accommodating when he got together with the brothers.

[13] Gal 2:10.

WHO AM I?

Abba Joseph asked Abba Poemen, 'Tell me, how can I become a monk?'

The old man said, 'If you wish to find peace both here and in the age to come, in every situation say "Who am I?" And *do not judge anyone*'.[14]

GREED AND DESIRE AND THEIR ROOTS IN OUR HEARTS

John of Lycopolis said, 'We must take great care concerning our feelings and our thoughts. We must be careful that no greed, or depraved desire, or empty longing, or anything that is not of God, put its roots down in our hearts. From such roots vain and unhelpful thoughts spring up rapidly and continuously and cause us much distress, nor do they cease when we are praying; they are not put to shame when we stand in the presence of God and pray for our salvation, but they take our attention captive and when we seem to be standing in prayer in the body we are wandering about in attention and thought and are distracted by various things.

'Therefore, if there is anyone who thinks that he has renounced the world and the works of the Devil, it is not enough to have renounced with the lips the possessions of lands and the affairs of this world; he must also renounce his own vices and profitless and empty pleasures. These are the things the Apostle is speaking about: *senseless and harmful desires that plunge people into their own destruction*'.[15]

[14] Lk 6:37.
[15] 1 Tim 6:9.

FLEEING

Abba Nisterus the Great was walking in the desert with a brother and when they saw a serpent they ran away. The brother said, 'Were you afraid, too, father?'

The old man said, 'I'm not afraid, child, but it's good for me to flee since then I won't have to flee the spirit of vainglory'.

SIXTY YEARS OF PRAYER DOWN THE ADMINISTRATIVE DRAIN

An anchorite became a bishop. This man, out of piety, would rebuke no one, patiently bearing everyone's faults. The bishop's administrator, however, was not managing the church's business as he was supposed to so some people said to the bishop, 'Why do you not rebuke the administrator for being negligent?'

The bishop postponed the rebuke to the next day; as a result, those who were opposed to the administrator, irritated with the bishop, came to see him. When the bishop learned about it, he hid himself somewhere and when those people came, they were unable to find him. They learned from the bishop's associates where he was hidden and they found him and said to him, 'Why did you hide yourself?'

He said, 'Because you wish to strip away in two days what it has taken me sixty years to accomplish by praying to God'.

UNABLE TO GRASP IT

A brother questioned Abba Moses, saying, 'I see something in front of me and I am not able to grasp it'.

The old man said to him, 'If you do not become dead like those who are in the tomb, you will not be able to grasp it'.

A THOUSAND COINS

One of the saints called Philagrius lived in Jerusalem and worked hard to earn his own bread. While he was standing in the market-place to sell his manual work, someone dropped a money pouch with a thousand coins in it. When the old man found it, he stood where he was, saying, 'Surely whoever lost it will come for it'.

And, indeed, the man did come back, weeping, and the old man took him aside and gave him the money pouch. That fellow took hold of the old man, wanting to offer him something, but the old man refused. Then the man proceeded to cry out, 'Come and see what this person of God has done!' The old man fled secretly and left the city in order that what he had done might not be made known and he be honored.

A HEART FILLED WITH COMPASSION

One time our all-holy father Abba John the Little took some baskets to Egypt in order to trade them for a little bread for himself, in particular for the needs of the body, and he sold them and filled a basket with bread in exchange for the price of the baskets.

While our father made preparations to walk back to the desert, an old woman came walking on the road. She was a poor widow and she was leading a blind child whom she served as a guide. He was her son to whom she had given birth blind. Our father Abba John watched them as they walked. He heard the blind child say to his mother, 'My mother, has God determined that we should have bread to eat today?' His mother groaned and wept, saying to him, 'My son, may the Lord see us and have mercy upon us through his caring providence'.

When our holy father heard this blind child and his mother, his heart was moved with the mercies of Christ who dwelled in him. He called to the woman and said to her, 'Come here', and when she came, our father said to her, 'Do you need these small loaves of bread, my mother?' She said to him, 'Oh yes, my father!' Our holy father, because he was moved with care for everyone, would forget his own needs in order to help others. He gave the breadbasket to the woman, placing his hope in Christ who lived in him and who would supply him with another portion of bread. The woman received the bread with joy and thanks. Moved by God, the woman was filled with great faith and said to our father, 'My holy father, I see that you are a holy one of God! This young boy that you see is my son, whom I bore like this. I ask Your Goodness to place your holy hands on his eyes so he may receive your blessing'.

Our holy father lifted his eyes to heaven; he groaned, his heart filled with compassion, and said, 'Lord, since you granted sight to the one born blind by the movement of your will,[16] which is powerful and perfect in mercy, now, Christ God, again let the assent of your holy will in every good thing be perfect for the well being of this child whom you created'.

Saying 'Amen', our holy father laid his hands on the eyes of the blind child and made the sign of the cross on them in the name of Christ. Immediately in that hour the blind child saw. On account of the joy and the miracle that happened, his mother cried out in a loud voice, 'Blessed is the Lord God of this holy old man and monk!' Because of her cry a multitude began to gather together to see. Because of this, our father *withdrew from this place to another*,[17] fleeing from human glory, and he disappeared from sight, Christ guiding him.

November 10
LEO THE GREAT, POPE, DOCTOR OF THE CHURCH (RC, A)

THE LION AND ITS BELLY

John the Little said, 'The lion is strong and on account of his belly falls into the trap and all of his strength is brought to nothing'.

[16] Jn 9.
[17] Mt 12:15, 14:13.

BE LIKE THE LION

Truly, the lion leaves the desert and erases his paw prints with his tail. If he prevails over the person who has come out after him, he goes up in complete confidence.

Now then, do not let your heart grow slack while you are in this world until you go up to the Lord in victory.

APATHEIA

The soul that has *apatheia* is not simply the one which is not disturbed by changing events but the one that remains unmoved at the memory of them as well.

November 11
THEODORE THE STUDITE (O)
MARTIN, BISHOP OF TOURS (RC, A)

A CULPABLE LACK OF FEAR

Abba Poemen said that Abba Sisoës said, 'There is a kind of shame that contains a culpable lack of fear'.

ONE VERSE OF ONE PSALM

When Abba Pambo came to the brothers he went and found an old man and said to him, 'Teach me a psalm', for he was illiterate, and the old man began to teach him this psalm: *I said, 'I will watch my ways so as to be unable to sin with my tongue'.*[18]

After the old man had given him the beginning of the text, Pambo stopped him, saying, 'My father, since I haven't yet learned the beginning of the text, I will not learn the rest'. And when Abba Pambo went to his cell, he spent eight years putting into practice the saying that he had learned, for he came into contact with no one, saying, 'Unless I first master my tongue, I will come into contact with no one lest I fall into sin on account of my tongue'.

After eight years, he went and paid a visit to the old man who had given him the psalm. The old man said to him, 'Pambo, why haven't we seen you until today? Why didn't you come to learn the psalm?'

Abba Pambo said to him, 'Since I hadn't learned the first verse, I didn't return to you to get the second since God had not given me the grace until now to learn it. In order not to act as if I despised you, I have come to visit you, my father. For if I learn the first verse, I will come to see you again'. And when he returned to his cell, he stayed there another ten years and did not come into contact with anyone.

---

[18] Ps 38:2 (LXX).

A SENATOR WHO RENOUNCED (ALMOST) EVERYTHING

Abba Cassian said, 'There was a senator who had renounced every-thing and distributed his possessions to the poor. He kept back some things for his own use, not wishing to accept the humil-ity that comes with total poverty and sincere submission to the cenobitic rule. Saint Basil, who is among the saints, offered this word to such a person: "You have lost your senatorial rank without making yourself a monk"'.

GET UP! LEAVE, IF YOU CAN!

Abba Macarius went up one time from Scetis to Terenuthis and went into a small building to sleep. There were some old polytheist corpses there and, taking one, he put it under his head as a pillow. When the demons saw his audacity, they were filled with jealousy and, wishing to terrify him, were calling out, as though address-ing a woman, 'So and so, come with us to the baths'. Another answered from beneath him, speaking as though from the dead, 'I have a stranger on top of me and I can't come!'

But the old man was not frightened; on the contrary, he knocked on the corpse, saying, 'Get up! Leave, if you can!'

When the demons heard this, they cried out in a loud voice, saying, 'You have defeated us!' And, put to shame, they fled.

November 13

SINS, JESUS, OR PEOPLE

Abba Elias said, 'People turn their minds either to their sins, or to Jesus, or to people'.

THOUGHTS AGAINST MY BROTHER, THOUGHTS AGAINST ME

Abba Isaac said, 'I have never allowed a thought against my brother who has grieved me to enter my cell; I have seen to it that no brother should return to his cell with a thought against me'.

HOW SHOULD ONE PRAY?

Abba Macarius was asked, 'How should one pray?'

The old man said, 'There is no need at all to make long discourses; it is enough to stretch out one's hands and say, "Lord, as you will, and as you know, have mercy". And if the conflict grows fiercer, say, "Lord, help!" He knows very well what we need and he shows us his mercy'.

THE JAWS OF THE ENEMY

One of the old men came to Abba Theodore and said to him, 'Look how such and such a brother has returned to the world'.

The old man said to him, 'Does that surprise you? No, rather be astonished when you hear that someone has been able to escape the jaws of the Enemy'.

BY ITS VERY NATURE

We have received no command to work and pass the night in vigils and to fast constantly. However, we do have the obligation to *pray without ceasing*.[19] Although the body, due to its weakness, does not suffice for such labors as these, which are calculated to restore health to the passionate part of the soul, these practices do require the body for their performance. But prayer makes the spirit strong and pure for combat since by its very nature the spirit is made to pray. Moreover, prayer even fights without the aid of the body on behalf of the other powers of the soul.

---

[19] 1 Thes 5:17.

WICKEDNESS ON TOP OF WICKEDNESS

Abba Poemen said, 'Wickedness does not do away with wickedness. If someone does you wrong, do good to him, so that by your action you destroy his wickedness'.

A USELESS VISIT

Abba Poemen said, 'If a brother comes to visit you and you realize that you have not profited by his visit, search your heart, and discover what you were thinking about before he came, and then you will understand why his visit was useless'.

THE IMPUTATION OF MADNESS

No one who loves true prayer and yet gives way to anger or resentment can be absolved from the imputation of madness. For he resembles a person who wishes to see clearly and for this purpose he scratches his eyes.

November 16

SMOKE SIGNALS

A certain brother, moved to anger against another brother, stood in prayer, asking for patience with his brother, that the temptation might pass him by without harm. Suddenly he saw smoke coming out of his mouth, and when this happened, his anger ceased.

ESPECIALLY BISHOPS

Numerous times Abba Theophilus the archbishop wished to take Abba Evagrius and make him bishop of Thmoui, but he would not agree to this and fled from the archbishop so he could not ordain him.

November 17

BLESSED IS THE MONK

Blessed is the monk who considers all persons as God—after God.

YOU KNOW YOUR WEAKNESS

You know your weakness. One person has one way, for another there is another way—to the cell for you!

BLOOD IN THE MOUTH

One of the old men came to see Abba Achilles and saw him spitting blood out of his mouth. He asked him, 'What's the matter, father?'

The old man said, 'Something a brother said has caused me grief; I struggled not to tell him and begged God to take it away from me and what he said became blood in my mouth. I spat it out and could breathe again, and I have forgotten what caused me the grief'.

November 18
ASSEMBLY OF THE COUNCIL OF NICAEA IN 325 (CO)
DEDICATION OF THE BASILICAS OF SAINT PETER
AND SAINT PAUL, ROME (RC)
HILDA, ABBESS OF WHITBY (A)[20]

PRAYER JOINED TO FASTING

Amma Syncletica said, 'Just as the most bitter medicine drives out poisonous creatures, so prayer joined to fasting drives evil thoughts away'.

[20] American Church calendar. November 19 elsewhere.

ACQUIRING EVERYTHING

She also said, 'Those who have endured the labors and dangers of the sea and then amass material riches, even when they have gained much, desire to gain even more and they consider what they have at present as nothing and reach out for what they have not got. We, who have nothing of that which we desire, wish to acquire everything through the fear of God'.

WE SAIL ON DARKNESS

She also said, 'Here below we are not exempt from temptations. For Scripture says, *Let the person who thinks that he stands take heed lest he fall.*[21] We sail on darkness. The psalmist calls our life a sea and the sea is either full of rocks, or very rough, or else it is calm. We are like those who sail on a calm sea, and those living in the world are like those on a rough sea. We always set our course by the sun of justice, but it can often happen that the person living in the world is saved in tempest and darkness, for he keeps watch as he ought, while we go to the bottom through negligence, although we are on a calm sea, because we have let go of the guidance of justice.'

[21] 1 Cor 10:12.

ABBA POEMEN WASHES HIS FEET

Abba Isaac came to see Abba Poemen and found him washing his feet. As he enjoyed freedom of speech with him, he said, 'How is it that others practice austerity and treat their bodies roughly?'

Abba Poemen said to him, 'We have not been taught to kill our bodies, but to kill our passions'.

WHAT MAKES A MONK?

Two brothers came to see Abba Pambo one day and the first asked him, 'Abba, I fast for two days, then I eat two loaves. Am I saving my soul, or am I going the wrong way?'

The second said, 'Abba, every day I get two pence from my manual work and I keep a little for my food and give the rest in alms. Shall I be saved or shall I be lost?'

They remained a long time questioning him and still the old man gave them no reply. After four days they had to leave and the priests comforted them, saying, 'Do not be troubled, brothers. God gives the reward. It is the old man's custom not to speak readily till God inspires him'.

So they went to see the old man and said to him, 'Abba, pray for us'.

He said to them, 'Do you want to go away?'

They said 'Yes'.

Then, giving his mind to their works and *writing on the ground*,[22] he said, 'If Pambo fasted for two days together and ate two loaves,

---

[22] See Jn 7:53-8:11.

would he become a monk that way? No. And if Pambo works to get two pence and gives them in alms, would he become a monk that way? No, not that way either'. He said to them, 'The works are good, but if you guard your conscience towards your neighbor, then you will be saved'.

They were satisfied and went away joyfully.

November 20

COMPUNCTION HAS TWO SIDES

Abba Poemen said, 'Compunction has two sides: it is a good work and a good protection'.

THE JAR OF COINS

The old men told the story about a certain gardener who labored and gave away all the fruits of his labor as alms and kept only enough to cover his expenses. But the thought insinuated itself to him, 'Gather together a few coins lest you grow old or infirm and need money for expenses', and so he gathered some coins together and filled a jar with them.

It so happened that he got ill and his foot became gangrened and he used up his coins *on doctors without it doing him any good*.[23] Finally, he went to an experienced doctor and he said to the

[23] See Mk 5:26.

gardener, 'If you don't amputate your foot, your whole body will become gangrened', so he thought it best to saw off his foot. But that night he came to himself and regretted his decision; groaning aloud, he said, 'Lord, remember the work I used to do, working and supplying the needs of the brothers!'

When he said this, an angel of the Lord stood before him and said, 'Where is the jar where you put the coins? And where is the hope that you treasured for them?'

Then he understood and said, 'I have sinned, Lord; forgive me. From now on I won't do anything like that'.

Then the angel touched his foot and it was healed at once, and he got up at dawn and went out to the field to work. So the doctor came at the appointed time with his instruments to saw off the gardener's foot and people told him, 'He went out at dawn to work in the field'. Then the doctor, astonished, went out to the field where he was working and when he saw him digging in the earth he gave glory to God who restored the gardener's health.

November 21
ENTRY OF THE THEOTOKOS INTO THE TEMPLE (O)
PRESENTATION OF THE BLESSED VIRGIN MARY (RC)

BE CONVERTED

Abba Poemen said, 'This voice cries out to a person to his last breath, "Be converted today"'.

HE WOULD SAY NO MORE

Abba Pambo was greater than many others in that if he was asked to interpret part of the Scriptures or a spiritual saying, he would not reply immediately, but he would say he did not know that saying. If he was asked again, he would say no more.

WITH ALL SAILS UNFURLED

In a parable the Lord spoke of the need for constant prayer and of the avoidance of discouragement.[24] Do not fall into despondency if at times you do not get what you ask for. Keep up your courage. It will come later. For the Lord went on to tell another parable: '*Though I have no fear of God and no respect for anyone, yet because this widow keeps bothering me, I will grant her justice*'.[25] The same thing will happen to those who cry out to God day and night—he will give them justice, and do it quickly. Take courage then, and persevere in your holy prayers with all sails unfurled.

[24] See Lk 18:1-8.
[25] Lk 18:4-5.

November 22
CECILIA, VIRGIN, MARTYR (RC, A)
C. S. LEWIS, APOLOGIST AND SPIRITUAL WRITER (A)

THIS FIELD BELONGS TO YOU

Abba Isaac, the priest of Kellia, said, I know a brother who was reaping in the field. He wanted to eat an ear of wheat and said to the field's owner, 'May I eat an ear?' When the owner heard this he was astonished and said to him, 'This field belongs to you, father, and you're asking my permission?' How conscientious the brother was!"

STEALING A CUCUMBER

It was said about Abba Zeno that he was walking in Palestine and when he got tired he sat down to eat near a cucumber-bed. This thought came to him: 'Take a cucumber for yourself and eat it; what's the big deal?' But in response he said to the thought, 'Thieves are taken away to punishment. Test yourself, therefore, to see if you can endure punishment from here on'.

So he got up and stood in the heat for five days and when he had fried himself, he said, 'I am unable to endure punishment'. So he said to his thought, 'If you are unable to endure punishment, do not steal the cucumber and eat it'.

YOUR WAY OF LIFE IS BETTER

One time Epiphanius, bishop of Cyprus, sent a message to Abba Hilarion, beseeching him, 'Come, that we may see each other before we leave the body'.

When he came, they rejoiced with one another. While they were eating, a fowl was brought to them. The bishop took it and gave it to Abba Hilarion. The old man said to him, 'Forgive me, Abba. Since I received the monastic habit I have not eaten meat'.

Epiphanius said to him, 'Since *I* received the monastic habit, I have not allowed anyone to go to sleep with something against me, nor *have I gone to sleep with something against anyone*'.[26]

The old man said to him, 'Forgive me. Your way of life is better than mine.'

November 23

IF MOSES HAD NOT

Abba Poemen said, '*If Moses had not led his sheep to Midian he would not have seen him who was in the bush*'.[27]

HAS SATAN ALWAYS DONE THIS?

A brother asked Abba Sisoës, 'Did Satan pursue people like this in the early days?'

---

[26] See Eph 4:26.
[27] See Ex 3:2-7.

447

The old man said to him, 'He does this more at the present time because his time is nearly finished and he is enraged'.

ONE WITH EVERYONE

A monk is a person who is separated from all and who is in harmony with all.

A monk is a person who considers himself one with all persons because he seems constantly to see himself in every person.

HOW WAS THE CITY?

The priest of Scetis, John the Little, went one time to the archbishop of Alexandria and when he returned to Scetis the brothers asked him, 'How was the city?'

He said to them, 'To tell the truth, brothers, I did not see anyone's face except that of the archbishop'.

When they heard this, they were amazed and were strengthened by what he had done to guard their own eyes from being distracted.

---

[28] November 25 on the RO calendar.

A MONK IN A TOMB IGNORED BY TWO DEMONS

Abba Daniel of Scetis related that a brother who was living in Egypt was walking along the road one time and, when evening overtook him, on account of the cold, went inside a tomb to sleep. Two demons were passing by and the one said to the other, 'Do you see how courageous this monk is, sleeping in a tomb? Come on, let's harass him'.

The other one replied, 'Why should we harass him? This guy is doing exactly what we want, eating and drinking and slandering and disregarding the monastic assembly. Let's ignore this guy and instead go afflict those who afflict us and who night and day wage war against us with their prayers'.

November 25
CATHERINE OF ALEXANDRIA, VIRGIN, MARTYR (RC, A)

NOT UNDERSTANDING

Abba Poemen said, 'Not understanding what has happened prevents us from going on to something better'.

THE FIRST OF ALL THE CONFLICTS

Abba Isaiah said, 'The first of all the conflicts comes with being away from home, especially while in solitude. The person who flees to another place abandons everything he calls his own, bringing with him perfect faith and hope and a heart steadfast against his own desires.

For the demons will surround and encircle you, by numerous means causing you to be fearful about temptations and grinding poverty or illnesses, whispering into your ear, "If you come to grief over things like this, what will you do when you don't have anyone who knows or cares about you?" But God's goodness will test and approve you so that your zeal and love for God may be made manifest'.

November 26
JOHN CHRYSOSTOM (CO)

TENDING THE NAME OF CHRIST

A brother asked Abba Macarius, 'Tell me the meaning of this saying, *the meditation of my heart is placed before you*'.[29]

The old man said to him, 'There is no better meditation than having this saving and blessed name of our Lord Jesus Christ continually within you, as it is written: *Like a swallow I will call and like a dove I will meditate*.[30] Thus it is with the person who worships God by tending the saving name of our Lord Jesus Christ'.

RUMINATING ON THE NAME OF CHRIST

A brother asked Abba Macarius, 'What work is best for the ascetic and the abstinent?'

[29] Ps 19:14, 49:3.
[30] Is 38:14 (LXX).

He responded and said to him, 'Blessed is the person who will be found tending the blessed name of our Lord Jesus Christ without ceasing and with contrition of heart. Of all the ascetic practices, none is better than this blessed nourishment if you ruminate on it at all times like the sheep: the sheep regurgitates and savors the sweet taste of its cud until it enters the interior of its heart and brings sweetness and good fatness to its intestines and to all its innards. Do you not see how beautiful its cheeks are, filled with the sweet cud that it ruminates in its mouth? May our Lord Jesus Christ also bless us with his sweet and rich name!'

November 27

WHY WE HAVE SO MUCH DIFFICULTY

Abba Poemen said, 'I will tell you why we have so much difficulty; it is because we do not care about our brother whom Scripture tells us to receive. Moreover, we do not remember *the woman of Canaan* who followed the Lord crying and begging for her daughter to be cured, and the Lord heard her and gave her peace'.[31]

GOD IS COMPASSIONATE

Three old men came to see Abba Sisoës, having heard about him. The first said to him, 'Father, how shall I save myself from *the river of fire?*'[32]

---

[31] See Mt 15:22.
[32] See Rev 20:14.

He did not answer him.

The second said to him, 'Father, how can I be saved from *the gnashing of teeth and the worm that will not die?*'[33]

The third said, 'Father, what shall I do, for the remembrance of *the outer darkness* is killing me?'[34]

By way of reply the old man said to them, 'For my part, I do not keep in mind the remembrance of any of these things, for God is compassionate and I hope that he will show me his mercy'.

Hearing this, the old men prepared to go back, offended. But the old man, not wishing to let them go away hurt, said to them, 'Blessed are you, my brothers. Truly, I envy you. The first speaks of the river of fire, the second of hell, and the third of darkness. Now if your spirit is filled with such remembrances, it is impossible for you to sin. What shall I do, then, I who am hard of heart and to whom it has not been granted so much as to know whether there is punishment for us? No doubt it is because of this that I am sinning all the time'.

They prostrated themselves before him and said, 'Now we have seen exactly that of which we have heard'.

November 28

ASCENDING THE LADDER

Amma Sarah said, 'I put out my foot to ascend the ladder, and I place death before my eyes before going up'.

[33] See Mt 8:12; Mk 9:48.
[34] See Mt 8:12.

ARE YOU EATING AT THIS HOUR?

There were two brothers in the cenobium who were great examples of the monastic life and each of them was considered worthy to see the grace of God upon his fellow brother. One time one of them left the cenobium on a Friday and saw someone eating early in the morning and he said to him, 'You're eating at this hour on Friday?'

The next day the synaxis took place and as was his custom the other brother gazed at the one who had left the monastery the day before and he saw that God's grace had left him and he was distressed. When he entered the cell he said to the one who had left, 'What have you done, brother? I did not see God's grace on you as I used to'.

In response the other said, 'I'm not aware that I've done any evil, either in word or in deed'.

His brother said to him, 'You didn't say something to anyone, either?'

He remembered and said, 'Yes. Yesterday I saw someone eating early in the morning and I said to him, "Are you eating at this hour on Friday?" That was my sin. But toil with me for two weeks and we will entreat God to forgive me'.

This they did and two weeks later the brother saw the grace of God once again come upon his brother and they were comforted and gave thanks to the good God.

SWEET AS HONEY IN MY MOUTH

I said to Onnophrius, 'My good and beloved father, at the beginning when you first came to this desert place, did you suffer from the weather?'

The blessed old man said to me: 'I suffered a great deal on numerous occasions from hunger and thirst and from the fiery heat outside during the day and the great frost at night. My flesh wasted away because of the dew of heaven. Now when God saw that I patiently endured in the good fight of fasting and that I devoted myself completely to ascetic practices, he had his holy angels serve me with my daily food; he gave it to me at night and strengthened my body. And the palm tree produced for me twelve bunches of dates each year, and I would eat one bunch each month.

'He also made the plants that grow in the desert sweet as honey in my mouth. For it is written, *A person shall not live by bread alone, but by every word which proceeds from the mouth of God shall a person live.*[35] If you do the will of God, he will care for you wherever you are, for he has said in the Holy Gospel: *Take no care for what you will eat or what you will drink or what you will clothe yourself with. Your father in heaven knows what you need without your asking him. Instead, seek his kingdom and his righteousness and these things will be added unto you*'.[36]

Now when I heard these things I was greatly amazed. I said to him, 'My holy father, where do you go for the Eucharist on the Sabbath and the Lord's day?'

He said to me: 'My holy father, an angel of God comes and gives me the Eucharist on the Sabbath and the Lord's day; and to everyone in the desert who lives there on account of God and

---

[35] Mt 4:4; Lk 4:4.
[36] Mt 6:31-33.

sees no human being, the angel comes and gives the Eucharist and comforts them. What's more, if they desire to see anyone, they are taken up into the heavenly places where they see all the saints and greet them, and their hearts are filled with light; they rejoice and are glad with God in these good things. Now when they are seen they are comforted and they completely forget that they have suffered. Afterwards, they return to their bodies and they continue to feel comforted for a long time. If they travel to another world through the joy which they have seen, they do not even remember that this world exists'.

When I heard these things I greatly rejoiced that I was worthy to hear them from him, and I forgot all the sufferings I had undergone while I was journeying through the mountain. The strength returned to my body and youthful vigor returned to my body and soul.

November 30
ANDREW THE APOSTLE, THE FIRST-CALLED (O, RC, A)
GREGORY THAUMATURGUS (CO)

CONTROLLING ANGER

A brother asked Abba Isidore, the priest of Scetis, 'Why are the demons so afraid of you?'

The old man said to him, 'Since I became a monk, I have practiced asceticism by not allowing anger to rise up in my throat'.

THE SUN HAS NOT SEEN ME ANGRY

Abba Cassian told about a certain Abba John, who had become superior of the monks, that he went to see Abba Arsenius, who had been living in the remotest desert for forty years. Since Abba John loved Abba Arsenius very much and, on account of this, could talk freely with him, he asked him a question: 'How have you lived a good life by living so long as an anchorite and by not being easily bothered by anyone?'

Abba Arsenius said, 'Since I have lived as a solitary, the sun has not seen me eating'.

Abba John said, 'Nor has it seen me angry'.

DECEMBER

ADVENT/CHRISTMAS/CHRISTMASTIDE

December 1
COSMAS AND DAMIAN, MARTYRS (CO)
CHARLES DE FOUCAULD, HERMIT (A)

WAIT A SECOND THERE

A brother received the monastic habit. He immediately withdrew to be by himself, saying, 'I am an anchorite'. The old men heard about it so they went to drive him out of his cell. They made him go around to the cells of the brothers, repenting and saying, 'Forgive me, I am not an anchorite but rather am a sinner and a novice'.

GLORIFYING GOD IN THE DESERT

One day, then, as Abba Bishoy sat in his cave with a divine hymn on his lips, the Saviour appeared to him, saying, 'Peace be with you, my beloved servant Bishoy'.

Bishoy got up, *filled with fear and trembling*.[1] 'Christ, my compassionate Saviour', he said, 'behold your servant'. What about me is good, Lord, when compared with your goodness? What is the reason for your condescending to come to me?'

The Lord said to him, 'Do you see this desert, in all its length and breadth? Through you I will fill it with monks glorifying my name'.

---

[1] 1 Cor 2:3, 2 Cor 7:15.

Bishoy, God's chosen, fell to the ground and said, 'All things, lord and master, are subject to your mighty hand and have their being at the same time as you will it. I entreat Your Goodness: Tell me who will provide those contending in this desert with what they need?'

He said, 'Believe me, I am telling the truth. If I find that they hold love as the mother of virtues and keep my commandments, no one will lack what he needs. I will take complete care of them'.

Then the divine Bishoy said to him, 'Once more I shall ask Your Goodness: How will they be able to avoid without difficulty the snares of the Enemy and his fearful assaults?'

The Saviour said, 'If, as I told you, they keep my commandments with humility and righteousness and a humble heart, not only will I make them immune to evil plots and the warfare that threatens them, I will also proclaim them inheritors of the eternal kingdom in the heavenly habitations'.

Having said these words, the Saviour ascended with glory into heaven while holy Bishoy from that time forward was seized with even greater fear, standing in awe of the Saviour's condescension towards him.

December 2

WHAT SHOULD I DO TO PLEASE GOD?

Someone asked Abba Antony, 'What practice should I observe in order to please God?'

The old man answered, 'Observe what I appoint for you: Wherever you go, always keep God in your sight; whatever you do, do it according to the witness of the Holy Scriptures; and wherever you settle, do not quickly move away. Observe these three things and you will be saved'.

LOOK AT THE STREET VENDOR

Some brothers asked Abba Macarius the Great, 'Are feelings of pity more important than works?'

He said to them, 'Yes'.

The brothers said to him, 'Persuade us'.

When Abba Macarius saw that they were fearful and timid, wanting to gladden them he said to them, 'Look at the street vendor who sells to a customer. He says to him, "I've given you a good deal", but if he sees that the customer is unhappy, he gives him back a little of his money and the customer goes away happy. It's the same with acts also: if they stand unhappy before God, the giver of good things, the true judge, our Lord Jesus Christ, his numerous acts of compassion move him and the acts leave with joy and rejoicing and gladness'.

December 3
FRANCIS XAVIER, PRIEST, MISSIONARY (RC, A)

OPENING THE DOOR

Another time, when the archbishop wanted to approach Arsenius, he first sent someone to see if the old man would open his door to

461

him. Arsenius sent word to him, saying, 'If you come, I will open my door to you; and if I open my door to you, I will open it to everyone, and then I will no longer live here'.

When the archbishop heard this, he said, 'If I drive him away by going to see him, I will no longer journey to see the saint'.

STAY AWAY FROM ARSENIUS

Blessed Archbishop Theophilus, in the company of a certain provincial governor, once approached Abba Arsenius. The archbishop asked Arsenius a question, wanting to hear a word from him.

After remaining silent a short while, the old man answered them, 'If I speak to you, will you heed what I say?'

They promised to heed what he told them, so the old man said to them, 'Do not go near wherever you hear Arsenius is'.

December 4
MERCURIUS, MARTYR (CO)
JOHN OF DAMASCUS, MONK, PRIEST (O, RC, A)
NICHOLAS FARRAR, DEACON (A)

THE CONFLICT OF THE HEART

Abba Antony said, 'The person who dwells in the desert and practices contemplative quiet is freed from three conflicts: those of hearing and speech and sight. He has only a single conflict: that of the heart'.

FISH HEADED FOR THE SEA

Abba Antony said, 'Just as fish die if they stay too long on dry land, monks who loiter outside their cells or spend their time with those living in the world lose the intensity of contemplative quiet. Therefore, like the fish headed for the sea, we must hasten to our cells lest in loitering outside we forget our interior watchfulness'.

ILLUMINATIONS RECEIVED IN SOLITUDE

Since Abba Bishoy was *always pushing forward to what lies ahead*,[2] he was not content with his former practices but insisted on finding other ones: to his former practice of fasting for one week he added another; fasting for two weeks, at the beginning of the third he would partake of a little bread with salt as his food. Even more remarkable is the fact that no one knew about his way of life equal to the angels except God alone, who sees what is hidden and has the unknown right before his eyes. And so his love for contemplative solitude became inexhaustible, but what he held dear seemed to be to offer prayers in solitude to God alone and to converse with him and be reconciled with the Supreme Judge and draw near to him through illuminations received in solitude.

[2] Phil 3:13.

December 5

FINDING PEACE

Abba Poemen said, 'If you take little account of yourself, you will have peace wherever you live'. He also said, 'If you are silent, you will have peace wherever you live'.

GOD'S POWER

Because no one among mortals lives without tasting death, the father of Abba Bishoy died and the care of the children fell to his most noble wife who suffered alone. Of all the children, the youngest was Bishoy and, because of his age, he gave his mother the most concern, so a kind-looking angel of the Lord appeared unexpectedly in the middle of the night. 'God, the father of orphans, has sent me', he said. 'Why do you appear so downhearted? Is it because you have to care for the children and think that you alone are responsible for all of them and God does not care about them? Do not be discouraged. Dedicate one of your sons to God Most High; through him, God's all-holy name, which is always glorified, will be glorified'.

She said, 'All my children are God's. May he take whomever is pleasing to him'.

The angel who appeared to her took Bishoy by the hand. 'This one', he said, 'pleases the Lord'.

She said, 'He is not capable of serving God; he is too young. Take one of the older ones instead, whoever is old enough'.

---

[3] Episcopal Church calendar.

The divine angel said to her, 'No, most noble of women, *God's power is accustomed to manifesting itself through the weak.*[4] This one is God's chosen; he will please God'.

Having said these words, he disappeared.

December 6

THE WAY THE FULLER CLEANS YOUR CLOTHES

Do not seek to avoid those who would give you a good drubbing. Though they kick you about and stretch you and hackle you like flax, yet after all this is the way the fuller cleans your clothes.

EATING OF THE FRUITS OF PARADISE

Abba Patermuthius was once transported physically to paradise, he said, and had seen a vast company of saints. He related how he had eaten of the fruits of paradise, and showed evidence of the fact. For he had brought his disciples a large choice fig, deliciously scented, to prove to them that what he had said was true. The priest Copres, who was telling this story, being at that time a young man, saw this fig in the hands of Patermuthius' disciples, and kissed it, and admired its scent. 'For many years', he said, 'it remained with his disciples, being kept as evidence of the father's visit to paradise. It

[4] See Lk 1:48.

465

was of enormous size. Indeed a sick person had only to smell it and he was at once cured of his illness'.

December 7
AMBROSE, BISHOP OF MILAN (O, RC, A)

TWO PAIRS OF SANDALS

Amma Theodora said, 'There was a monk who, because of the great number of his temptations, said, 'I will go away from here'.

As he was putting on his sandals, he saw another monk who was also putting on his sandals and this other monk said to him, 'Is it on my account that you are going away? Because I go before you wherever you are going'.

WING FEATHERS ON A LUMP OF WOOD

They said of Abba Pambo that his face never smiled. So one day, wishing to make him laugh, the demons stuck wing feathers on to a lump of wood and brought it in, making an uproar and saying, 'Go, go!'

When he saw them, Abba Pambo began to laugh and the demons started to say in chorus, 'Ha! Ha! Pambo has laughed!'

But in reply he said to them, 'I have not laughed, but I made fun of your powerlessness, because it takes so many of you to carry a wing'.

LET THE SHADE SUFFICE

Abba Evagrius said, 'I paid a visit to Abba Macarius at the hottest time of the day. I was burning with thirst and said to him, 'I am very thirsty, my father'.

'He said to me, "Let the shade suffice. There are numbers of people on the road right now who are burning who have no shade"'.

A MOTHER GIVES HER CHILD A SWEET

A brother asked Abba Macarius, 'My father, guide me concerning *what is sweet and what is salty*'.[6]

Abba Macarius said to him, 'They say that if the mother of a small child places the child on the ground, she puts some kind of sweet in his hand for him to lick so he won't vex his mother. The vexing can be likened to sin and pleasure while the sweet, on the other hand, represents our Lord Jesus Christ, the blessed name, the true pearl, for it is written in the Holy Gospel that *the kingdom of heaven is like a merchant who is looking for precious jewels. Therefore, when he found a valuable jewel, he went and sold what he possessed and bought it. So he gave up what he owned, his heart's desires, and wanted only the precious stone, that is, our Lord Jesus Christ, king of kings and lord of lords*'.[7]

---

[5] Not on the American calendar.
[6] Jm 3:11.
[7] Mt 13:45, 1 Tim 6:15, Rev 17:14.

YOU CAN BE SURE

Pray not to this end, that your own desires be fulfilled. You can be sure they do not fully accord with the will of God. Once you have learned to accept this point, *pray instead your will be done in me*.[8] In every matter ask him in this way for what is good and for what confers profit on your soul, for you yourself do not seek this so completely as he does.

WHAT SEEMED GOOD TO ME

Many times while I was at prayer, I would keep asking for what seemed good to me. I kept insisting on my own request, unreasonably putting pressure on the will of God. I simply would not leave it up to his Providence to arrange what he knew would turn out for my profit. Finally, when I obtained my request I became greatly chagrined at having been so stubborn about getting my own way, for in the end the matter did not turn out to be what I had fancied it would.

[8] See Mt 6:10.

THINGS CONTRARY TO NATURE

Abba Poemen said, 'God has given this way of life to Israel: to abstain from things that are contrary to nature, that is, anger, rage, envy, hatred, slander against one's brother, and the remaining vices of *the old self*'.[9]

THE WORLD

A brother asked Abba Isaiah, 'How ought I maintain contemplative quiet in my cell?'

The old man answered, 'In order to maintain contemplative quiet in your cell, you have to abandon yourself before God and do everything in your power to resist every thought sown by the Enemy. This, indeed, is what it means to flee the world'.

The brother said, 'What is the world?'

The old man answered, '"The world" is the distractions that come from *things*; "the world" is doing things that are contrary to nature and fulfilling your own fleshly desires; "the world" is thinking that you are going to remain in this present age; "the world" is having more concern for your body than for your soul and rejoicing in those things you leave behind. I have not said these things of my own accord; no, it is the apostle John who says these things: *Do not love the world or things in the world*'.[10]

---

[9] Rom 6:6.
[10] 1 Jn 2:15.

PERMEATED THROUGH AND THROUGH

A person who has established the virtues in himself and is entirely permeated with them no longer remembers the law or commandments or punishment. Rather, he says and does what excellent habit suggests.

WHAT THE WOLF CRIED OUT

It was said about Abba Macarius the Great that one time when he was working the harvest with the brothers, a wolf opened its mouth and let out a great cry, its eyes staring up to heaven to the Lord. The saint stopped and smiled with tears in his eyes.

When the brothers saw him, they were amazed. They threw themselves down at his feet, beseeching him, 'We beseech you, our father, tell us why you were staring with tears in your eyes'.

While he stared with tears in his eyes, his face shone like fire, like the rays of the sun, on account of the grace of our Lord Jesus Christ that was in him. He said to them, 'Didn't you hear what this wolf cried out?'

They said to him, 'What was that, our father?'

He said to them, 'He cried up to the lover of humanity, to the compassionate one alone, who possesses the treasuries of numerous mercies, our Lord Jesus Christ, saying, "If you are not going to care about me and provide me with my food, at least tell me why I am suffering. You were the one who created me". If even flesh-eating beasts have understanding and cry up to the goodness of our Lord Jesus Christ and he nourishes all of them, then how will he not care about us, who are rational beings, with his bountiful mercy and compassion?'

As the luminary and light-giver was saying these things to the brothers, the wolf stood with its mouth agape. Afterwards, the beast went to the place where God had prepared food for it and all the brothers prostrated themselves and venerated the holy feet of our righteous father, the Spiritbearer Abba Macarius the Great, giving glory to our Lord Jesus Christ.

December 12
OUR LADY OF GUADALUPE (RC)[11]
JANE FRANCES DE CHANTAL, RELIGIOUS (RC)

DID YOU SEE ANYTHING HERE?

A brother came to the cell of Abba Arsenius in Scetis. Waiting outside the door, he saw the old man entirely like a flame. (The brother was worthy of this sight.) When he knocked, the old man came out and saw the brother marveling. He said to him, 'Have you been knocking long? Did you see anything here?'

The other answered 'No'.

So then Arsenius talked with him and sent him away.

I DO NOT KNOW

One day some old men came to see Abba Antony. In the midst of them was Abba Joseph. Wanting to test them, the old man

---

[11] American Church calendar.

suggested a text from the Scriptures, and, beginning with the youngest, he asked them what it meant. Each gave his opinion as he was able. But to each one the old man said, 'You have not understood it'.

Last of all he said to Abba Joseph, 'How would you explain this saying?' and he replied, 'I do not know'. Then Abba Antony said, 'Indeed, Abba Joseph has found the way, for he has said "I do not know"'.

December 13
ANDREW THE APOSTLE (CO)
HERMAN OF ALASKA (RO)
LUCY, VIRGIN AND MARTYR (RC, A)

LORD, YOU SEE MY WEARINESS

It was said about Abba Macarius that one time as he was going up from Scetis to Egypt he was carrying some baskets. When he grew weary, he sat down. He raised his eyes up to heaven and said, 'Lord, it is you who see my weariness', and after he said this, he found himself at the Nile with the baskets.

ANTONY TAMES THE BEASTS IN THE DESERT

Later, when the brothers learned about the place, like children thinking of their father, they took care to send him what he needed. But Antony saw that some of them, out of their concern to bring him bread, were putting themselves to great trouble and were wearing themselves out. Wishing to spare the monks this burden, he reflected on this and asked some of those who came to see him to bring him a hoe and an ax and a little grain. Once supplied with these, he surveyed the land around the mountain. Finding a very small piece suitable for tilling, he farmed it, and having a sufficient supply of fresh water, he sowed the ground. By doing this, each year he had bread from there, rejoicing that he would not be bothering anyone about bread, and he made sure that he would not be a burden in anything.

Later, however, when he once again saw people coming to see him, he also planted a few vegetables so that those coming to visit might have a little relief from the hardships of that rugged journey. At first, however, the wild beasts in the desert would come along on account of the water and would often harm what he had planted and tilled. But Antony, with grace and dexterity, captured one of the beasts and said to all of them, 'Why do you harm me when I do you no harm? Go away, and in the name of the Lord do not come near here anymore!' From that day on, as though they were afraid because of what he had commanded, the beasts no longer came near the place.

December 14
JOHN OF THE CROSS, PRIEST, POET, AND DOCTOR (RC, A)

CLEANSING THE SOUL

The drugs that purge the body do not remain within the body of the patient. The virtues, however, cleanse the soul but yet remain in the person who has been purified.

THE TRUE AND GOOD TENT

The *true and good tent*[12] shall be the person of God who sits in it. A wise person in his cell is the true and perfect 'tent with the golden urn in it, with manna, and *Aaron's rod that budded, and the tablets of the covenant*'.[13]

MY BOOK

A certain member of what was then considered the circle of the wise once approached the just Antony and asked him: 'How do you ever manage to carry on, Father, deprived as you are of the consolation of books?'

His reply: 'My book, my dear philosopher, is the nature of created things, and it is always at hand when I wish to read the words of God'.

December 15

PARADISE REGAINED

When I had traveled some days' distance, I came upon a well of water. I sat down for a little while because I was tired and there were large trees growing by the well. When I had rested awhile

---

[12] See Heb 9:11.
[13] See Heb 9:11, 9:4.

and slept a bit, I stayed there and walked among the trees. I was amazed and thought to myself, 'Who planted these here?' There were date-palms laden with fruit, and citron and pomegranate and fig trees and apple trees and grapevines, nectarine trees and other trees that gave off a sweet fragrance. The well produced water and watered all the trees growing there.

Now while I was marveling at the trees and looking at them and their fruit, suddenly four young men appeared in the distance, handsome in their appearance. They were dressed in fine sheepskin garments which they wore wrapped around them. When they came up to me they said to me, 'Greetings, Paphnutius, our beloved brother!' I prostrated myself at their feet and greeted them, but they raised me up and embraced me. They were very much at peace and were like those who come from the other world, so much joy and comfort did they bring to me. They set about gathering fruit from the trees and they placed it in my mouth. And as for me, my heart rejoiced because of the affection they showed toward me. I spent seven days with them eating fruit from the trees.

I asked them, 'Where have you come here from and what region are you natives of?'

They said to me: 'Our brother, God has sent you to us so we can tell you about our whole manner of life, for we ourselves are natives of a city of Egypt called Pemje. Our fathers were magistrates of the city and they sent us to school to have us educated. Now we were all in school together where we were like-minded fellows. When we had finished our education in the school we were sent to college. When we had been thoroughly and well educated in all the wisdom of this world, we then wanted to be instructed in the wisdom of God. Now it happened one day when we were talking together about these things, a good inspiration stirred us to action. The four of us rose and set off into the desert so we could live in quiet contemplation until we saw what the Lord had determined for us. We took with us a few loaves of bread, enough for seven days'.[14]

---

[14] Continued on December 16.

PARADISE REGAINED[15]

The four young men continued: 'Now when we had gone some distance into the desert, an ecstatic vision suddenly came upon us: a man, wholly of light, took us by the hand and brought us here. Now when we had come to this place we found a holy man of God, and the angel of the Lord entrusted us to him and for a year of days he set about teaching us to be servants of God. When the year was finished, the holy and blessed old man died and we remained alone here. Our lord brother, we confess to you in the Lord that it has been sixty years and we have not known the taste of bread or any other kind of food except the fruit from these trees which we live on. When we wish to see each other we gather here each week to see one another. We spend the whole night of the Lord's day together and afterwards each of us goes and lives his own ascetic life'.

I said to them, 'Where do you gather for the Eucharist?'

They said to me, 'We assemble right here for that purpose, and every Sabbath an angel of God comes and gives us Communion on the Sabbath and on the Lord's day'.

Now I stayed with them and greatly rejoiced. They said to me, 'On the seventh day of the week an angel of the Lord will give Communion to us and to you together, and the person who receives Communion from the hand of that angel will be washed clean from all sin and the Adversary will in no way have power over him'.

Now while we were talking together I smelled a powerful fragrance whose like I had never smelled. As soon as the fragrance washed over us we got up and stood and praised God. Afterwards the angel came and gave us Communion together by means of the body and blood of the Lord. Now because of the fearful sight

[15] Continued from December 15.

I had seen I became like those who are asleep. The angel blessed us and ascended into heaven as we watched him with our eyes. When he had gone, they brought me to my senses and said to me, 'Be strong and resolved and be a person of determination'. Immediately I became sober-minded like those recovering from the influence of wine. And we spent the whole night of the Lord's day standing and praying until morning.

December 17
THE THREE YOUNG MEN: ANANIAS, AZARIUS AND MISAEL (O)
O SAPIENTIA / O WISDOM (RC, A)[16]

LIKE LIONS AND A MOTHER BEAR

Now then, you who are poor, you shall look boldly upon your enemies like *the roaring lions and like a bear that has had her cubs taken away from her*.[17]

NO MAN IS AN ISLAND

Abba Poemen said that Abba Theonas said, 'Even if a person acquires a virtue, God does not grant him grace for himself alone'.

He knew that he was not faithful in his own labor, but that if he went to his companion, God would be with him.

[16] The 'Great O' pre-Nativity Antiphons on the Magnificat begin today.
[17] See Prv 28:15; 2 Sam 17:8.

HOW LONG SHALL WE GO ON LIKE THIS?

Abba Paul the Barber and his brother Timothy lived in Scetis. They often used to argue. So Abba Paul said, 'How long shall we go on like this?'

Abba Timothy said to him, 'I suggest you take my side of the argument and in turn I will take your side when you oppose me'.

They spent the rest of their days in this practice.

MARY NEEDS MARTHA

A brother went to see Abba Silvanus on the mountain of Sinai. When he saw the brothers working hard he said to the old man, '*Do not labor for the food that perishes.*[18] *Mary has chosen the better part*'.[19]

The old man said to his disciple, 'Zacharias, give the brother a book and put him in a cell without anything else'.

So when the ninth hour came, the visitor watched the door, expecting someone would be sent to call him to the meal. When no one called him, he got up, went to find the old man, and said to him, 'Have the brothers not eaten today?' The old man replied that they had.

Then he said, 'Why did you not call me?'

The old man said to him, 'Because you are a spiritual person and do not need that kind of food. We, being carnal, want to eat, and

[18] Jn 6:27.
[19] Lk 10:42.

that is why we work. But you have chosen the better part and read the whole day long and you do not want to eat carnal food'.

When the brother heard these words, he made a prostration, saying, 'Forgive me, abba'.

The old man said to him, 'Mary needs Martha. It is really thanks to Martha that Mary is praised'.

December 19
O ROOT OF JESSE

DO NOT JUDGE YOURSELF

Abba Poemen said that Abba Paphnutius used to say, 'During the whole lifetime of the old men, I used to go see them twice a month, although it was a distance of twelve miles. I told them each of my thoughts and they never answered me anything but this: "Wherever you go, do not judge yourself and you will be at peace"'.

HOW SHOULD WE CONDUCT OURSELVES?

When Abba Romanus was at the point of death, his disciples gathered around him and said, 'How should we conduct ourselves?'

The old man said to them, 'I do not think I have ever told one of you to do something without having first made the decision not to get angry if what I said were not done. And so we have lived in peace all our days.'

BREAD FROM GOD

Now when I saw that it was not God's will that I remain there, I stretched out my hands and prayed to the Lord and suddenly the man who had come to me the first time and had strengthened me came to me again as he had done the first time. He said to me, 'Paphnutius, our Lord has informed me today that you were coming to us in this place. You're the first person we've seen in sixty years'. When we had spent some time talking with each other, finally they said to me, 'Brother, strengthen yourself with a little bread, for you have come a great distance. The Lord has determined that we are to remain together for a few days and we will rejoice with you, our beloved brother'.

Now while we were talking together, five loaves of bread were brought in, warm and fresh as though straight from the oven; furthermore, in quick succession other dishes were brought in. We sat down and ate together and he said to me, 'See, we have been here sixty years, and four loaves of bread have been allotted to us each day, and these came to us from God. Now since you have come to us today, look, a fifth loaf has been brought for you. We have never known where they came from, but when we come in we find them sitting here'.

When we finished eating together we spent the whole night in prayer until morning. When morning came, I entreated them to let me stay with them until the day of my death. They said to me, 'Our fellow-laborer, it has not been determined that you should stay here. Rather, rise and go to Egypt and tell those whom you see that the brethren here keep them in their thoughts, and it will profit those who listen'.

Now I entreated them to tell me their names but they refused to say them. I tried to force them, but again they would not tell me their names. They answered and said, 'The one who has given names to everything and who knows everything, he is the one who knows our names. Now, then, our brother, remember us until we see you in the house of God. Be careful that you not allow the world to deceive you as it has done to so many'.

When they finished saying these things, they blessed me and bid me farewell, and I left their mountain.

THE ROYAL PATH

Abba Benjamin said to his disciples, 'Walk on the royal path and measure off the miles'.

PILGRIMAGE

Abba Tithoës used to say, 'Pilgrimage means that a person should control his own tongue'.

JUST LIKE ANTONY

A brother asked an old man, 'What shall I do, father? Nothing I do is monastic. I'm careless and neglectful about eating and drinking and sleeping and I'm prone to disgraceful thoughts and being

481

troubled a lot. I go from one job to another and one thought to another'.

The old man said, 'Stay in your cell and do what you can without worrying about it. I think that the little bit you're doing now is just like the great works that Abba Antony used to do in the desert and I believe that whoever stays in his cell for the sake of the name of God and guards his conscience will himself also be found where Abba Antony is'.

December 22
O KING OF NATIONS

THE GRACE OF THE CELL

The angels entered Lot's house.[20]
The angel entered the house of Tobias and Tobit and his wife.[21]
He also entered the house of Manoah.[22]

Now, then, give yourself to the grace of the cell. All healing will take place for you there.

---

[20] See Gen 19:3.
[21] See Tob 5:10, 5:18.
[22] See Jdg 13.

ACCIDIE WILL WEIGH DOWN YOUR SOUL

Amma Theodora said, 'It is good to live in peace, for the wise person practices *perpetual prayer*.[23] It is truly a great thing for a virgin or a monk to live in peace, especially for the younger ones. However, you should realize that as soon as you intend to live in peace, at once evil comes and weighs down your soul through *accidie*, faintheartedness, and evil thoughts. It also attacks your body through sickness, debility, weakening of the knees, and all the members. It dissipates the strength of soul and body, so that one believes one is ill and no longer able to pray. But if we are vigilant, all these temptations fall away'.

December 23
O EMMANUEL

WHAT WOULD YOU SAY THEN?

One day when Abba John the Little was sitting in front of the church, the brothers were consulting him about their thoughts. One of the old men who saw it became a prey to jealousy and said to him, 'John, your vessel is full of poison'.

Abba John said to him, 'That is very true, abba; and you have said that when you see only the outside. But if you were able to see the inside, too, what would you say then?'[24]

---

[23] See 1 Thes 5:17.
[24] Lk 11:39, Mt 23:27.

A WONDERFUL BOOK

While Father Copres was telling us about the signs and wonders performed by Abba Patermuthius, one of our party, overcome with incredulity at what was being said, dozed off. And he saw a wonderful book lying in the father's hands, inscribed in letters of gold. And beside the father stood a white-haired man who said to him in a threatening manner, 'Are you dozing instead of listening attentively to the readings?' He immediately woke up and, in Latin, told the rest of us who were listening to Copres what he had seen.

December 24
CHRISTMAS EVE

IF

Abba Pambo said, 'If you have a heart, you can be saved'.

THE DESIRE FOR POSSESSIONS

Abba Isidore of Pelusia said, 'The desire for possessions is dangerous and terrible, knowing no satiety; it drives the soul which it controls to the heights of evil. Therefore let us vigorously drive it away from the beginning. Once it has become master it cannot be overthrown'.

THINGS

An old man said, 'Just as grass does not grow at all on a well-traveled road, even if you sow seed on the road, because the ground is trampled down, so it is with us: Live quietly, apart from *things*, and you will see plants growing that you had no knowledge of because they were within you and you were trampling them down'.

CHRIST THE COMPASSIONATE POTTER

Abba Macarius said: The potter who sits working the earth first takes care to fashion vessels decorated with colorful motifs that become honored at the morning and evening meals of emperors and are even honored by the priestly order of the Church. After making these, *he fashions other vessels that are ugly and inferior*[25] for use as chamber pots and for birthing stools for the newborn and innocent. After making these, he loads the furnace and fires them. Truly I say that just as he prays for the precious and decorated vessels, he also prays for those that are ugly and inferior because they are works of his hand.

It is the same with our Lord Jesus Christ, who possesses the treasuries of numerous mercies, who alone is compassionate with his good Father and the Holy Spirit: just as he rejoices over the person who is honored and adorned with the pure progress of virtue and abstinence, he also rejoices over the conversion of some-one who is inferior, that is, the sinner, as it is written, *There will be rejoicing in heaven in the presence of the angels of God over one sinner,*

[25] Rom 9:21, 2 Tim 2:20.

if he repents.[26] He also said, *I do not desire the death of the sinner so much as his conversion and his life.*[27] When he took on this flesh, he also willingly accepted its griefs. On account of this, our Lord Jesus Christ also says, *I have not come to invite the righteous to repentance but sinners.*[28]

December 26
STEPHEN, DEACON AND MARTYR (RC, A)

SINGING THE SANCTUS WITH THE ANGELS

It was revealed to Abba Antony in his desert that there was one who was his equal in the city. He was a doctor by profession and whatever he had beyond his needs he gave to the poor, and every day he sang the Sanctus with the angels.

GIVING YOUR LIFE FOR YOUR NEIGHBOR

Abba Poemen said, '*No one has greater love than this, to lay down one's life for one's friends.*[29] In truth, if someone hears an evil saying, that is, one that harms him, and in his turn wants to repeat it, he must fight in order not to say it. Or if someone is taken advantage of and he bears it, without retaliating at all, then he is giving his life for his neighbor'.

[26] Lk 15:7.
[27] Ezek 33:11, 1 Tim 2:4, 2 Pet 3:9.
[28] Mt 9:13.
[29] Jn 15:13.

December 27

PROTOMARTYR STEPHEN (O)

JOHN, APOSTLE AND EVANGELIST (RC, A)

GOD HAS THE POWER

Now it happened one year that some people came to Abba Aaron filled with fear. They continued to entreat him to petition Christ to send them water to save the people. They were terrified because the proper time for the rising of the waters had passed. He had compassion on them and prayed to God, saying, 'God, do not forsake the work of your hands, man and beast. For indeed you created us all from your blood and you deigned to come into the world. For our salvation you had a human birth. We know that with you nothing is impossible. God, do not forget the lives of the poor, lest they sin with their lips before you. For I remember what the wise man Solomon said, *Give me neither wealth nor poverty*.[30] Whether God causes the waters to rise or not, it is for our refreshment alone.

'The merciful person is like *the ladder that Jacob saw*: its foot was planted firmly on the earth while its top reached to heaven, and the angels of God supported it, that is to say, the Father of mercy.[31] Consider that the Lord said *these little ones*, that is to say, those who are of little account.[32] And again, as he said, *When you prepare a dinner or supper, do not invite your neighbors or your kin, but call the poor and the blind and the lame because they have nothing to offer you in exchange*.[33] Therefore, let us show mercy, for mercy allows one to triumph over judgement'.[34]

[30] Prv 30:8.
[31] See Gen 28:12.
[32] Mt 10:42, 18:6, 10, 14, etc.
[33] Lk 14:12-14.
[34] Jm 2:13.

Now when the holy man Abba Aaron had said these things, he prayed and dismissed them in peace, saying, 'God will make the river fill with water, and he will bring it up to its proper level. Do not be afraid, and do not be unbelieving. You say that the time for the rising of the water has passed. Nevertheless, believe that God has the power to do everything'. And they got up and left in peace.

Now the following evening the holy one went to the river and prayed, saying, 'Lord, you are the same yesterday, and today, and for-ever. *It was you who burst open the rock and water flowed forth and you gave it to the people to drink.*[35] Therefore, I entreat you today to send the river's water over the entire land so the poor among your people have enough food and bless you and your holy name'.

The holy man Abba Aaron spent the whole night praying and calling on God concerning the river's water. And so it was that the water rose and continued to rise, filling the river, and it did not subside for a day, until all of our fields had gotten water. And so there was abundance and plenty that year through the prayers of the holy man, as it is written, *The prayer of a righteous person is powerful and effective.*[36]

December 28
THE HOLY INNOCENTS (RC, A)

OUR BODIES ARE LIKE CLOTHING

It was said about one of the fathers that he had come from the world and was besieged by thoughts of his own wife and so he

[35] Ex 17:6
[36] Jm 5:16.

told this to the fathers. When they saw that he was a worker and that he did more than what they told him to do, they placed so many ascetic practices on him that his body was weakened and he could no longer stand up.

By the providence of God, one of the fathers, a foreigner, paid a visit to Scetis. When he came to the father's cell he saw that it was open and he walked on by, amazed that no one came out to meet him. But then he turned around and knocked, saying to himself, 'Perhaps the brother is ill'. Knocking, he went in and found the brother ill and said to him, 'What's wrong, father?'

The father explained to him, 'I am from the world and now the Enemy wages war against me with thoughts of my wife. I told the fathers and they laid various ascetic practices on me and, doing them, I became weak and the warfare increases'.

When the old man heard these things, he was saddened and said to him, 'The fathers are powerful men and did well in placing these ascetic practices on you. But if you will listen to my humble suggestion, cast off these practices and take a little food at the proper time and, performing your little synaxis, *cast your worries upon the Lord*,[37] for you are not able to accomplish this by your own labors. To be sure, our bodies are like clothing: if we take care of them, they will last, but if we neglect them, they fall into tatters'.

The father listened to him and did what he said and within a few days the warfare withdrew from him.

[37] Ps 54:23.

A WIDOW, A CORPSE, AND A DEPOSIT

Abba Sisoës said: When I was at Scetis with Macarius, we went up, seven of us, to bring in the harvest. Now a widow cried out behind us and would not stop weeping. So the old man called the owner of the field and said to him, 'What is the matter with the woman that she goes on weeping?'

'It is because her husband received a deposit in trust from someone and he died suddenly without saying where he had hidden it, and the owner of the deposit wants to take her and her children and make slaves of them'.

The old man said to him, 'Tell her to come to us when we take our mid-day rest'.

The woman came, and the old man said to her, 'Why are you weeping all the time like this?'

She replied, 'My husband, who had received a deposit on trust from someone, has died and when he died he did not say where he had put it'.

The old man said to her, 'Come, show me where you have buried him'.

Taking the brothers with him, he went with her. When they had come to the place, the old man asked the dead man, 'So and so, where have you put the deposit?'

The corpse replied, 'It is hidden in the house, at the foot of the bed'.

The old man said, 'Rest again, until the day of resurrection'.

When the brothers saw this, they were filled with fear and threw themselves at his feet. But the old man said to them, 'It is not for my sake that this has happened, for I am nothing, but it is because of the widow and the orphans that God has performed this miracle.[38] This is what is remarkable, that God wants the soul to be without sin and grants it all it asks'.

He went to tell the widow where the deposit was. Taking it, she returned it to its owner and thus freed her children. All who heard this story gave glory to God.

December 30

IF TEMPTATION HAPPENS UPON YOU

The fathers used to say, 'If temptation happens upon you in the place where you are living, do not leave the place where temptation has come to you; otherwise, wherever you go, you will find there right in front of you what you are fleeing. Instead, be patient until the temptation passes so that your departure causes no one scandal and so your withdrawal from the community does not cause any hardship for those who live there.'

A FLASK OF WINE FOR A NEIGHBOR

When Abba Poemen went one time into Egypt to live, he happened to have as his neighbor a brother who had a wife. The old man knew about it and never reproached him. One night the woman happened to give birth and when the old man learned about it he summoned his youngest brother and said, 'Take with you a flask of wine and give it to our neighbor; he has need of it today'. (The brothers did not know why he was doing this.)

---

[38] Jm 1:27.

The brother did as the old man had ordered him and the married brother benefitted from this action and was moved to compunction; a few days later he left his wife, having provided her with whatever she might need, and went and spoke to the old man, 'From today on I am a penitent, father'. And he went and lived by himself in a cell near the old man and went to see him very frequently and the old man illuminated for him the way to God and gained him for the Lord.

December 31
MELANIA OF ROME, ASCETIC (O)
SYLVESTER, POPE (RC)
JOHN WYCLIF, REFORMER (A)

DO NOT SPEAK EVIL OF ANYONE

A brother questioned Abba Hierax, saying, 'Give me a word. How can I be saved?'

The old man said to him, 'Sit in your cell. If you are hungry, eat; if you are thirsty, drink. Only do not speak evil of anyone, and you will be saved'.

GUARD YOUR CONSCIENCE

A brother asked Abba Joseph, saying, 'What should I do? I do not have the strength to bear evil, nor to work for charity's sake.'

The old man said to him, 'If you cannot do any of these things, at least guard your conscience from all evil with regard to your neighbor and you will be saved'.

APPENDIX:

HOLY DAYS

ASH WEDNESDAY

PALM SUNDAY

HOLY WEEK

MAUNDY THURSDAY

GOOD FRIDAY

EASTER

PENTECOST

Ash Wednesday

BREAD AND ASHES

It was said of Abba Isaac that he ate the ashes from the incense offering with his bread.

DEAD TO THE WORLD

Abba Cassian said: There was a monk living in a cave in the desert. His relations according to the flesh let him know, 'Your father is very ill, at the point of death. Come and receive his inheritance'.

He replied to them, 'I died to the world before he did and the dead do not inherit from the living'.

FLEE FROM PEOPLE

Abba Isaiah questioned Abba Macarius, saying, 'Give me a word'.

The old man said to him, 'Flee from people'.

Abba Isaiah said to him, 'What does it mean to flee from people?'

The old man said, 'It means to sit in your cell and weep for your sins'.

Palm Sunday

SHORT AND SIMPLE

Abba Paul said, 'Keep close to Jesus'.

BREAD AND CHEESE

One time a magistrate came to visit Abba Simon. The clergy went on ahead and said to the old man, 'Abba, get ready. The magistrate has heard of you and is coming for your blessing'.

So he said, 'Yes, I will prepare myself'. Then he put on a rough habit and, taking some bread and cheese in his hands, went and sat in the doorway to eat it.

When the magistrate arrived with his retinue and saw him, he despised him and said, 'Is this the anchorite of whom we have heard so much?' And they went away at once.

Monday in Holy Week

EVEN IF I WERE ASHES THROWN TO THE WIND

Abba Poemen used to say this about Abba Isidore: Every night he plaited a bundle of palms and the brothers pleaded with him, saying, 'Rest a little, for you are getting old'.

But he said to them, 'Even if Isidore were burned, and his ashes thrown to the winds, I would not allow myself any relaxation because the Son of God came here for our sake'.

MACARIUS, THE THIEF, AND THE RECALCITRANT CAMEL

They said of Abba Macarius that a thief went into his cell when he was away. Macarius went back to his cell and found the thief loading his things onto a camel. So Macarius went into the cell, picked up his things, and helped him load them onto the camel. When the loading was finished, the thief began to beat the camel to make it get up, but in vain. Seeing that it did not get up, Abba Macarius went inside his cell, found a small hoe there, picked it up, and put it onto the camel, saying, 'Brother, the camel wants to have this'.

Then the old man kicked it, saying, 'Get up'. At once the camel got up and went forward a little because of his command. Then it lay down again and refused to get up until it was completely unloaded; and then it set off.

Tuesday in Holy Week

AS FOR ME

A brother went to Abba Matoës and said to him, 'How is it that the monks of Scetis did more than the Scriptures required in loving their enemies more than themselves?'

Abba Matoës said to him, 'As for me, I have not yet managed to love those who love me as much as I love myself'.

A TORN CLOAK

A soldier asked Abba Mius if God accepted repentance.

After the old man had taught him many things, he said to the soldier, 'Tell me, my dear, if your cloak is torn do you throw it away?'

The soldier replied, 'No. I mend it and use it again'.

The old man said to him, 'If you are so careful about your cloak, will not God be equally careful about his creature?'

Wednesday in Holy Week

TAKING UP THE CROSS

Abba Nilus said, '*Go, sell all that belongs to you and give it to the poor*[1] and, *taking up the cross*,[2] deny yourself; in this way you will be able to pray without distraction'.

[1] Mk 10:21.
[2] See Lk 14:27.

THE DOG AND THE HARE

An old man was asked how the zealous monk should not have his feelings hurt if he sees others turning back to the world and he said, 'It's profitable to observe dogs as they chase after hares: when one of them sees the hare he gives chase; the others see only the dog giving chase and run after him for a while but finally turn back to where they were. Only the dog that saw the hare keeps up the chase until he catches it: he is not deterred from pursuing his objective by the dogs that turned back nor does he worry about cliffs or woods or thistles; even when he's in the middle of thorns and is getting all scraped up, he does not stop. It's the same with whoever is seeking Christ our master: that person focuses unceasingly on the cross, leaping over every obstacle that gets in his way until he reaches the Crucified'.

Thursday in Holy Week
Maundy Thursday / Holy Thursday

WASHING THE FEET OF EVILDOERS

It was said of Abba John the Persian that when some evildoers came to him, he took a basin and wanted to wash their feet. But they were filled with confusion, and began to do penance.

WASHING CHRIST'S FEET

One time, while Abba Bishoy was praying in his cave, the Saviour visited him with two angels, *as he had the patriarch Abraham*,[3] and said, 'Greetings, Bishoy! Today we will be enjoying your hospitality if you oblige and welcome us'.

Bishoy eagerly welcomed them, emulating the hospitality of that patriarch. He did not busy himself with food and drink, however, but rather possessed a pure disposition. So he welcomed the Omnipresent One; then, putting water in a basin, *he washed your undefiled feet in imitation of you*.[4] It happened this way: Bishoy eagerly busied himself with showing hospitality while the Lord, demonstrating his love for humankind, accepted his hospitality. (Nothing that a person does in offering hospitality shows more kindness and forbearance than to wash the feet of those who come to visit.)

'*Peace be with you, my chosen one*',[5] said the Saviour, and then he disappeared.

Good Friday

I WISH I COULD WEEP LIKE THAT

Abba Joseph related that Abba Isaac said, 'I was sitting with Abba Poemen one day and I saw him in ecstasy. I was on terms of great

[3] See Gen 18.
[4] See Jn 13:1-11.
[5] See Jn 14:27.

freedom of speech with him so I prostrated myself before him and begged him, saying, 'Tell me where you were'.

He was forced to answer and he said, 'My thought was with Saint Mary, the Mother of God, as she wept by the cross of the Saviour. I wish I could always weep like that'.

CARRYING CHRIST'S CROSS

Pachomius went with his brother to an island to cut rushes for mats. And as he was keeping vigil alone, praying to be taught *the whole will of God*,[6] an angel appeared to him from the Lord, just *as one appeared to Manoah and his wife about the birth of Samson*.[7] The angel said to him, 'The will of God is to minister to the human race in order to reconcile them to himself'. He said this three times and went away.

Pachomius thought about the voice he had heard and was re-assured. Then he began to receive those who came to him. After appropriately testing them and their parents, he clothed them in the monks' habit. He introduced them to the life gradually. First, they had to *renounce all the world, their parents, and themselves, and follow the Saviour who taught doing so*,[8] for this is *to carry the Cross*.[9] Being well taught by him according to the Scriptures, *they bore fruits worthy of their vocation*.[10]

[6] Rom 12:2.
[7] Jdg 13:3-11.
[8] Lk 14:26-27, 33.
[9] Lk 14:27.
[10] Eph 4:1.

LAYING A NEW FOUNDATION

Abba Moses asked Abba Silvanus, 'Can a person lay a new foundation every day?'

The old man said, 'If he works hard, he can lay a new foundation at every moment'.

I HEARD THE VOICES OF ANGELS SINGING HYMNS

Abba Onnophrius said, 'Now go to Egypt, my son, and persevere in the good work'.

I immediately fell to the ground and said to him, 'Bless me, my father, that I may stand before God and as I have been worthy to see you on earth so may I be worthy to see you in the other world before the Lord Jesus Christ'.

He said to me, 'My son, may God not cause you to grieve about anything and may he strengthen you in his love, so that your eyes may see the light of his divinity, that you neither turn away nor fall but succeed in the work which you have undertaken. May the angels shelter you and deliver you and may no accusation fall on you when you come to meet God'.

When he had finished saying these things, he rose and prayed to God with sighs and many tears. Afterwards he lay down on the ground and completed his stewardship of God, and he gave up his spirit[11] into the hands of God on the sixteenth of Paone. And I heard the voices of angels singing hymns before the blessed Abba Onnophrius and there was great gladness when he came to meet God.

---

[11] Mt 27:50.

Now I took off the cloak I was wearing and tore it in two: the one piece was for a burial shroud and with the other piece I covered myself so I would not stay naked. When I set his body down in a cleft in the rock, I heard the voices of a multitude of angels rejoicing and crying out, 'Alleluia!' I said my prayer over him and I rolled several stones over him. I stood up and prayed a second time and immediately the palm tree that had fed Abba Onnophrius fell down. Now I was greatly amazed at what had happened. I ate what was left of the bread and I drank the water that we had left.

Easter Sunday

SEEK AND DO NOT SEEK

Abba Sisoës said, 'Seek God, and do not seek where he dwells'.

A CHRISTIAN

An old man said, 'A Christian is one who imitates Christ'.

BLESSED BE CHRIST!

Blessed be Christ who gives you the victory![12]

[12] See 1 Cor 15:57.

UNTIL THE SUN SHONE

It was said about Abba Arsenius that on Saturday evenings, preparing for the glory of Sunday, he would turn his back on the sun and stretch out his hands in prayer towards the heavens till once again the sun shone on his face. Then he would sit down.

Pentecost

FERVENT IN THE SPIRIT

Abba Macarius the Great said, 'It is fitting that the monk be purified from every passion of the flesh and every stain and that he not allow his thoughts to commingle with evil thoughts at all; instead, he should *be fervent in the Spirit at all times*'.[13]

A BASKET WITH THREE HANDLES

A certain old man, living in a village near the borders of Egypt, fell because of ignorance. He asserted that the duality of the Holy Trinity should be worshipped, that is, the Father and the Son, but that the Spirit should not be called 'God'. A large number followed him in thinking this way. God, however, did not want the old man's ascetic labor and sweat to be vainly squandered so he revealed the

[13] Rom 12:11.

504

old man's ideas to the divine Bishoy, as well as showing him the region and location where the old man lived.

Bishoy immediately got up and made a number of large baskets with three handles. He went to see that man and, when he found him, pretended to be a stranger. Many of the simpler people there shared the old man's wicked opinion. When those with him saw the three-handled baskets, not knowing who Bishoy was or where he was from, they were utterly astonished and had no idea how the baskets had been made. They asked him what they were and what he wanted to do with them.

'I want to sell them', he said.

'And why', they then asked, 'did you make them with three handles?'

'Because I am a friend and lover of the supremely holy Trinity', he said, 'it is incumbent upon me to represent through my work the persons of the Trinity and to praise the Trinity in a three-fold fashion by making these three signs representing it. That one Nature expresses itself in three Persons. If someone understands this differently, he does not think correctly and should not hold such an opinion. Each basket has one nature with three *hypostases*, for in each of the three handles the entire essence of each basket manifests itself equally. In this way, then, the immaterial Nature and superessential Godhead is manifested in three forms or persons— the Father with the Son and the Holy Spirit—and the whole essence abides in each. Concerning the three, neither more nor less is spoken of, seeing that one does not claim to be greater in nature than another.'

TRANSLATORS AND CONTRIBUTORS

APOSTOLOS N. ATHANASSAKIS is James and Sarah Argyropoulos Chair in Hellenic Studies and has taught at the University of California in Santa Barbara for nearly four decades. He has translated Hesiod, the Homeric Hymns, and the Orphic Hymns, and has done extensive work in the field of classical linguistics. For many years, he has collaborated with Tim Vivian to produce translations of the early Desert Fathers.

JOHN EUDES BAMBERGER OCSO is the retired abbot of Our Lady of the Genessee Abbey in upstate New York. A medical doctor, he did his psychiatric residency at Georgetown University. For many years he has lectured on the Fathers of the Church and monastic spirituality in various monasteries, especially of the Cistercian-Trappist Order in Asia, Africa, Latin America, and Europe. In active retirement, he serves as editor of *Cistercian Studies Quarterly* while living as a hermit at the abbey.

JOHN CHRYSSAVGIS studied in Athens and Oxford. Having taught in Sydney and Boston, he currently serves as theological advisor to the Ecumenical Patriarch on environmental issues. His recent publications include *In the Heart of the Desert, Letters from the Desert, John Climacus: From the Egyptian Desert to the Sinaite Mountain, The Reflections of Abba Zosimas,* and *Barsanuphius and John: Letters.* He lives with his family in Brunswick, Maine.

STEPHEN EMMEL has been Professor of Coptology at the University of Münster (Germany) since 1996. He began his career in the 1970s as a member of the international team that conserved and published the Nag Hammadi Codices in the Coptic Museum in Cairo. He earned his Ph.D. in Religious Studies at Yale University in 1993 with a dissertation on the Coptic monastic leader and author Shenoute. He has been active in the International Association for Coptic Studies since its foundation in

1976, serving as Secretary since 2000. His numerous publications include *Shenoute's Literary Corpus*.

AELRED GLIDDEN OSB entered Saint Gregory's Abbey in 1975 and made his solemn profession six years later. Appointed Novice Master in 1982, he became prior in 1989, and was ordained to the priesthood in 1992. He has published an article on the historical work of his patron, Aelred of Rievaulx, and is the author of 'Abbot Primate, Benedictine' in the *Encyclopedia of Monasticism*.

MAGED S.A. MIKHAIL is Assistant Professor of History at California State University, Fullerton. He specializes in the Late Roman Empire and the Early Islamic Caliphate. He has published 'On Cana of Galilee: A Sermon by Patriarch Benjamin I', *Coptic Church Review* 23.3 (2002) 66-93, and 'Some Observations Concerning Edibles in Late Antique and Early Islamic Egypt', *Byzantion: Revue Internationale des Études Byzantines* 70 (2000) 105-121.

BIRGER A. PEARSON, Professor Emeritus of Religious Studies, University of California, Santa Barbara, holds a Ph.D. from Harvard (1968) and a Teol. Dr. *h.c.* from Uppsala (2002). He is the author of *Ancient Gnosticism: Traditions and Literature* (2007), and *Gnosticism and Christianity in Roman and Coptic Egypt*.

LUKE (ROBERT, PACHOMIOS) PENKETT, an Orthodox priest, is a solitary hieromonk of the Monastère Sainte-Présence, Brittany. He lectures internationally and has published works on the Desert Fathers and Orthodox Spirituality.

NORMAN RUSSELL is an independent scholar and translator. He is the author of *The Doctrine of Deification in the Greek Patristic Tradition* (2004) and has translated several works by the contemporary Greek theologians and philosophers, Christos Yannaras and Stelios Ramfos.

ARMAND VEILLEUX OCSO has served as abbot of Notre-Dame de Mistassini in his native Canada; of Holy Spirit Abbey, Conyers, Georgia; and currently of Notre-Dame de Scourmont in Belgium. His work on *La liturgie dans le cénobitisme pachômien* and his translations of all documents relating to the life and tradition of Pachomius have vastly enhanced our knowledge of this fourth-century cenobite.

TIM VIVIAN is an Assistant Professor of Religious Studies at California State University, Bakersfield. He is the author of numerous books and articles on early Christian monasticism, including *The Life of Antony* (with Apostolos N. Athanassakis) and *Words to Live By: Journeys in Ancient and Modern Egyptian Monasticism* (both Cistercian Publications).

BENEDICTA WARD SLG is a Reader in the History of Spirituality at Oxford University and a member of the Sisters of the Love of God, a contemplative Anglican religious community. Her studies and translations of work in both the British and the desert traditions have introduced many readers to these two very different but complementary spiritualities.

GLOSSARY

*Words followed by an asterisk
are cross-referenced in the Glossary.*

A

Abba
The aramaic word for 'father' used by Jesus and Paul in the New Testament (Mk 14:36, Rom 8:15, Gal 4:6), transferred as a title of respect to respected or venerated monks. See Amma.★ See Apa.★

Abbess
The assistant to the Superior of a women's monastery.

Abbot
From 'abba',★ the head of a monastery.

Acedia/Accidie
Greek *akêdia*, the Latin *acedia*, 'the noonday demon', spiritual torpor, listlessness. See Evagrius of Pontus, 'The Noonday Demon', at April 20 and Amma Theodora's saying on December 22.

Adversary, the
Satan, the Devil.

Agape
Greek: 'love'. The word was used in the early Church for a communal meal, often combined with or following Communion. In early monasticism the term also refers to such a meal, often on Saturday, when the anchoritic★ and semi-anchoritic★ monks would leave their cells and gather in a central location.

Amente	The coptic term for Hell.
Amma	'Mother'; used of venerable female monks. See Abba.★
Anchorite	From the greek verb *anachōrein*, 'to withdraw'. Anchorites were monks who lived by themselves or with only a disciple or two.
Apa	The aramaic word for 'father' used by Jesus and Paul in the New Testament (Mk 14:36, Rom 8:15, Gal 4:6), transferred as a title of respect to respected or venerated monks. See Amma.★ See Abba.★
Apatheia	From the greek word *pathos*, meaning 'incident, accident, change', then 'calamity', 'disease', then 'emotion, passion'. *Apatheia* literally means to be 'without passion', a much-desired state. Passions:★ For the monks, disordered desires that distract a person (literally 'draw [him] away from') from following God. See 'Apatheia' at November 10.
Apollo	Apollo was born around 305, and lived most of the fourth century. His monastic activity centered around Hermopolis Magna★ in the Thebaid★ (Shmoun; al-Ashmunein in the Middle Sa'id) between modern-day al-Minya and Asyut (Lycopolis). According to *Historia Monachorum* 8.2, 'when he was eighty years old he established on his own a great monastery of five hundred perfect men' at Bawit, about fifteen miles south of Hermopolis (which is mentioned in this story).
Apophthegmata Patrum	*The Sayings of the [Desert] Fathers [and Mothers].*
Apostle, the	The Apostle Paul, a common designation for Paul in early and medieval Christianity.
Arabia of Egypt	This phrase probably indicates the 'arabian desert', that is, the desert places east of the Nile; the western desert was called the 'libyan desert'.

Archimandrite	The archimandrite (a term still in use) is the head of a monastery or, by extension, a senior celibate priest. See hegumenos.
Arsenius, Abba	Arsenius lived from approximately 360 to 449. He had been tutor to the princes Arcadius and Honorius but in 394 came to Scetis* and lived in the community of Abba John the Little.*
Artaba	Coptic *ertob* comes from the Persian by way of Greek *artabê*, a measure ranging from 24 to 42 *choinikes*, roughly equivalent to english quarts. A *choinix* of grain was considered one person's daily allowance.
Ascesis/ascetic	Literally in Greek 'training, exercise', a term from athletics adopted by monks to mean 'spiritual training, regimen'.
Athanasius	Lived about 296 to 373. Archbishop of Alexandria and author of the *Life of Antony*.
Aswan	A city in the south of Egypt, the capital of the Aswan Governorate. It stands on the east bank of the Nile at the first cataract.

Β

Barbarians	Nomadic tribes from the west (the libyan desert) invaded Scetis* a number of times in the fifth and sixth centuries. The first invasion took place in 407–408.
Basil (the Great)	Lived roughly 330 to 379. Bishop of Caesarea in Asia Minor (now Turkey), theologian and ascetic writer.
Bishoy, Abba	Also Pshoi in Coptic and Paesius in Greek. A fourth-century egyptian monk who gathered a community around him in Scetis.*
Black man	See Ethiopian(s).*
Blessed	Greek *makarios*, often used to pun on Macarius'* name.

Bread	Hard, dry bread would be kept for long periods of time and moistened for eating; see *Life of Antony* 12.4.
Brother	In monastic parlance, a 'brother' was a monastic, not a familial, brother; a fellow-monk.
Brothers, Spiritual	'Spiritual brothers', *agapētoi*, were the male companions of *subintroductae*, female village ascetics who shared living accommodations with male ascetics.★
Brought to shore	'Brought' in 'brought to shore' is *esōthē*, literally 'was saved'.

C

Cannibals	See D. R. MacDonald, ed., *The Acts of Andrew and Matthias in the City of the Cannibals* (Atlanta: Scholars Press, 1990).
Cappadocian Fathers	Designation for Basil the Great★, Gregory of Nazianzus★, and Gregory of Nyssa★.
Cassian, Abba	Cassian (lived *c.* 360 to 435) visited Egypt in the late fourth century and later wrote two great monastic books, the *Institutes* and *Conferences*, describing monastic life to Latin readers by drawing on his experience in Egypt.
Cell	A monastic dwelling, either of one room or two rooms. In the latter, the back room was used for prayer and sleep and the front room for work and greeting visitors.
Cells, the	See Kellia.★
Cenobium	A greek word for a monastic community where the male or female monks lived together under an abbot★ and a Rule,★ as distinct from anchorites★ and semi-anchorites★.
Children in Ephesus	In his translation of *Qur'an*, Surah 18:25 ('The Cave'), Ahmed Ali includes a note: 'There is also

the famous cave near Ephesus in Turkey known as the Cave of Seven Sleepers where, it is said, seven Christians slept two hundred years to escape persecution by the Romans'. On the Seven Sleepers of Ephesus, see the on-line article in the 1910 *Catholic Encyclopedia*: <http://www. newadvent.org/cathen/05496a.htm>.

Citizen

Coptic/Greek: *politeutēs*. *Politeia*, 'citizenship', came also to mean a monastic 'way of life'.

Confidence

'Complete confidence' translates the Greek *parrēsia*, an important virtue in the New Testament—especially in John and Paul— which passed into monasticism.

Constans

Roman Emperor 323-350.

Constantine

'The Great'. Became emperor in 312 and died in 337. He legalized Christianity in the Roman Empire.

Constantius

Constantius II, Roman Emperor from 324 to 361.

Contemplation

In Greek *theōria*, literally 'seeing', 'beholding'. The higher level of ascetic* practice, gained through *hesychia*, 'contemplative silence', 'quiet contemplation'; meditation whose goal is union with God.

D

Daniel, Abba

A sixth-century monk and hegoumen,* monastic leader, of Scetis.*

Deceitful One

Satan, the Devil.

Diocletian

Roman Emperor from 284 to 305. He instituted the last great persecution of the Church, especially virulent in Egypt.

Domitius

See Maximus.*

513

Duke	Latin *dux*: in the fourth century a roman military commander in frontier areas.

E

Eating early	The usual meal time for anchorites★ and semi-anchorites★ was the ninth hour, about mid-afternoon.
Edified	The verb meaning 'to be edified' and 'to build' is the same in Greek: *oikodomein*.
Egypt	In monastic parlance, the 'civilized' places away from Scetis,★ that is, Alexandria or Babylon (Old Cairo) or other settled areas.
Eighth hour	About 2 PM.
Enaton	The Enaton, or Ennaton, nine miles west of Alexandria, was one of the most famous monastic settlements of the sixth and seventh centuries; it was a collection of monasteries, hermitages, and churches, rather than a single monastery.
Enemy, the	Satan.
Epiphanius	Bishop of Salamis on Cyprus, who lived *c.* 315 to 403. A writer against heresy and supporter of monasticism.
Ethiopian(s)	The belief that the Devil and demons took the form of Ethiopians was common in early monastic literature; as Lucien Regnault points out, 'the form that they seem to have especially effected was that of male or female Ethiopians, whose swarthy color evoked the blackness of malice'. For references, see Tim Vivian and Apostolos N. Athanassakis, trans., *The Life of Antony* 6.1 (Kalamazoo: Cistercian Publications, 2005) and n. 49 (p. 71).
Evagrius	Evagrius (346 to 399) came to Egypt, to Nitria★ and Kellia,★ in 382 and lived there until his death. The first great monastic theologian.

514

F

Father

A spiritual father. The term also hearkens back to the father-son advice in the Wisdom literature of the Hebrew Bible.

Foster father

Tropheus, translated here as 'foster father', was used of Christ. For Clement of Alexandria, the Logos is both mother and father and instructor and foster father. The word could also designate someone who gave money to the poor, which may also be its meaning here.

Fourth hour

About 10 AM.

G

Gate of the Sun

The 'Gate of the Sun' was the eastern gate of the walled city of Alexandria. No trace of it remains, but the location can be established with some degree of certainty. The Gate of the Sun was believed by pre-Christians to be 'guarded' by the Sun divinity. Evidently most travellers from Egypt to Alexandria entered through the Gate of the Sun, which was built by Antoninus Pius (AD 138-161) and marked the formal boundary of the fortified city. The Sun Gate stood near a quarter filled with hostels and accommodations for travellers and also functioned, not surprisingly, as the 'red light' district. A church was established by the gate dedicated to Saint Metras, an alexandrian martyr who was dragged out of the city and stoned during the reign of Decius (249-251)

Gregory of Nazianzus

One of the 'Cappadocian Fathers'★ (along with Basil the Great★ and Gregory of Nazianzus★), he lived from 329 to 389 and was briefly bishop of Constantinople.

Gregory of Nyssa

Lived from about 330 to 395. One of the 'Cappadocian Fathers'.

H

Habit

Monastic clothing, often given as a sign of entrance into the monastic life. Cassian details its symbolic meaning in *Institutes* 1.1

Hegoumen(os)

From Greek *hēgoumenos*, 'ruler' or 'leader'. The head of a monastery. See also Archimandrite.

Hermopolis Magna

Modern el-Ashmunein, on the west bank of the Nile in the Thebaid, between al-Minya and Asyut (the greek Lycopolis).

Hesychast

From Greek *hēsychia*, 'silence, quiet, stillness, tranquility', an important monastic term meaning interior stillness, contemplative peace. A hesychast was one who practiced hēsychia.

Hour, this

The normal time for eating was the ninth hour, about 3 PM., but could be later on Friday or put off until the synaxis★ on Saturday.

Hypostasis
(pl.: *hypostases*)

A concrete manifestation of an abstract reality: being, substance, reality. For its many nuances, with patristic citations, see Lampe,★ 1454-1461.

I

Inner Cell

Many monastic dwellings consisted of two rooms: a front room for work and receiving guests and a back room for prayer and sleep.

Isaiah of Scetis

Died 491. A monk of Scetis★ who later moved to Gaza. The author of the *Ascetic Discourses*.

J

Jani

Sa el-Hagar in modern Egypt.

Jeremiah

The Monastery of Abba Jeremiah. Marie Drew-Bear, *Le nome Hermopolite: Toponymes et sites* (American Studies in Papyrology 21; Missoula, Montana: Scholars Press, 1979) 132, identifies two monasteries dedicated to Apa Jeremiah, one south of Antinoë, and the other, the monastery for women, which she believes had no connection with the other.

John, Abba	Abba John the Little, a famous fourth-century monk of Scetis.★ Sometime around 407 he fled barbarian incursion into Scetis and went to Klysma (Suez).
Justin	Justin became emperor in AD 518 and ruled until 527, when he was succeeded by Justinian I★.
Justinian I	Roman Emperor from 527 to 565.

K

Kellia	Kellia (Cells) was a monastic settlement about eighteen kilometers south of Nitria.
Keration	A small coin.
Klysma	Suez.
Kosack	Wolfgang Kosack, *Historisches Kartenwerk Ägyptens*. Bonn, 1971.

L

Lampe	W. G. H. Lampe, ed., A *Patristic Greek Lexicon* (Oxford: Clarendon, 1961).
Laura (lavra)	A semi-anchoritic★ community, like that of Kellia,★ where the monks lived apart in individual cells and gathered together on Saturdays and Sundays for communal meals, instruction, and liturgies. The term was used in Palestine rather than in Egypt, one sign that the *Apophthegmata* were assembled in the former locale. From Greek *laura*, 'path, lane'.
Leave	A circumlocution or euphemism for 'die'.
Listlessness	See *Acedia*.★

517

Longinus	A well-known monk of the Enaton,★ a monastic community at the ninth milestone west of Alexandria.
LXX	Septuagint; Greek translation of the Hebrew Bible/Old Testament.

ᴍ

Macarius of Alexandria	A fourth-century monk especially associated with Nitria.★
Macarius the Great (Macarius of Scetis/ Macarius of Egypt)	In this volume 'Macarius' indicates Macarius of Egypt. He lived from about 300 to 399 and was one of the great monastic leaders and founders of Scetis.★
Maximus & Domitius	Two anonymous young men who came to Scetis★ and lived in the settlement of Macarius the Great.★ Later coptic tradition conflated them with Maximus and Domitius, sons of the emperor.
Matins	The Office★ recited during the darkness of the night. Also called Vigils or Nocturns.
Meditation	Coptic/Greek *meletē* meant to meditate on Scripture, that is, to quietly utter with one's lips the words of Scripture, most commonly the Psalms.
Melania	Melania the Elder (*c.* 342 to 410) journeyed to Egypt and eventually co-founded (with Jerome) a double monastery (for men and women) on the Mount of Olives.
Menas	An egyptian martyr of the third to fourth centuries whose story was apparently combined with that of a christian soldier killed under Diocletian.★ A famous pilgrimage center southwest of Alexandria grew up at his reputed birthplace.
Metanoia	Literally: 'repentance'. A *metanoia* at this period was probably an act of prostration. See Repentance.★

Moses, Abba	Called Moses 'the Black' because he was from Ethiopia. He was a robber who repented and became a monk, eventually a priest, and great monastic leader of Scetis.★
Mother	See Amma.★
Mother Archimandrite	The head of a monastery for women, the superior.
Movement(s)	In his first letter, Antony speaks of the soul's movements; see Samuel Rubenson, *The Letters of St. Antony: Monasticism and the Making of a Saint* (Minneapolis: Fortress, 1995) 197-202.
Mountain	In monastic parlance, 'mountain' (Coptic *toou* and Greek *oros*) signifies a place away from the fertile and inhabited Nile flood plain.
Mysteries, holy	Communion, the Eucharist.

N

Ninth hour	The ancients reckoned the beginning of each day at sun-up, roughly 6 AM., depending on the time of the year. The ninth hour, then, was approximately 3 PM, mid-afternoon and the usual time for the one daily meal.
Ninth milestone	See Enaton.★
Nitria	A famous monastic settlement northwest of Scetis.★
Nome	An administrative division of Egypt.
Noumia	The greek word *noumion* (plural: *noumia*) is an adaptation of the latin word *nummus* (plural: *nummi*), generally 'a piece of money, coin, money' or, more specifically, a roman silver coin, the *sestercius*.
Nubians	Those of (black) african descent who lived in upper (southern) Egypt and Nubia.

O

Office
An 'office' (latin: *officium*, occupation) indicates a prayer service at a set time during the day, whether recited by the monks individually or together in community. The 'Divine Office' refers to the series of daily services.

Oktokaidekaton
The monastic settlement eighteen miles east of Alexandria.

Old man
An old, or at least an experienced monk, a spiritual advisor. A term of great respect.

Oxyrhynchus
Coptic Pemje, el-Bahnasa in modern Egypt, a city in Upper Egypt, located about one hundred sixty kilometres south-southwest of Cairo, in the governorate of Al-Minya. An important monastic area in Late Antiquity.

P

Pachomius
Lived from *c.* 290 to 346. Great monastic leader in Upper (southern) Egypt and founder of cenobitic★ monasticism.

Palamon
An anchorite★ who trained Pachomius★ after the latter's conversion.

Pambo, Abba
Pambo (*c.* 303–373) was an early monk of Nitria.

Paone
The tenth coptic month, June 8 to July 7 (Gregorian).

Paphnutius
Coptic: *pa-pnoute*, 'he of God'. In *Alphabetical Apophthegmata*★ Macarius 28 and 37, Paphnutius is described as 'the disciple of Abba Macarius'. In the *Life of Macarius of Scetis* 36, he is described as 'the holy man Abba Paphnutius, who was the greatest of the saint's disciples. It was he who assumed the fatherhood in the holy places after Abba Macarius'. There were a number of known monks named Paphnutius, including the Paphnutius to whom the *Life of Onnophrius* is attributed.

Paraclete	From the greek verb *parakalein* meaning both 'to comfort' and 'to exhort'; used in Jn 14:26 of the Holy Spirit, the 'Advocate', 'Comforter'.
Passion/s	The monks considered 'passions' to be disordered desires that distract a person (literally 'draw [him] away') from following God. The word should not be equated with the modern English 'passion', as in 'a passion for' or 'a passionate kiss'. See *apatheia*.★
Paul of Tamma	A middle egyptian monk of the fourth-fifth centuries who wrote a number of works (see Abbreviations/Sources in this volume).
Pelusia	Or Pelusium, a city in the eastern Nile delta.
Pemje	Oxyrhynchus.★
Pempton	A monastic settlement at the fifth milestone west of Alexandria.
Perfected	To have died, with the theological and spiritual meaning of having reached the conclusion of a christian life.
Pernouj	Nitria.★
Philae	Philae or Pilak (Egyptian: 'remote place or the end or the angle island') or Arabic *Anas el Wagud*, an island in the Nile River and the previous site of an ancient egyptian temple complex in southern Egypt. The complex is now located on the nearby island of Agilika.
Philoponoi	Literally, 'those who love hard work'; *philoponoi* were laymen with particular duties in the Church.
Philosophy	The use of 'philosophy' to designate the monastic life is common in early monastic literature.
Poemen, Abba	A famous monk of Scetis★ in the fourth-fifth centuries and around whose name gathered

numerous sayings collected in the *Apophtheg-mata Patrum*★ or *Sayings of the [Desert] Fathers.*

Poor

Coptic: *pebiēn. Ebiēn* can mean either 'poor' or 'wretched', literally or metaphorically, and can be the equivalent of the Greek *penēs, ptōchos,* or *talaipōros.* 'O wretch' or 'you wretch' in English does not quite fit, although *ebiēn* may suggest that the monk is wretched in the eyes of the world, and thus the term may be a self-designation. In Paul of Tamma, *On the Cell* 69, the monk is the one who 'withdraws' (*anachōri*); he is 'poor and wretched'—and 'blessed', a son of God'; in Paul of Tamma, *On the Cell* 97, 'poor man' seems to be a synonym for 'monk'. See 2 Cor 8:9, where Paul calls Christ 'poor'.

Pope

The term 'pope' (from 'papa', 'father') was originally—and is still— used for the bishop of Alexandria.

Poverty

In Greek 'poverty' (*aktēmosunē*) and 'possessed' (*ekektēto*) are related etymologically (*ktaomai*); 'poverty' is literally 'lack of possessions'. In monastic parlance, it almost always means voluntary poverty. See poor.★

Practical

In evagrian thought, *praktikos* 'starts from acute observation of the psychology of the solitary, the vices which threaten him, [and] the ascesis★ that purifies his heart and thoughts' (J. Gribomont, *Encyclopedia of the Early Church* s.v. EVAGRIUS of Pontus, I.306a).

Precentor

On this official, who had important duties in the monastery, see Cyril of Scythopolis, *Life of Sabas* 43, and John Moschus, *The Spiritual Meadow* 50.

Prefect

Various kinds of roman officials. A prefect's office, department, or area of control was called a prefecture.

Procurator	Procurators were agents of the emperor in the civil administration and were posted to minor roman provinces such as Judea.
Prophecy	In the *Life of Bishoy* IX (February 13), 'prophecy' refers to the book of the prophet Jeremiah, not to a particular prophecy by the seer; for this use of the word, see Lampe,★ 1193A (III).
Prophets, Two Great	Isaiah and Jeremiah.
Prostration	See *Metanoia*.★

R

Repentance	Probably prostrations, elsewhere called *metanoias*,★ literally 'repentances'. This egyptian practice appears to have traveled to Syria. John of Ephesus, in his 'Lives of Thomas and Stephen' (*Lives of the Eastern Saints* 13, *Patrologia Orientalis* 18.204), describes one act of penance this way: 'During every [interval], he would make thirty Egyptian metunâyê [*metanoiai*] which are called prayers, until he accomplished five hundred during the night with the service of matins, and these I myself on many nights secretly counted'.
Resurrection, Church of	*Hagian Anastasin.* The late-antique pilgrim Egeria many times in her diary mentions the *Anastasis*, which was part of Constantine's Basilica of the Holy Sepulcher in Jerusalem. As one of her modern editors notes, 'Moving from west to east, we find first the Anastasis, or sanctuary of the Resurrection, a church in the round, in the center of which was the grotto of the Holy Sepulchre' where, in Daniel's vision, the young man is sitting on the stone. See George E. Gingras, trans., *Egeria: Diary of a Pilgrimage*, Ancient Christian Writers, 38 (New York: Newman, 1970) 24.
Right, on your	The 'Instructions of Saint Pachomius' 56 declare to the monk that 'demons come to you from the

right, while to all other men they clearly come from the left'. See Armand Veilleux, trans., *Pachomian Koinonia* (Kalamazoo: Cistercian, 1982) 3:39. See also Zech 3:1 where Satan stands at Joshua's right hand in order 'to accuse him'.

Rule   The monastic Rule, or governing ordinances of a monastic community or monastery.

S

Sanctus   A hymn of adoration beginning 'Holy, Holy, Holy'.

Scetis   The Wadi al-Natrun has been the site of continuous monastic life for over 1600 years. Its ancient name, Scetis, comes from the Coptic *shi hêt*, 'to weigh the heart', a very appropriate name for a place long dedicated to silence, prayer, and contemplation. The Wadi itself has a well-watered strip of oases about 20-25 miles long that runs in a northwesterly direction. Its southeast end is about forty miles northwest of Cairo.

Semi-anchorites   Monks who lived alone during the week but gathered with others for a meeting on Saturday and church on Sunday.

Shmoun   Egyptian Khemenu; Hermopolis Magna★ of the Greeks and the Ashmunen of the Arabs.

Signal   At a monastery a signal (the *krouma*, or *krousma*) was given by striking metal or wood to call the monks together for the divine office [see office★] or some other occasion.

Sister   The feminine equivalent of brother.★ A spiritual sister, a fellow (female) monastic.

Solidus/pl. *Solidi*   A roman gold coin introduced by Constantine★ in 309–310 to replace the *aureus* as the main gold coin of the Roman Empire. The name *solidus* had previously been used by Diocletian★

(284–305) for the gold coin that he introduced, which is different from the *solidus* introduced by Constantine. The coin was struck at a theoretical value of 1/72 of a roman pound (about 4.5 grams). *Solidi* were wider and thinner than the *aureus*. Interestingly, the word *soldier* is ultimately derived from *solidus*, referring to the *solidi* with which soldiers were paid.

Son
: A spiritual son. The term also hearkens back to the father-son advice in the Wisdom literature of the Hebrew Bible.

Stillness
: Greek *hesychia*,★ contemplative quiet, outer and inner silence and peace.

Saint Mark's Outside-the-City
: The church associated with the *martyrium* of Saint Mark the Evangelist in Boukolou (Baucalis). By the third century the city had shrunk, and the church had become a suburban one.

Steward
: The monk in a monastery or monastic settlement who was in charge of business matters.

Synaxis
: Either the weekly meeting of semi-anchorites★ on Saturday-Sunday, or a meeting in general.

Syncletica, Amma
: Almost nothing is known of Amma Syncletica, a female monk of the fourth-fifth centuries. According to the *Coptic Encyclopedia* (2192a-2192b), 'the little' that may be known about Syncletica 'is furnished by a *Vita sanctae Syncleticae* [*Life of Saint Syncletica*], that at a late date was arbitrarily attributed to Athanasius of Alexandria'.★ The few biographical details are stereotypically hagiographical and it is impossible to determine if any are historical. 'The most important part of the *Vita* reports the teaching that she gave to the virgins who came to visit her or, as it seems, lived beside her. The alphabetical *Apophthegmata Patrum*★ has eighteen apothegms under her name, all of them extracts from the *Vita*. If we are to accord any historical value

to the *Vita*, Syncletica would have lived in the fourth century.'

T

Tartarus

In classical greek mythology, Tartarus is either a deep, gloomy place, a pit or abyss used as a dungeon of torment and suffering that resides within Hades or the entire underworld with Hades being the hellish component. In Plato's *Gorgias*, souls are judged after death and those who received punishment are sent to Tartarus. In 2 Pet 2:4, 'God did not hold back from punishing the angels that sinned, but, by throwing them into Tartarus, delivered them into pits of dense darkness to be reserved for judgement'.

Tashenthosh

A monastery in the eastern Nile delta; see Wolfgang Kosack, *Historisches Kartenwerk Ägyptens* (Bonn: Rudolf Habelt, 1971) 90, and in that same volume, 'Karte des koptischen Ägypten' 6C (grid number).

Tempter, the

Satan, the Devil.

Tetrapylōn

The Tetrapylon, attested only in christian sources from late antiquity, was evidently an arched structure located in the center of Alexandria. No trace of it remains. See Christopher Haas, *Alexandria in Late Antiquity: Topography and Social Conflict* (Johns Hopkins, 1997) 193 and 368, note 27. The city of Aphrodisias had a sixteen-columned tetrapylon.

Thebaid

The division of Egypt into two parts, Lower and Upper Egypt, goes back to pharaonic antiquity. The Sa'id, Upper Egypt, may be divided into (a) the lower Sa'id (or Lower Thebaid), from Cairo to al-Bahnasa (Oxyrhynchus); (b) the middle Sa'id (or Thebaid), from al-Bahnasa to Akhmim; and (c) the Upper Sa'id (or Upper Thebaid), from Akhmim to Aswan (*Coptic Encyclopedia*: 2080a-2080b).

Thebes	A great egyptian city, it was located about eight hundred kilometres south of the Mediterranean, on the east bank of the Nile. Thebes was the capital of Waset, the fourth upper egyptian nome.*
Theophilus	Archbishop of Alexandria, AD 385-412.
Timothy	Archbishop of Alexandria from 381-85.
Tremissis	A small gold coin worth one third of the *aureus*. The *keration*★ was another small coin. According to John Moschus, *Spiritual Meadow* 184, twenty-four *keratia* equaled one *tremissis*.

Virtues	The Virtues were an important spiritual concept to the early monks. They tried to cultivate them in themselves and in others. The Virtues were sometimes grouped together: *Pistis* (Faith), *Elpis* (Hope), *Agapē* (Love) and *Parthenia* (Virginity), *Thbbio* (Humility), *Tbbo* (Chastity), *Mntrmrash* (Gentleness), *Gratia* (Grace), *Hypomonē* (Patience), and *Sophia* (Wisdom).

Wadi	In Egypt a strip of land amid the arid desert with a good water supply and water table.
Wicked One	The context seems to suggest that the Devil is being referred to. 'Wicked' (*pethoou*), which is lacking in the Septuagint, is singular and thus probably refers to Satan.
World, the	As Abba Isaiah says, '"The world" is the distractions that come from *things*'. See his long definitions under March 10 and December 10 ('The World'). See also 'The Fruits of the Spirit' at June 2.

ABBREVIATIONS, SOURCES, & BIBLIOGRAPHY

[DS] Daniel of Scetis   *Witness to Holiness:Abba Daniel of Scetis*, ed.Tim Vivian. Kalamazoo: Cistercian Publications, 2008.

[H] Hyperechius   *Exhortation to the Monks*, trans. Tim Vivian (unpublished).

[IS] Isaiah of Scetis   *Isaiah of Scetis:Ascetic Discourses*, trans.John Chryssavgis & Pachomios (Robert) Penkett. Kalamazoo: Cistercian Publications, 2002.

[LA] Life of Antony   *The Life of Antony*, trans.Tim Vivian & Apostolos N.Athanassakis. Kalamazoo: Cistercian Publications, 2003.

[LB] Life of Bishoy   Unpublished. Translated by Tim Vivian from the text edited by I. V. Pomialovskii, *Zhitie prepodobnogo Paisiia Velikogo i Timofeia Patriarkha Alexandriiskogo* [*The Life of the Blessed Paisios and Timothy, Patriarch of Alexandria*], *Zapiski istoriko-filologicheskogo fakul'teta SPb U* [*Journal of the Historical-Philological Department of Saint Petersburg University*], 2 [3?], vol. 50 (1902) 1-61.

[LDF] The Lives of the Desert Fathers   *The Lives of the Desert Fathers: The* Historia Monachorum in Aegypto, trans. Norman Russell. Oxford: Mowbray–Kalamazoo: Cistercian Publications, 1981.

[LE] Life of Evagrius   *Four Desert Fathers: Pambo, Evagrius, Macarius of Egypt, and Macarius of Alexandria. Coptic Texts Re-*

lating to the Lausiac History of Palladius, trans. Tim Vivian. Crestwood, New York: Saint Vladimir's Seminary Press, 2004.

[LJL] Life of John the Little — Maged S. A. Mikhail and Tim Vivian, 'Life of Saint John the Little', *Coptic Church Review* 18:1 & 2 (Spring/Summer, 1997) 1-64.

[LL] Life of Longinus — *Words to Live By: Journeys in Ancient and Modern Monasticism*, trans. Tim Vivian. Kalamazoo: Cistercian Publications, 2005.

[LM] Life of Macrina — 'Life of Macrina', trans. Joan M. Petersen, in Joan M. Petersen, ed., *Handmaids of the Lord: Holy Women in Late Antiquity and The Early Middle Ages*. Kalamazoo: Cistercian Publications, 1996.

[LMA] Life of Macarius of Alexandria — *Four Desert Fathers: Pambo, Evagrius, Macarius of Egypt, and Macarius of Alexandria. Coptic Texts Relating to the Lausiac History of Palladius*, trans. Tim Vivian. Crestwood, New York: Saint Vladimir's Seminary Press, 2004.

[LMG] Life of Macarius the Great — *Four Desert Fathers: Pambo, Evagrius, Macarius of Egypt, and Macarius of Alexandria. Coptic Texts Relating to the Lausiac History of Palladius*, trans. Tim Vivian. Crestwood, New York: Saint Vladimir's Seminary Press, 2004.

[LMS] Life of Macarius of Scetis — *Saint Macarius the Spiritbearer: Coptic Texts Relating to Saint Macarius the Great*, trans. Tim Vivian. Crestwood, New York: Saint Vladimir's Seminary Press, 2004.

[LMD] Life of Maximus & Domitius — Tim Vivian, 'The Bohairic Life of Maximus and Domitius', *Coptic Church Review* 26: 2 & 3 (2005) 34-63.

[LO] Life of Onnophrius — *Paphnutius: Histories of the Monks of Upper Egypt and the Life of Onnophrius*, trans. Tim Vivian. Kalamazoo: Cistercian Publications, 1993.

[LP] Life of Pambo — *Journeying into God: Seven Early Monastic Lives*, trans. Tim Vivian. Minneapolis: Fortress Press, 1996.

[LPN] Life of Pambo of Nitria	*Four Desert Fathers: Pambo, Evagrius, Macarius of Egypt, and Macarius of Alexandria. Coptic Texts Relating to the Lausiac History of Palladius,* trans. Tim Vivian. Crestwood, New York: Saint Vladimir's Seminary Press, 2004.
[LPT] Life of Paul of Tamma	*Words to Live By: Journeys in Ancient and Modern Monasticism,* trans. Tim Vivian. Kalamazoo: Cistercian Publications, 2005.
[MVC] *Le manuscrit de la version Copte*	*Le manuscrit de la version Copte en dialecte sahidique des 'Apophthegmata Patrum',* ed M. Chaîne. Cairo: Imprimerie de l'institut français d'archéologie orientale, 1960. Trans. Tim Vivian (unpublished)
[PBL] Bohairic Life of Pachomius	*Pachomian Koinonia 1: The Life of Saint Pachomius and His Disciples,* trans. Armand Veilleux. Kalamazoo: Cistercian Publications, 1980. Pp. 23-295.
[PGL] First Greek Life of Pachomius	*Pachomian Koinonia 1: The Life of Saint Pachomius and His Disciples,* trans. Armand Veilleux. Kalamazoo: Cistercian Publications, 1980. Pp. 297-423.
[PH] Paphnutius, Histories	*Paphnutius: Histories of the Monks of Upper Egypt and the Life of Onnophrius,* trans. Tim Vivian. Kalamazoo: Cistercian Publications, 1993.
[PLO] Paphnutius, Life of Onnophrius	*Paphnutius: Histories of the Monks of Upper Egypt and the Life of Onnophrius,* trans. Tim Vivian. Kalamazoo: Cistercian Publications, 1993.
[PTC] Paul of Tamma: On the Cell	*Words to Live By: Journeys in Ancient and Modern Monasticism,* trans. Tim Vivian. Kalamazoo: Cistercian Publications, 2005.
[PTE] Paul of Tamma: Letter (Epistle)	*Words to Live By: Journeys in Ancient and Modern Monasticism,* trans. Tim Vivian. Kalamazoo: Cistercian Publications, 2005.
[PTH] Paul of Tamma: On Humility	*Words to Live By: Journeys in Ancient and Modern Monasticism,* trans. Tim Vivian. Kalamazoo: Cistercian Publications, 2005.

[PTL] Paul of Tamma: Life	*Words to Live By: Journeys in Ancient and Modern Monasticism*, trans. Tim Vivian. Kalamazoo: Cistercian Publications, 2005.
[PTP] Paul of Tamma: On Poverty	*Words to Live By: Journeys in Ancient and Modern Monasticism*, trans. Tim Vivian. Kalamazoo: Cistercian Publications, 2005.
[SDF] Sayings of the Desert Fathers	*The Sayings of the Desert Fathers*, trans. Benedicta Ward. Kalamazoo: Cistercian Publications, 1975.
[SM] Sayings of Macarius	*Saint Macarius the Spiritbearer: Coptic Texts Relating to Saint Macarius the* Great, trans. Tim Vivian. Crestwood, New York: Saint Vladimir's Seminary Press, 2004.
[SA] Systematic Apophthegmata	Tim Vivian and Apostolos N. Athanassakis, 'On Perfection: Chapter One of the Greek Systematic Apophthegmata', *Hallel* 26:2 (2001) 98-107; 'Serving the Lord: Chapter Six of the Greek Systematic Apophthegmata, "Concerning Voluntary Poverty"', *American Benedictine Review* 53:2 (June 2002) 193-209; 'Spiritual Direction from the Early Monastic Mothers and Fathers on Observing a Holy Lent: Chapter Three of the Greek *Systematic Apophthegmata*, "On Compunction"', *Sewanee Theological Review* 44:1 (Christmas 2000) 60-78.
[VM] Virtues of Macarius	*Saint Macarius the Spiritbearer: Coptic Texts Relating to Saint Macarius the* Great, trans. Tim Vivian. Crestwood: St. Vladimir's Seminary Press, 2004.
[WLB] Words to Live By	'Words to Live By', in *Words to Live By: Journeys in Ancient and Modern Monasticism*, trans. Tim Vivian. Kalamazoo: Cistercian Publications, 2005.

SOURCES

29 SDF Syncletica 10; SDF Syncletica 14
30 PTC 94; PTC 33

MAY
1 LJL 26; VM 19
2 SM 2; SA VII.40
3 LJL 35; VM 20
4 SA IV.52; SA IV.47
5 VM 16; LA 3.5-7
6 LA 5:1-7
7 SDF Antony 4; LDF I.13, 18-21
8 SDF Simon 1; LE 24
9 SA VIII.2; LA 84.1-6
10 SA V.13; SA V.14
11 SA II.8; VM 82
12 SDF Poemen 61; VM 61
13 SDF Antony 25; LPN 8
14 LMA 2
15 SDF Theodora 10; SDF Elias 7
16 SA I.27; DS I.2
17 SDF Poemen 27; SDF Poemen 155
18 PTC 39; SDF Arsenius 39
19 SA VI.3; SA VII.51
20 P 119-122
21 SDF Evagrius 5; EPP 35; SDF Poemen 156
22 PGL 4-6
23 SDF Isaiah 6; SDF Isaiah 5
24 SDF Antony 1; LJL 48
25 VM 17; MG 8
26 SA I.2; SDF Macarius the Great 3
27 SDF Poemen 132; VM 14
28 SA IV.59; SA IV.60; LE 14
29 SA VI.28; SDF John the Dwarf 1
30 SA IX.21; SDF Poemen 67
31 SDF Macarius the Great 36; SDF Joseph of Panephysis 7

JUNE
1 LB XLI
2 SDF Arsenius 4

3 PTC 25-26; LMS 26; SDF Macarius 19
4 PTC 30; EPCP 20; SA IX.23
5 SA IV.97; SA V.32
6 SDF Antony 9; SDF Poemen 28; WLB 31
7 SDF Antony 19; LA 16:1-7
8 SM 28; LJL 49
9 PTC 33; SA V.16
10 SA VIII.7; LMA 10
11 SA II.12; SA II.11
12 SA II.6; P 123
13 SA IX.11; LDF I.32-35
14 VM 67; VM 37
15 LA 55.4-11
16 SDF Poemen 105; LA 17:1-7
17 EPCP 22; PTC 44-45; SDF Poemen 148
18 SDF Poemen 157; SDF Poemen 158; EPP 14
19 SA VIII.31; SA IV.100
20 SDF Poemen 160; SDF Sarmatas 1; SDF Poemen 159
21 LE 28
22 PTC 47-49; SDF Pambo 3
23 PLO 11
24 SDF Poemen 106; PTC 76-77
25 SA VI.16; SA VII.11
26 SA VII.52
27 SDF Pambo 6; SDF Sisoës 1
28 SDF Poemen 69; LA 60.1-3, 10-11
29 SDF Sisoës 6; SA IV.101
30 SDF Isidore of Pelusia 1; SDF Joseph of Panephysis 11

JULY
1 PTC 51-55; SDF Moses 2; SDF Moses 3
2 SA IV.35; SM 31
3 LMA 11
4 SDF Antony 31; LA 81
5 SA IX.1; SA IX.12

535

14 VM 77; IS 8
15 SDF Poemen 94; SDF
   Euprepius 2
16 PTC 34-35; WLB 27
17 SDF Syncletica 16; SDF
   Syncletica 24; EPP 48
18 P 109-115
19 P 109-115
20 PTC 91; LA 20.1-9
21 WLB 28; SA IX.14
22 SDF Poemen 96; SA VII.7
23 SA VIII.17; LJL 60
24 SDF John the Dwarf 25; SA
   VII.58
25 VM 45; EPCP 43; SA VII.6
26 SA IV.69; SA IV.70
27 LMA 23
28 SA VIII.22; SA VIII.23
29 PTC 100-102; Macarius the
   Great 18
30 LB XIV-XV

OCTOBER
1 PTL 3; SM 26
2 IS 8(87); SA VIII.24; SA VIII.25
3 SDF Daniel 5; LMA 8
4 PTC 1; SA IX.20
5 WLB 19; SA VI.4
6 VM 7; VM 71
7 PH 47-49
8 PTC 6; LDF I.22-28 (Rufinus)
9 DS I.5
10 SA IX.15; SA VIII.6
11 EPCP 60; SM 13
12 SDF Antony 37; VM 69
13 SDF Tithoës 3; SA II.32; SDF
   Arenius 29
14 SDF Poemen 97; WLB 21
15 SDF Syncletica 14; SDF
   Syncletica 9
16 PTC 20; PTC 45; EPCP 44-45
17 PTL
18 PTC 7; LE 17

19 SA VI.24; SA VII.37
20 PTC 12; SDF Poemen 124
21 SDF Poemen 85; LPN 10
22 SDF Matoës 13; SM 11
23 LB XVI-XVIII
24 PTC 9; VM 55
25 PTC 95; EPP 65; P 16
26 SDF Macarius of Alexandria 2;
   SDF Nisterus 5
27 SA IX.19; P 103-104
28 SA IX.3; LPN 12
29 SDF Isidore of Pelusia 2; SA
   VII.6
30 LJL 24; LJL 25
31 SDF Olympius 2; SDF John the
   Dwarf 18

NOVEMBER
1 LJL 53; PTP 5-9
2 LMD
3 PTC 112-117; SA IV.1
4 VM 41; VM 42
5 PGL 6; MVC 78; SA VIII.27
6 SA IX.8; LDF I.22-28 (Rufinus)
7 SA VIII.15; SA IX.23
8 SDF Moses 11; SA VI.19
9 LJL 64
10 PTC 7-8; EPP 67
11 SDF Poemen 82; LPN 2
12 SA VI.14; SA VII.15
13 SDF Elias 5; SDF Isaac, Priest of
   the Cells; SDF Macarius 19
14 SDF Theodore of Pherme 8;
   EPP 49
15 SDF Poemen 177; SDF Poemen
   175; EPCP 64
16 SA IV.65; LE 19
17 EPCP 123; PTC 65; SA IV.9
18 SDF Syncletica 3; SDF
   Syncletica 10; SDF Syncletica
   25
19 SDF Poemen 184; SDF Poemen
   2

20 SDF Poemen 39; SA VI.25
21 SDF Poemen 192; SDF Poemen 9; EPCP 88
22 SA IV.22; SA IV.17; SA IV.15
23 SDF Poemen 195; SDF Sisoës 11; EPCP 124-125
24 SA IV.66; DS II.1
25 SDF Poemen 200; SA VII.8
26 VM 35; VM 34
27 SDF Poemen 204; SDF Sisoës 19
28 SA Sarah 6; SA IX.18
29 LO 16-18
30 SA IV.24; SA IV.26

DECEMBER
1 MVC 70; LB XIII
2 SA I.1; VM 25
3 SA II.7; SA II.6
4 SA II.2; SA II.1; LB X
5 SDF Poemen 81, SDF Poemen 84; LB III
6 EPCP 140; LDF X.21-22
7 SDF Theodora 7; SDF Pambo 13
8 VM 78; VM 12
9 EPCP 31; EPCP 32
10 SA IV.61; SA I.21; SA II.15
11 EPP 70; VM 36

12 SDF Arsenius 27; SDF Antony 17
13 VM 81; LA 50.4-9
14 EPP 85; PTC 67-68; EPP 92
15 LO 28-30
16 LO 31-33
17 PTC 23; SDF Poemen 151
18 SDF Paul the Barber 1; SDF Silvanus 5
19 SDF Paphnutius 3; SDF Romanus 1
20 LO 25-27
21 SA VII.5; SDF Tithoës 2; SA VII.41
22 PTC 57-58; SDF Theodora 3
23 SDF John the Dwarf 8; LDF X.26-27
24 SDF Pambo 10; SDF Isidore of Pelusia 6
25 SA II.33; VM 38
26 SDF Antony 24; SDF Poemen 116
27 P 132-135
28 SA V.45
29 SDF Macarius the Great 7
30 SA VII.39; SA IX.20
31 SDF Hierax 1; Joseph of Panephysis 4

HOLY DAYS

Ash Wednesday	SDF Isaac, Priest of the Cells; SDF Cassian 8; SDF Macarius the Great 27
Palm Sunday	SDF Paul the Great 4; SDF Simon 2
Monday in Holy Week	SDF Isidore the Priest 5; SDF Macarius the Great 40
Tuesday in Holy Week	SDF Matoës 5; SDF Mius 3
Wednesday in Holy Week	SDF Nilus 4; SA VII.42
Thursday in Holy Week	SDF John the Persian 3; LB LXIX
Good Friday	SDF Poemen 144; PGL 23-24
Holy Saturday	SDF Silvanus 11; LO 21-24
Easter Sunday	SDF Sisoës 40; SA I.37; PTC 99; SDF Arsenius 30
Pentecost	VM 56; LB XLI

WORD INDEX

A

Aaron, Abba 123, 210-211, 241,
 272-273, 302-303, 321,
 364-366, 411-412, 487-488
abba 8, 27, 38, 42, 46, 49, 55, 68, 84,
 102, 105, 132, 135, 166, 176-177,
 181-182, 202, 215, 222-223, 234,
 257-259, 266, 272, 283, 294,
 309-310, 323, 332, 335, 348, 376,
 417, 425, 442, 447, 479, 483, 496,
 509-511, 513, 519, 521
Abraham Abba 60
Adam 25, 49, 152, 382, 425
afflict 132, 327, 449
affliction 80, 92, 118, 214, 216, 267,
 308, 341-342
Agathon, Abba 79, 117, 223, 385
Alexandria 12, 34, 44, 52, 54, 80, 84,
 86, 166, 181, 190, 204, 237, 258,
 267, 277, 285-286, 300-301, 308,
 345, 374-375, 383, 410, 413,
 448-449, 464, 511, 514-515, 518,
 520-522, 525-530, 536
Alexandrian 140-141, 345, 374
alms 55, 172, 176, 259, 276, 287, 299,
 320, 323, 442-443
altar 265, 309, 335
Amma 166, 509-510, 519, 525
Ammoës, Abba 383
Ammonas, Abba 18, 117, 298, 300,
 369
Amoi, Abba 415

Amoun 121, 260
Anatolius 405
anchorite 24, 27, 29, 150-151,
 167-168, 197, 231, 254-255,
 295, 298-299, 358, 375-376,
 429, 456, 459, 496, 510, 512,
 514, 520
Andronicus, Abba 390, 391
angels 7, 17, 37, 64-65, 74, 88, 99,
 100, 113-114, 129, 136, 145,
 162, 208, 211, 216, 251-252,
 255, 288, 308, 315-316, 323,
 328, 369, 376, 378, 383, 409,
 413, 444, 455, 463-464,
 476-477, 482, 486, 500-501, 526
angels of God 42, 485, 487
 angels singing hymns 502
Anoub, Abba 79, 170
Antony, Abba 37, 39, 40, 50-51,
 53-54, 56, 67-68, 87, 109, 113,
 129, 143, 149, 175, 196, 198,
 203, 218, 234-235, 244, 246,
 269-270, 292, 314, 367,
 394-395, 424, 460, 462-463,
 471-472, 482, 486
apatheia 433, 510, 521
Apollo, Abba 75-77
apparitions 130, 314-315
archbishop 75, 80, 86, 129, 196, 207,
 237, 240, 277, 301, 360,
 374-375, 437, 439, 448,
 461-462, 511, 532

549

SCRIPTURE INDEX

HEBREW BIBLE

LXX = the Septuagint, the Greek translation of the Hebrew Bible/Old Testament

2 KINGS

10:10	194
17:23	284

EZRA

28:2	195

JOB

40:16 LXX	195
40:26	426
42	202
42:5	120

PSALMS

2:11	100
19:14	450
22	288
23:2	288
24:18 LXX	120
25:18	120
27:1	423
37:11	247
38:2 LXX	434
38:18	111
39:14	288
45:12	118
49:3	450
50:10 LXX	120
51:3	150
51:8	120
54:23	489
90:10	236
96:10	282
119:103	255
124:8	426
141:2	288

PROVERBS

3:6	423
4:23	341
20:26 LXX	209
25:8 LXX	272

28:15	477
29:23	120
30:8 LXX	128, 487

ECCLESIASTES (QOHELET)

2:18-19	247
4:7-8	247
6:1-2	247

SONG OF SOLOMON

1:7	288
1:41	141
2:3	326

ISAIAH

1:17	302
5:8	365
6:5	120
10:15	170
14:4	195
38:14 LXX	450
40:1	53
40:3	368
40:12	45
40:31 LXX	255
41:10	119
48:21	255
58	83
66:2	120, 397
66:24	195

EZEKIEL

3:3	255
33:11	111, 163

DANIEL

3	139
6:5-6	54
33:11	153

MICAH

2:2	365

APOCRYPHA/DEUTEROCANONICAL BOOKS

TOBIT		SIRACH [ECCLESIASTICUS]	
5:10	482	4:6	120
5:18	482	5:14	230
		6:6	53
JUDITH		6:15	307
6:17	195	7:17	195
		11:1	120
		42:20	291

NEW TESTAMENT

MATTHEW		9:2	202
3:3	368, 423	9:6	288
3:11	415	9:9-10	422
4:4	454	9:13	486
4:9	315	10:9	273
4:10	315	10:10	128
4:19	315	10:23	82
5:4	341	10:37	193
5:5	247	10:38	409
5:7	365	10:42	487
5:9	33, 388	11:11	254
5:21-22	272	11:12	409
5:27-28	272, 392	11:28	211
5:31-32	272	11:29	247
5:38-39	272	12:31-32	201
5:43-44	272	12:15	432
6:3	119	12:33	229
6:5	392	12:36	233
6:10	468	12:37	276
6:14	365	13:14	37
6:31-33	454	13:31	192
6:34	52	13:45	467
7:1	144, 151, 392	14:13	432
7:7	317	16:23	315
7:18	229	17:20	192, 201
7:24	190	18:6	487
8:12	202, 230, 452	18:10	487